SPIDER-MAN

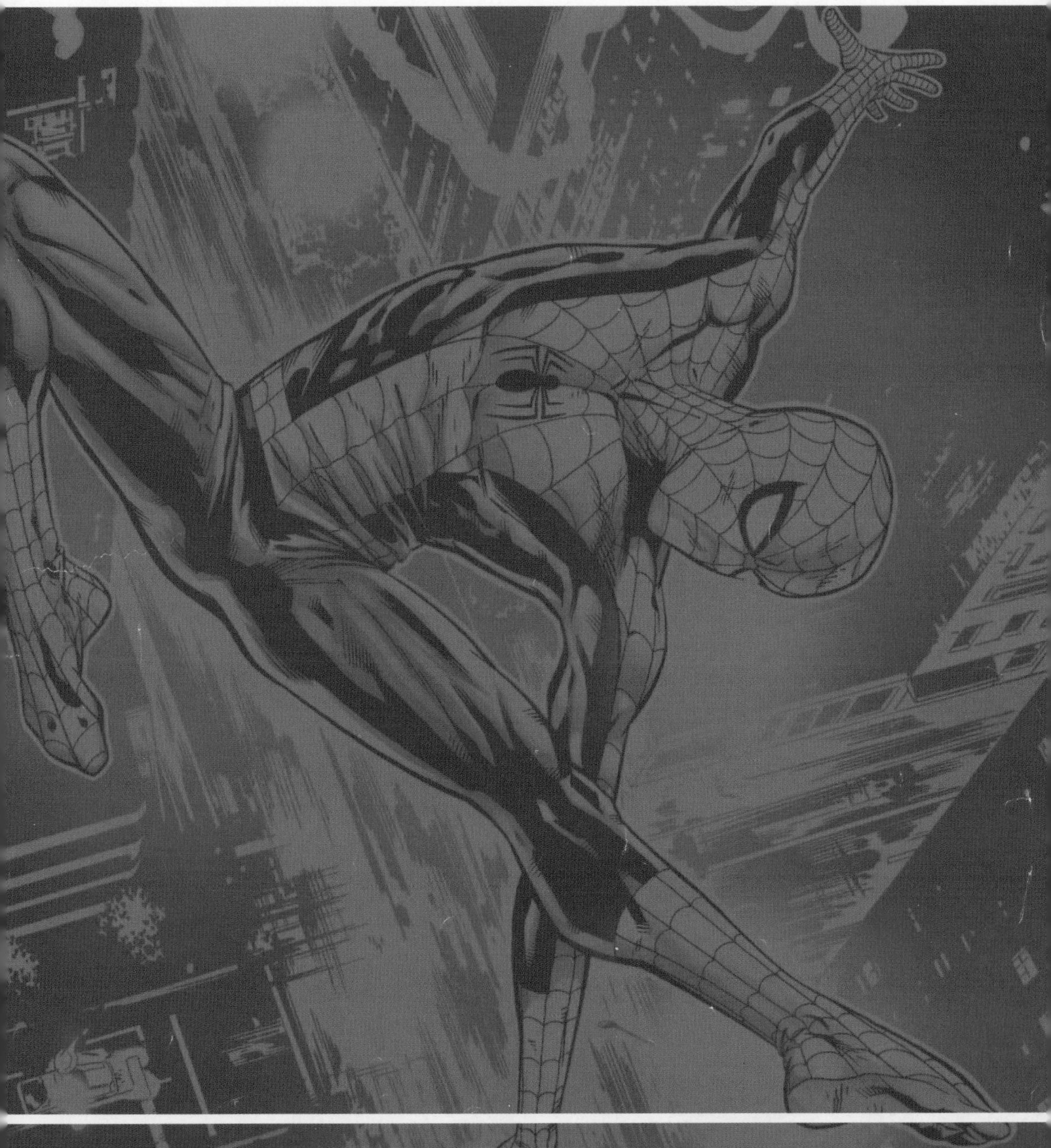

COLLECTION EDITOR: **JENNIFER GRÜNWALD**
ASSISTANT EDITORS: **ALEX STARBUCK & NELSON RIBEIRO**
EDITOR, SPECIAL PROJECTS: **MARK D. BEAZLEY**
SENIOR EDITOR, SPECIAL PROJECTS: **JEFF YOUNGQUIST**
SENIOR VICE PRESIDENT OF SALES: **DAVID GABRIEL**
SVP OF BRAND PLANNING & COMMUNICATIONS: **MICHAEL PASCIULLO**
COVER & BOOK DESIGN: **JEFF POWELL**

EDITOR IN CHIEF: **AXEL ALONSO**
CHIEF CREATIVE OFFICER: **JOE QUESADA**
PUBLISHER: **DAN BUCKLEY**
EXECUTIVE PRODUCER: **ALAN FINE**

SPIDER-MAN: SEASON ONE. Contains material originally published in magazine form as AVENGING SPIDER-MAN #1. First printing 2012. ISBN# 978-0-7851-5820-2. Published by MARVEL WORLDWIDE, INC., a s
of MARVEL ENTERTAINMENT, LLC. OFFICE OF PUBLICATION: 135 West 50th Street, New York, NY 10020. Copyright © 2011 and 2012 Marvel Characters, Inc. All rights reserved. $24.99 per copy in the U.S. and
Canada (GST #R127032852); Canadian Agreement #40668537. All characters featured in this issue and the distinctive names and likenesses thereof, and all related indicia are trademarks of Marvel Characte
similarity between any of the names, characters, persons, and/or institutions in this magazine with those of any living or dead person or institution is intended, and any such similarity which may exist is purely coi
Printed in the U.S.A. ALAN FINE, EVP - Office of the President, Marvel Worldwide, Inc. and EVP & CMO Marvel Characters B.V.; DAN BUCKLEY, Publisher & President - Print, Animation & Digital Divisions; JOE C
Chief Creative Officer; DAVID BOGART, SVP of Business Affairs & Talent Management; TOM BREVOORT, SVP of Publishing; C.B. CEBULSKI, SVP of Creator & Content Development; DAVID GABRIEL, SVP of Publish
& Circulation; MICHAEL PASCIULLO, SVP of Brand Planning & Communications; JIM O'KEEFE, VP of Operations & Logistics; DAN CARR, Executive Director of Publishing Technology; SUSAN CRESPI, Editorial C
Manager; ALEX MORALES, Publishing Operations Manager; STAN LEE, Chairman Emeritus. For information regarding advertising in Marvel Comics or on Marvel.com, please contact John Dokes, SVP Integrated
Marketing, at jdokes@marvel.com. For Marvel subscription inquiries, please call 800-217-9158. **Manufactured between 2/27/2012 and 4/2/2012 by R.R. DONNELLEY, INC., SALEM, VA, USA.**

10 9 8 7 6 5 4 3 2 1

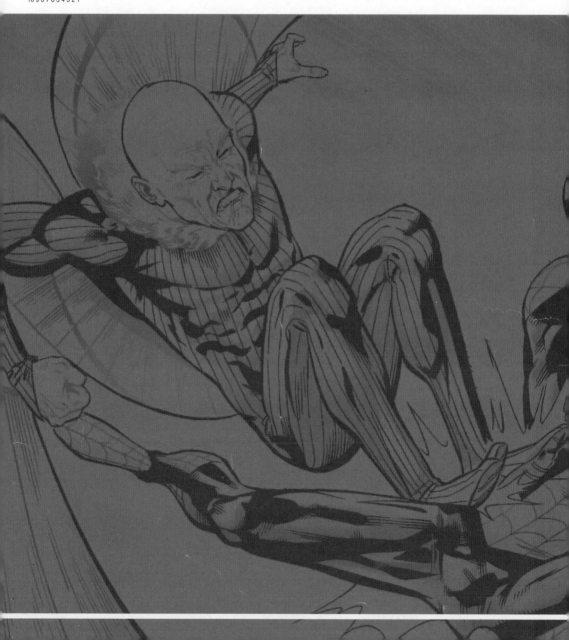

SPIDER-MAN

WRITER
CULLEN BUNN

PENCILER
NEIL EDWARDS

INKER
KARL KESEL

COLORIST
DAVID CURIEL

LETTERER
VC'S CLAYTON COWLES

COVER ARTIST
JULIAN TOTINO TEDESCO

ASSISTANT EDITOR
ELLIE PYLE & RACHEL PINNELAS

EDITOR
STEPHEN WACKER

EXECUTIVE EDITOR
TOM BREVOORT

INSPIRED BY *AMAZING FANTASY #15*
BY STAN LEE AND STEVE DITKO

SEASON ONE

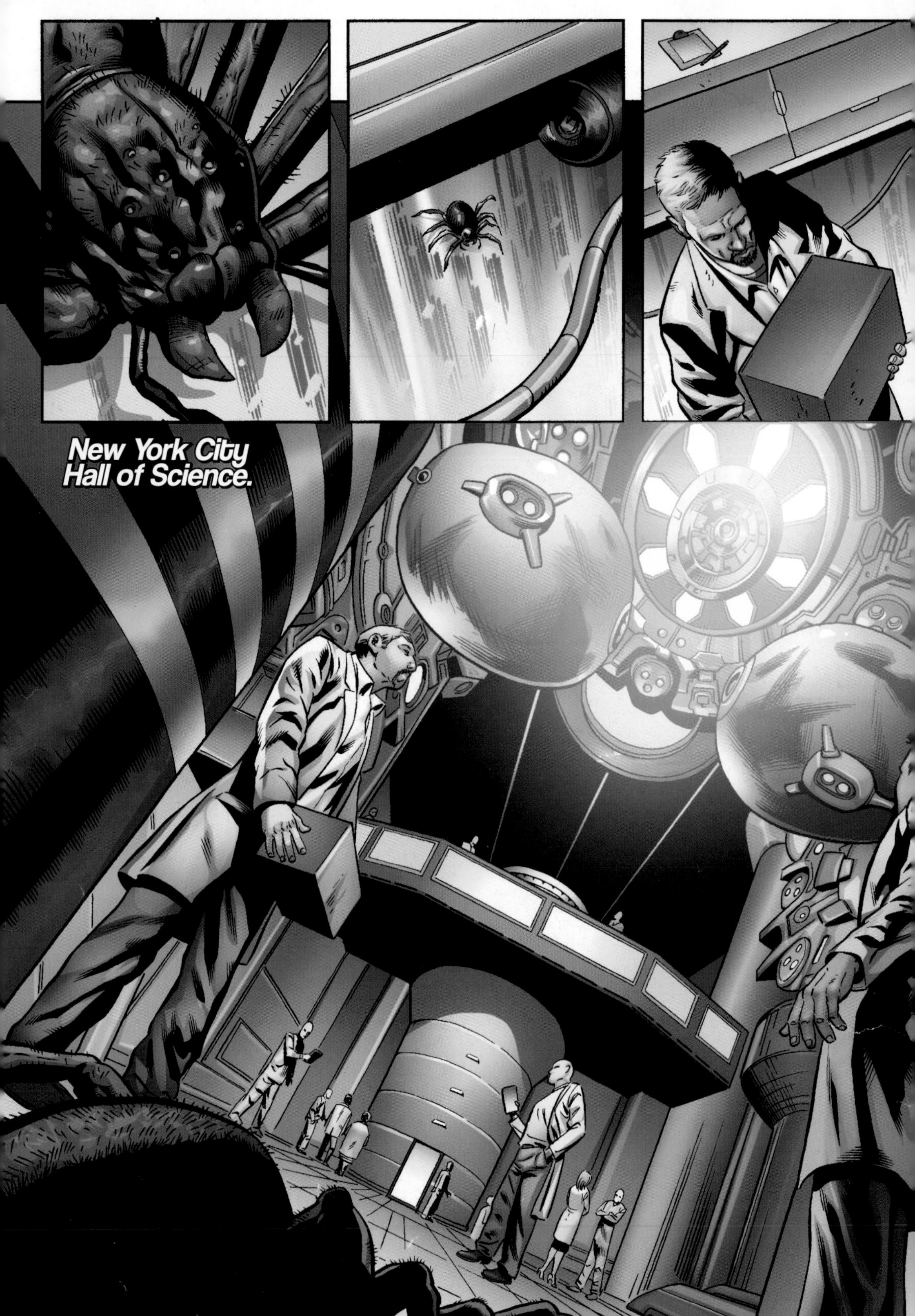
New York City
Hall of Science.

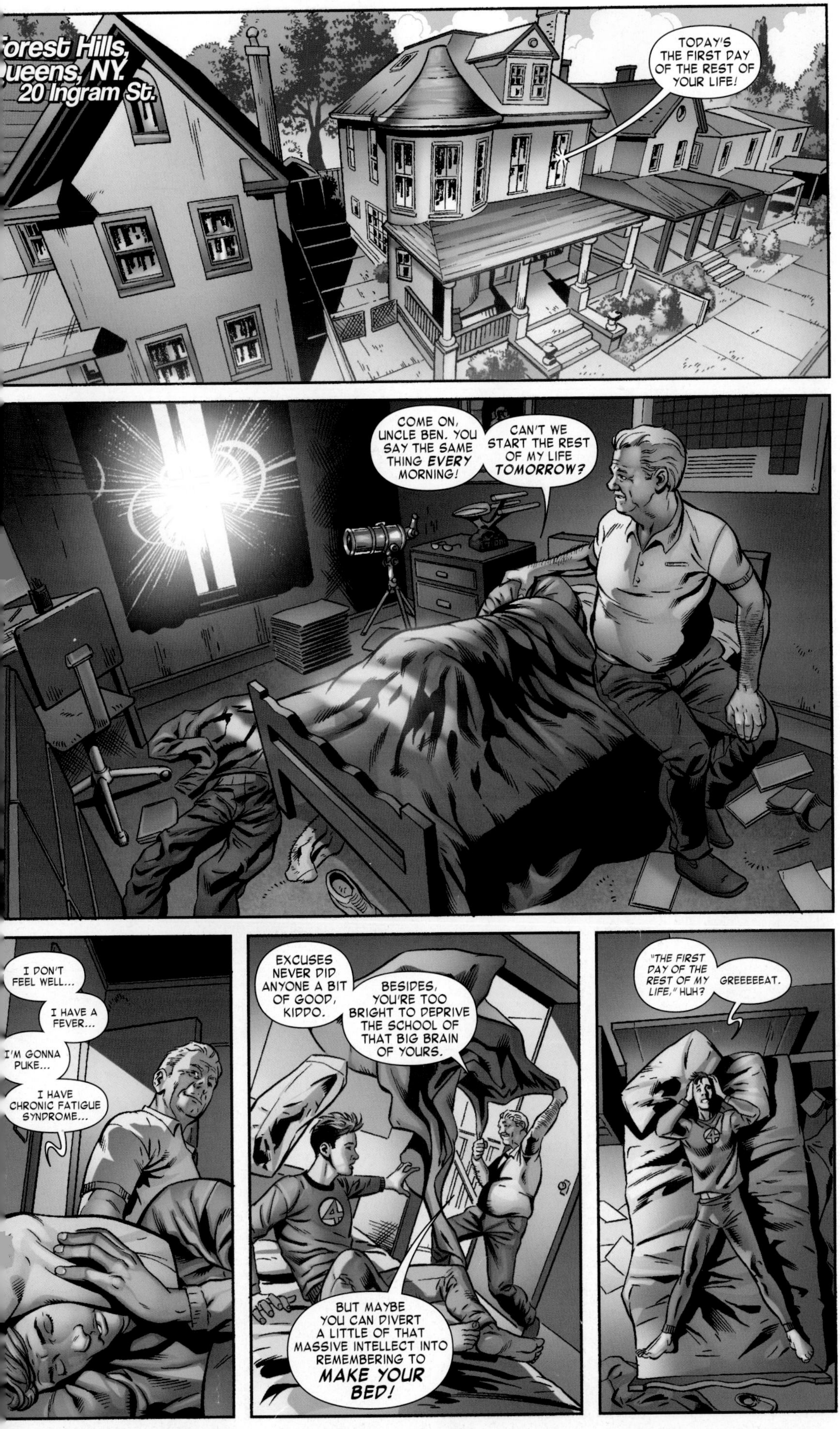
Forest Hills,
Queens, NY.
20 Ingram St.
TODAY'S THE FIRST DAY OF THE REST OF YOUR LIFE!
COME ON, UNCLE BEN. YOU SAY THE SAME THING EVERY MORNING!
CAN'T WE START THE REST OF MY LIFE TOMORROW?
I DON'T FEEL WELL...
I HAVE A FEVER...
I'M GONNA PUKE...
I HAVE CHRONIC FATIGUE SYNDROME...
EXCUSES NEVER DID ANYONE A BIT OF GOOD, KIDDO.
BESIDES, YOU'RE TOO BRIGHT TO DEPRIVE THE SCHOOL OF THAT BIG BRAIN OF YOURS.
BUT MAYBE YOU CAN DIVERT A LITTLE OF THAT MASSIVE INTELLECT INTO REMEMBERING TO MAKE YOUR BED!
"THE FIRST DAY OF THE REST OF MY LIFE," HUH?
GREEEEEAT.

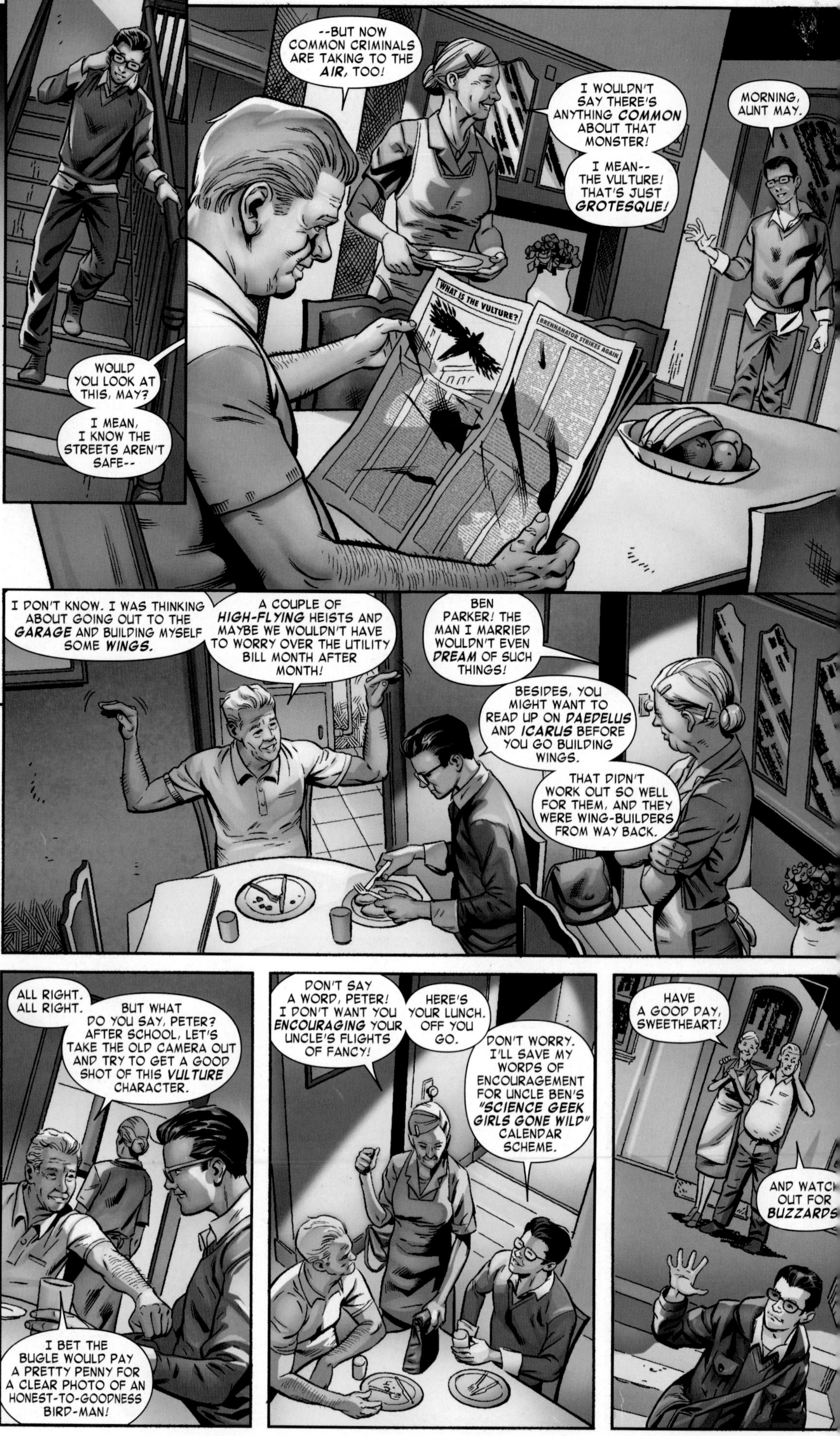
WOULD YOU LOOK AT THIS, MAY?
I MEAN, I KNOW THE STREETS AREN'T SAFE--
--BUT NOW COMMON CRIMINALS ARE TAKING TO THE AIR, TOO!
I WOULDN'T SAY THERE'S ANYTHING COMMON ABOUT THAT MONSTER!
I MEAN-- THE VULTURE! THAT'S JUST GROTESQUE!
MORNING, AUNT MAY.
WHAT IS THE VULTURE?
BRENNANATOR STRIKES AGAIN
I DON'T KNOW. I WAS THINKING ABOUT GOING OUT TO THE GARAGE AND BUILDING MYSELF SOME WINGS.
A COUPLE OF HIGH-FLYING HEISTS AND MAYBE WE WOULDN'T HAVE TO WORRY OVER THE UTILITY BILL MONTH AFTER MONTH!
BEN PARKER! THE MAN I MARRIED WOULDN'T EVEN DREAM OF SUCH THINGS!
BESIDES, YOU MIGHT WANT TO READ UP ON DAEDELUS AND ICARUS BEFORE YOU GO BUILDING WINGS.
THAT DIDN'T WORK OUT SO WELL FOR THEM, AND THEY WERE WING-BUILDERS FROM WAY BACK.
ALL RIGHT. ALL RIGHT.
BUT WHAT DO YOU SAY, PETER? AFTER SCHOOL, LET'S TAKE THE OLD CAMERA OUT AND TRY TO GET A GOOD SHOT OF THIS VULTURE CHARACTER.
I BET THE BUGLE WOULD PAY A PRETTY PENNY FOR A CLEAR PHOTO OF AN HONEST-TO-GOODNESS BIRD-MAN!
DON'T SAY A WORD, PETER! I DON'T WANT YOU ENCOURAGING YOUR UNCLE'S FLIGHTS OF FANCY!
HERE'S YOUR LUNCH. OFF YOU GO.
DON'T WORRY. I'LL SAVE MY WORDS OF ENCOURAGEMENT FOR UNCLE BEN'S "SCIENCE GEEK GIRLS GONE WILD" CALENDAR SCHEME.
HAVE A GOOD DAY, SWEETHEART!
AND WATCH OUT FOR BUZZARDS

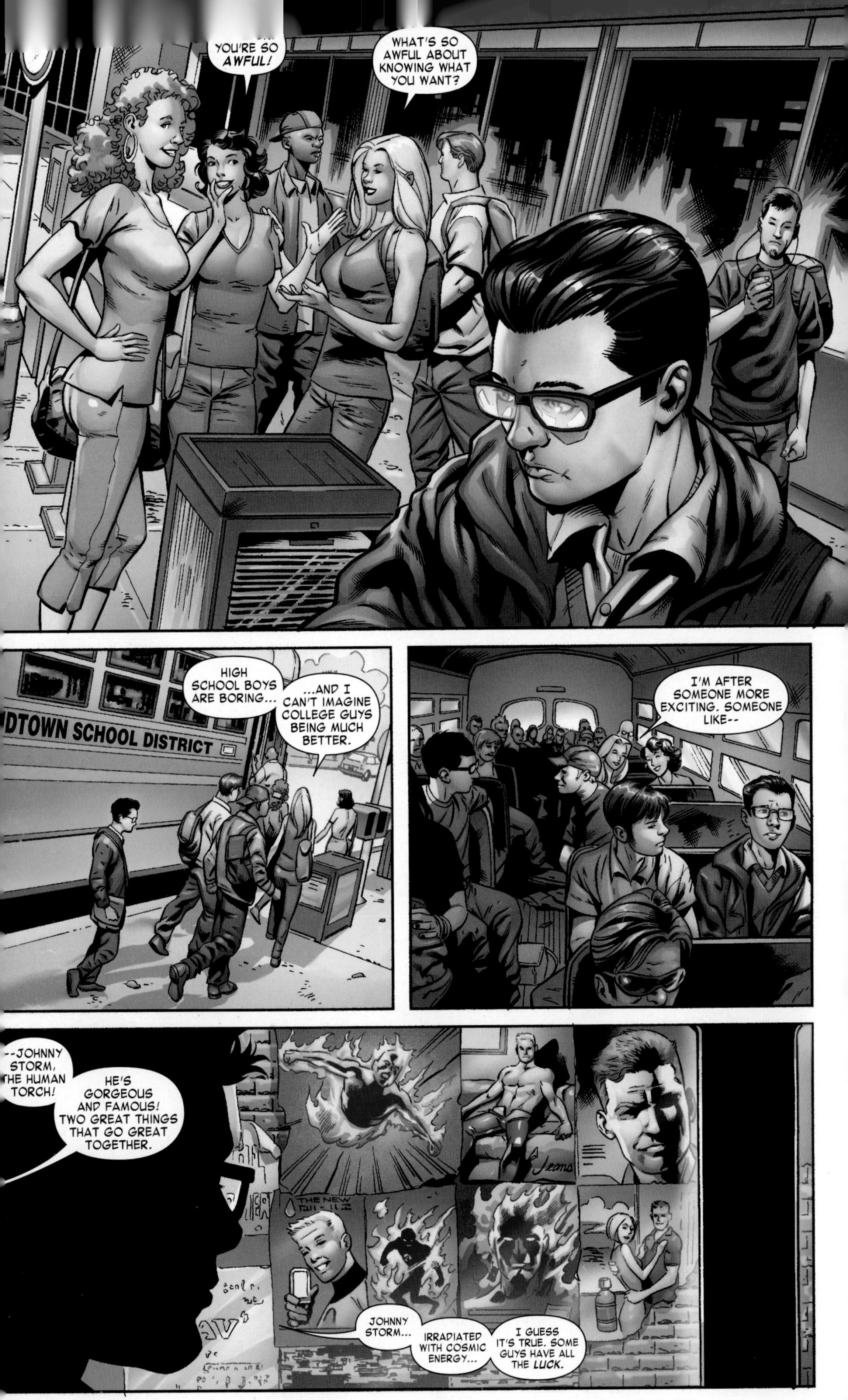
YOU'RE SO AWFUL!
WHAT'S SO AWFUL ABOUT KNOWING WHAT YOU WANT?
HIGH SCHOOL BOYS ARE BORING...
...AND I CAN'T IMAGINE COLLEGE GUYS BEING MUCH BETTER.
DTOWN SCHOOL DISTRICT
I'M AFTER SOMEONE MORE EXCITING. SOMEONE LIKE--
--JOHNNY STORM, THE HUMAN TORCH!
HE'S GORGEOUS AND FAMOUS! TWO GREAT THINGS THAT GO GREAT TOGETHER.
JOHNNY STORM...
IRRADIATED WITH COSMIC ENERGY...
I GUESS IT'S TRUE. SOME GUYS HAVE ALL THE LUCK.

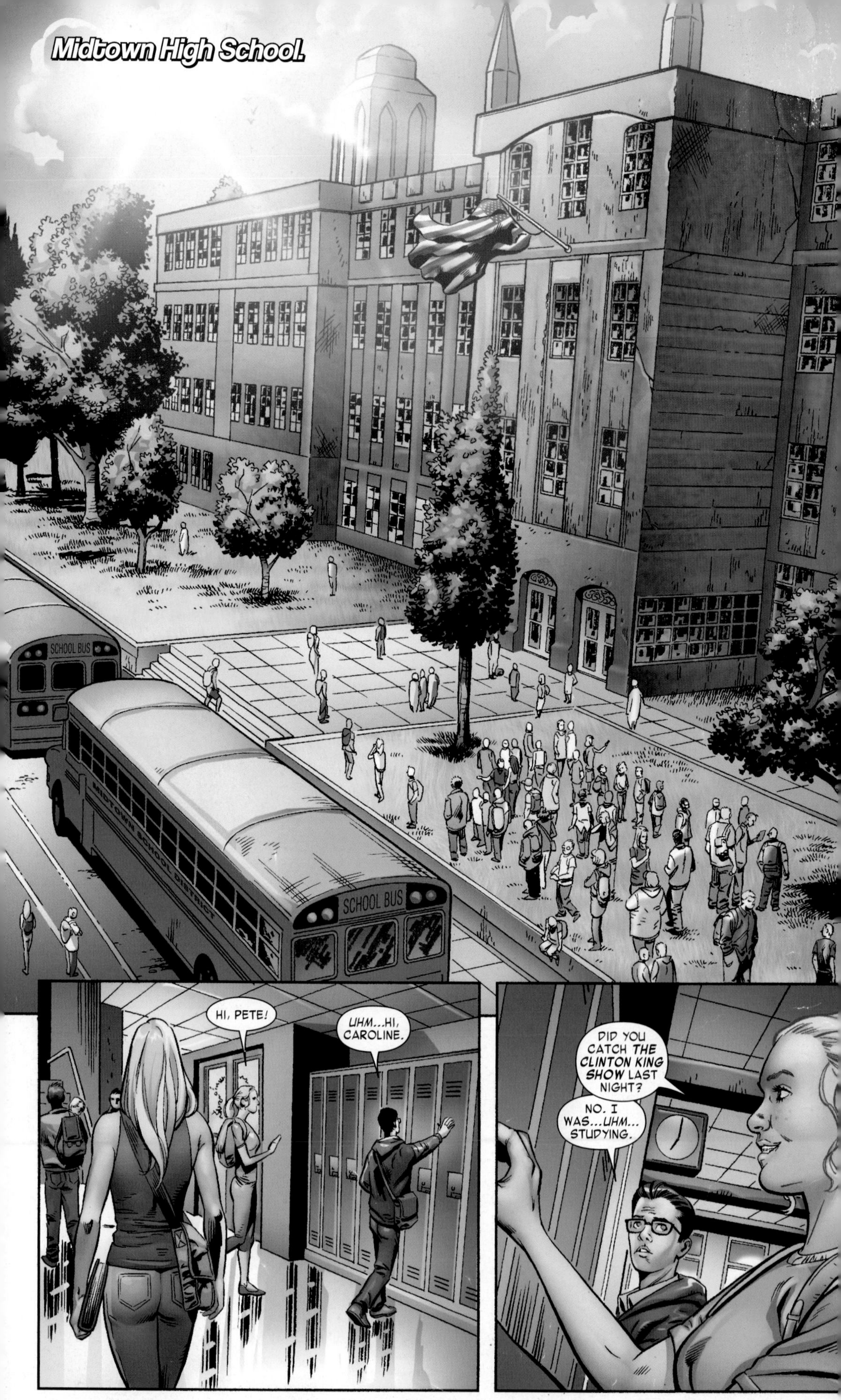
Midtown High School.
SCHOOL BUS
MIDTOWN SCHOOL DISTRICT
SCHOOL BUS
HI, PETE!
UHM...HI, CAROLINE.
DID YOU CATCH THE CLINTON KING SHOW LAST NIGHT?
NO. I WAS...UHM... STUDYING.

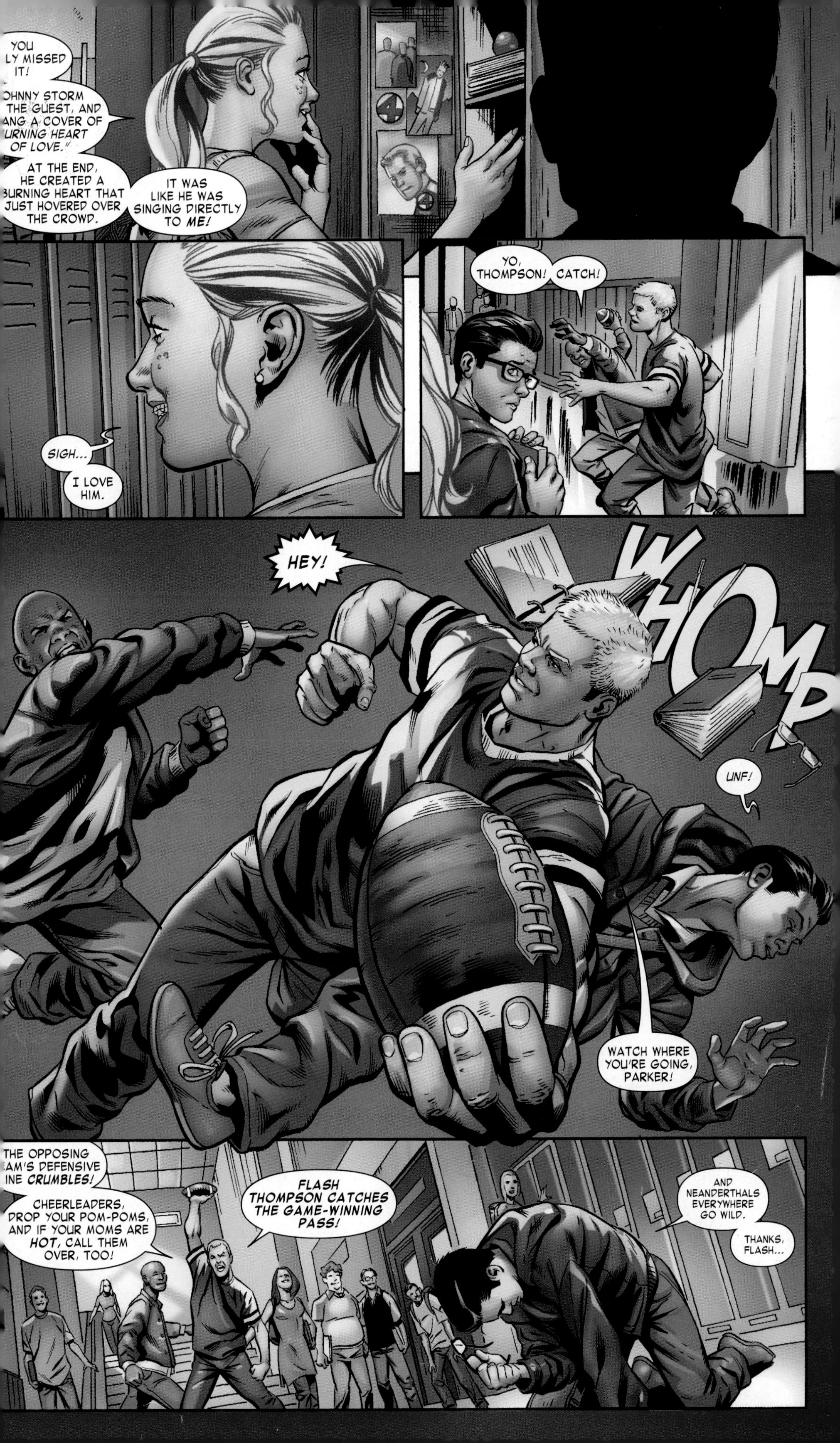
YOU
LY MISSED
IT!
OHNNY STORM
THE GUEST, AND
ANG A COVER OF
URNING HEART
OF LOVE."
AT THE END,
HE CREATED A
BURNING HEART THAT
JUST HOVERED OVER
THE CROWD.
IT WAS
LIKE HE WAS
SINGING DIRECTLY
TO ME!
SIGH...
I LOVE
HIM.
YO,
THOMPSON!
CATCH!
HEY!
WHOMP
UNF!
WATCH WHERE
YOU'RE GOING,
PARKER!
THE OPPOSING
EAM'S DEFENSIVE
INE CRUMBLES!
CHEERLEADERS,
DROP YOUR POM-POMS,
AND IF YOUR MOMS ARE
HOT, CALL THEM
OVER, TOO!
FLASH
THOMPSON CATCHES
THE GAME-WINNING
PASS!
AND
NEANDERTHALS
EVERYWHERE
GO WILD.
THANKS,
FLASH...

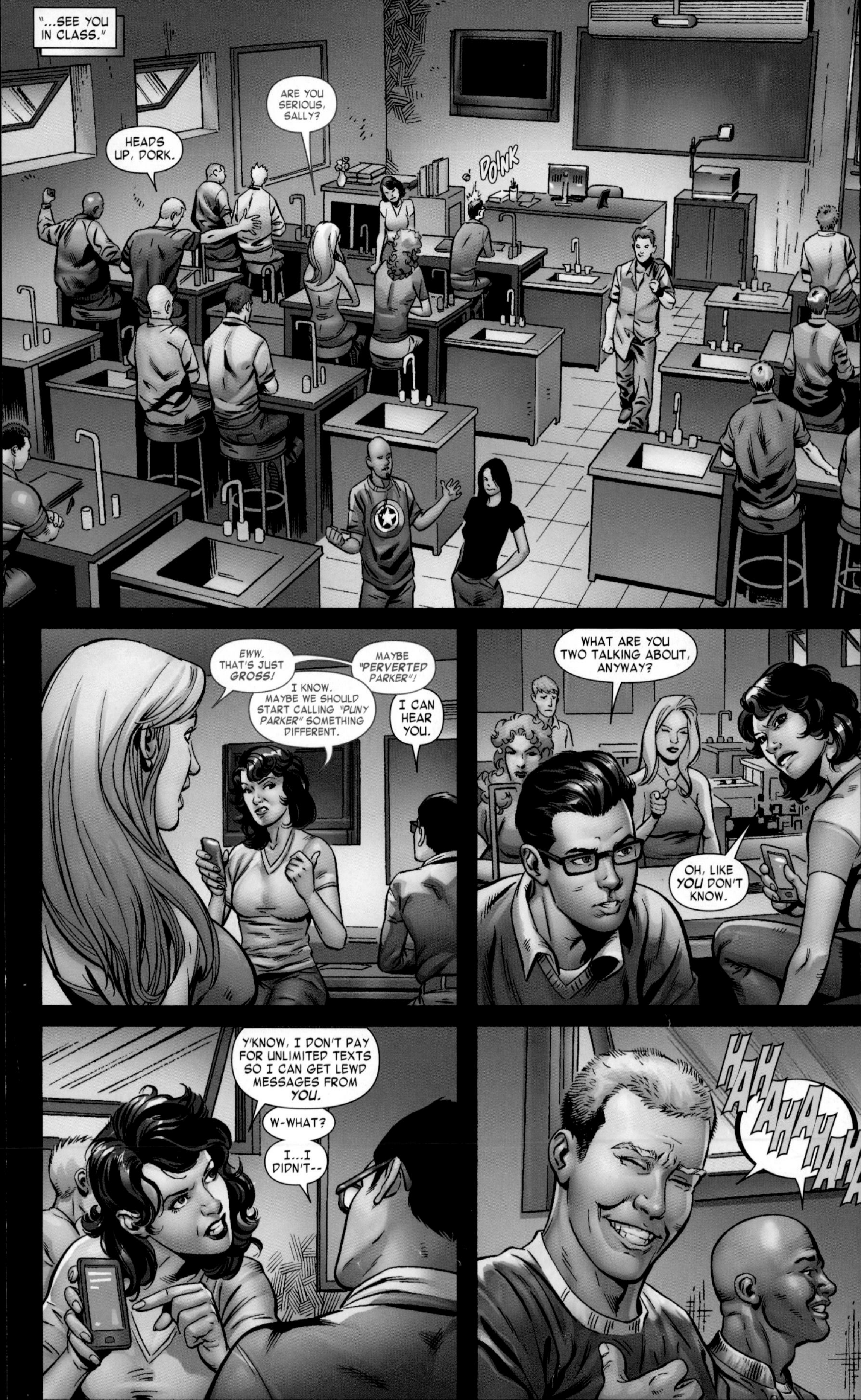
"...SEE YOU IN CLASS."
HEADS UP, DORK.
ARE YOU SERIOUS, SALLY?
DOINK
EWW. THAT'S JUST GROSS!
I KNOW. MAYBE WE SHOULD START CALLING "PUNY PARKER" SOMETHING DIFFERENT.
MAYBE "PERVERTED PARKER"!
I CAN HEAR YOU.
WHAT ARE YOU TWO TALKING ABOUT, ANYWAY?
OH, LIKE YOU DON'T KNOW.
Y'KNOW, I DON'T PAY FOR UNLIMITED TEXTS SO I CAN GET LEWD MESSAGES FROM YOU.
W-WHAT?
I...I DIDN'T--
HAHAHAHAHAHAHA

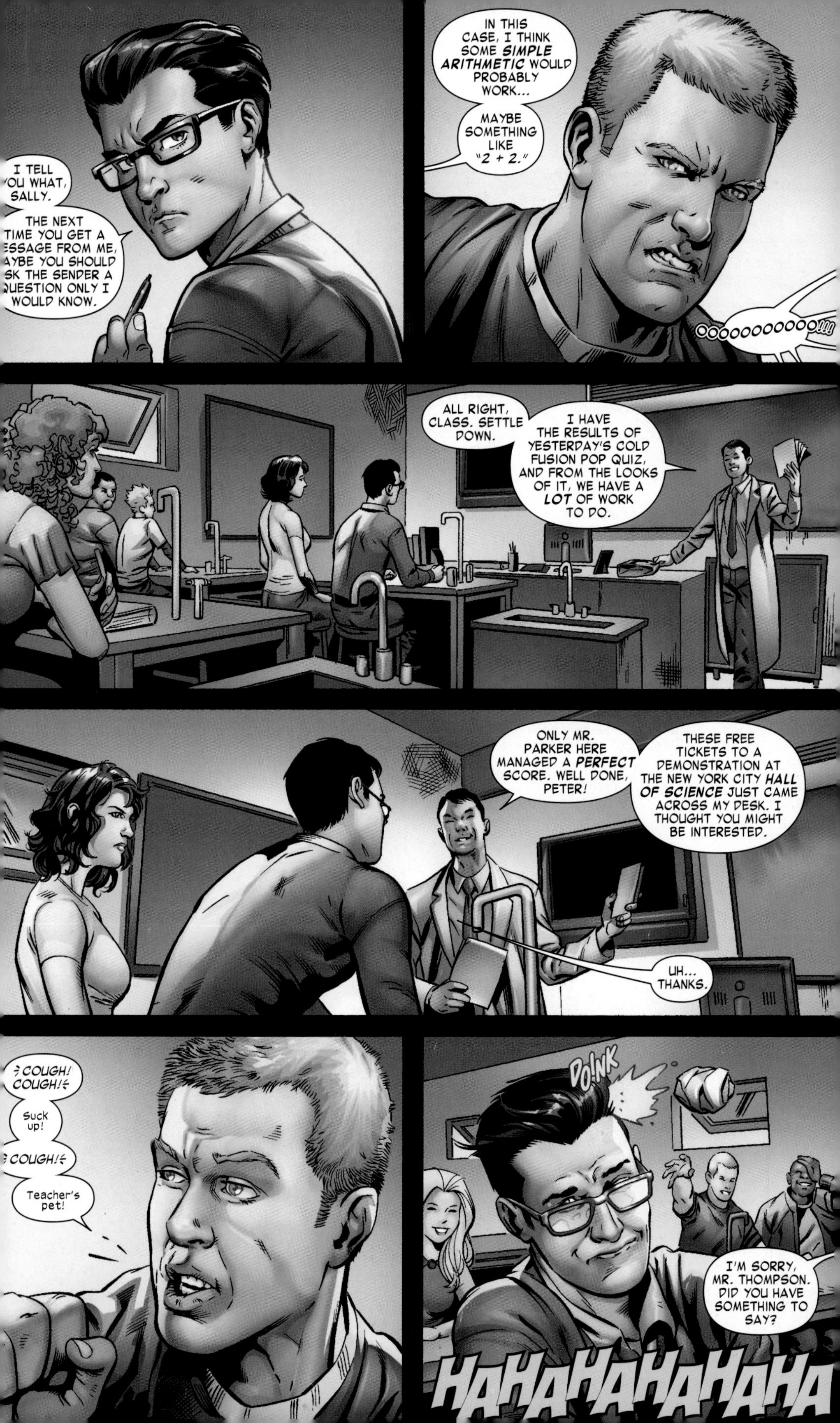
I TELL YOU WHAT, SALLY.
THE NEXT TIME YOU GET A ESSAGE FROM ME, AYBE YOU SHOULD SK THE SENDER A QUESTION ONLY I WOULD KNOW.
IN THIS CASE, I THINK SOME SIMPLE ARITHMETIC WOULD PROBABLY WORK...
MAYBE SOMETHING LIKE "2 + 2."
OOOOOOOOOO!!!
ALL RIGHT, CLASS. SETTLE DOWN.
I HAVE THE RESULTS OF YESTERDAY'S COLD FUSION POP QUIZ, AND FROM THE LOOKS OF IT, WE HAVE A LOT OF WORK TO DO.
ONLY MR. PARKER HERE MANAGED A PERFECT SCORE. WELL DONE, PETER!
THESE FREE TICKETS TO A DEMONSTRATION AT THE NEW YORK CITY HALL OF SCIENCE JUST CAME ACROSS MY DESK. I THOUGHT YOU MIGHT BE INTERESTED.
UH... THANKS.
COUGH! COUGH!
Suck up!
COUGH!
Teacher's pet!
DOINK
I'M SORRY, MR. THOMPSON. DID YOU HAVE SOMETHING TO SAY?
HAHAHAHAHAHAHA

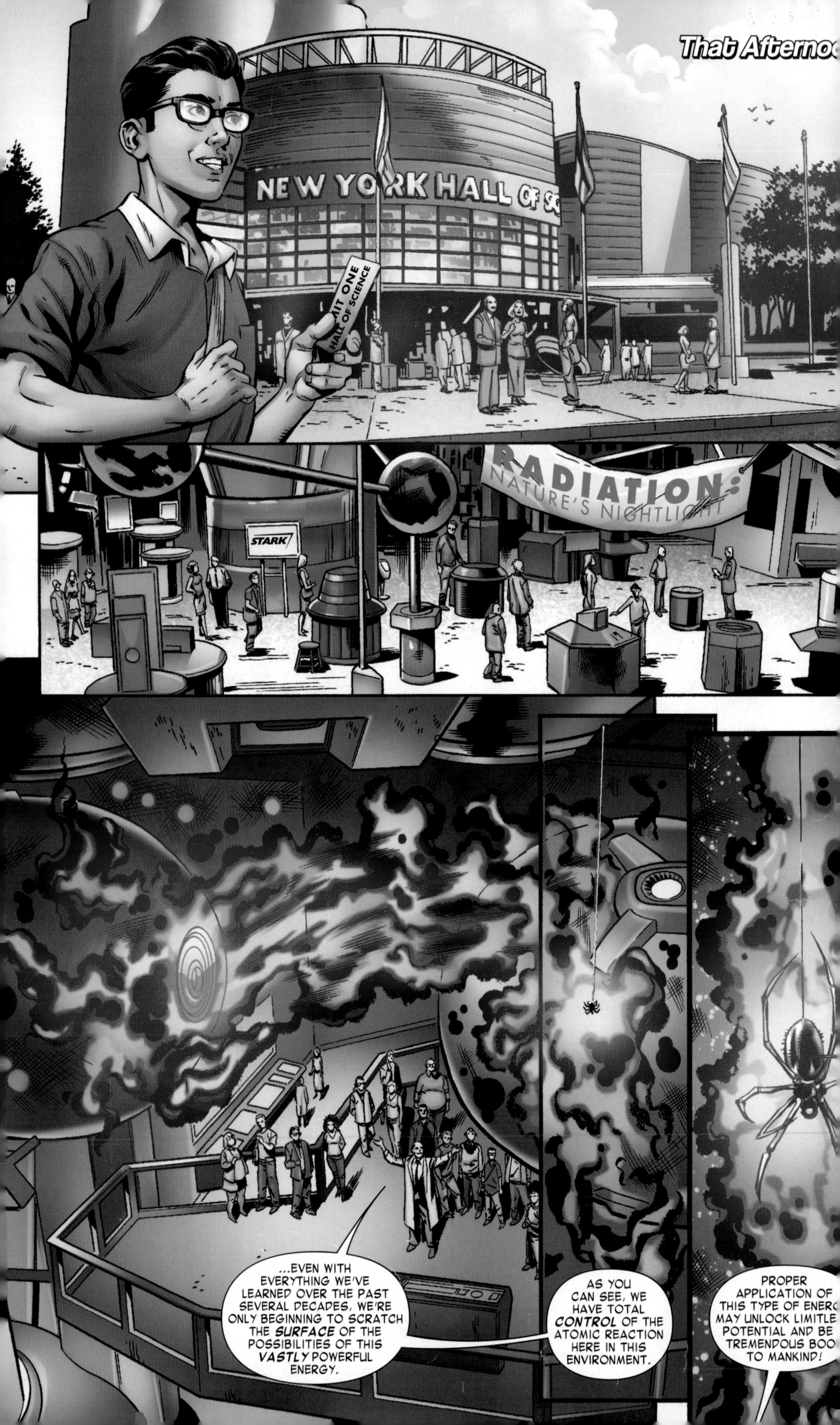
That Afterno
NEW YORK HALL OF SC
ADMIT ONE HALL OF SCIENCE
STARK
RADIATION: NATURE'S NIGHTLIGHT
...EVEN WITH EVERYTHING WE'VE LEARNED OVER THE PAST SEVERAL DECADES, WE'RE ONLY BEGINNING TO SCRATCH THE SURFACE OF THE POSSIBILITIES OF THIS VASTLY POWERFUL ENERGY.
AS YOU CAN SEE, WE HAVE TOTAL CONTROL OF THE ATOMIC REACTION HERE IN THIS ENVIRONMENT.
PROPER APPLICATION OF THIS TYPE OF ENERG MAY UNLOCK LIMITLE POTENTIAL AND BE TREMENDOUS BOO TO MANKIND!

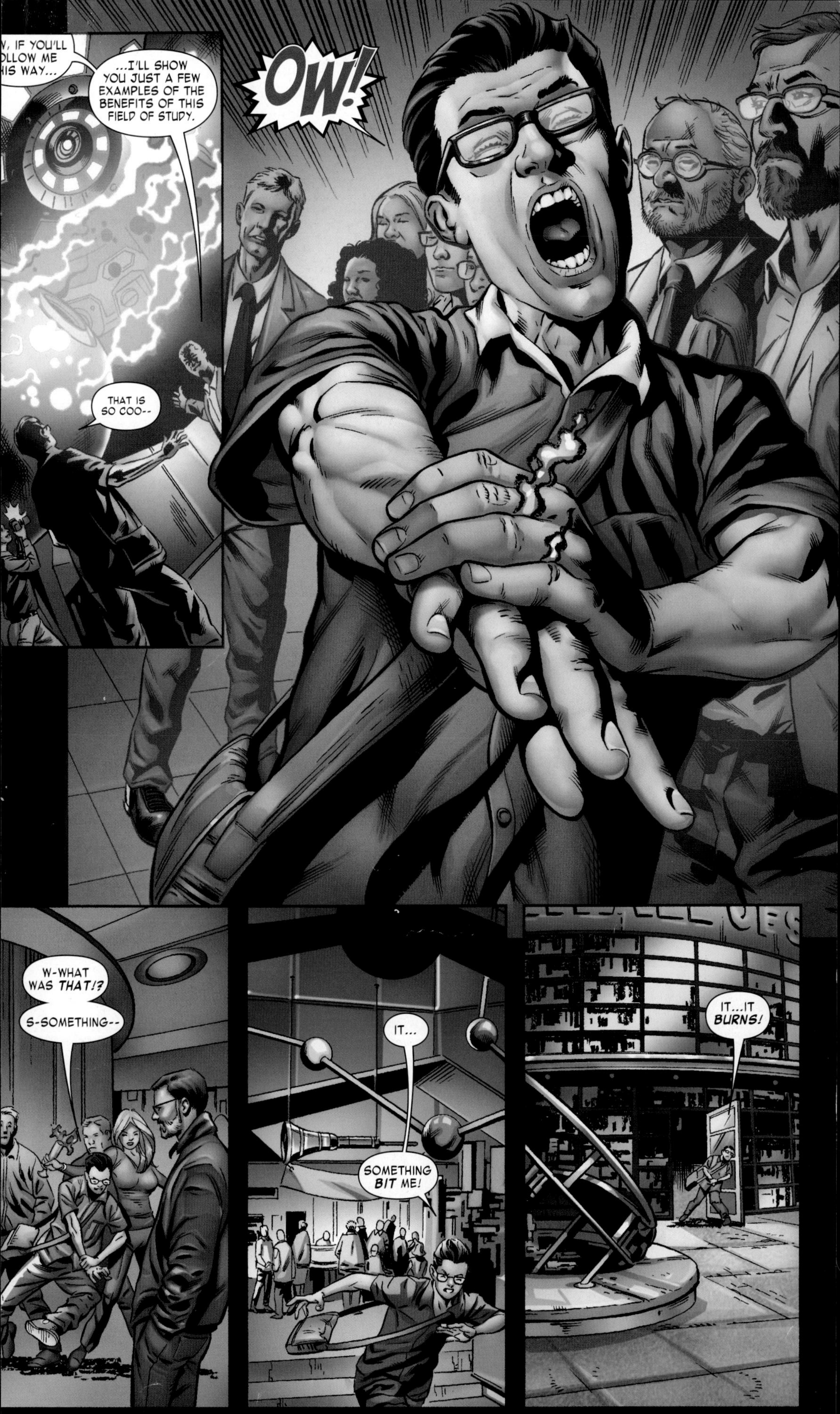
W, IF YOU'LL OLLOW ME HIS WAY...
...I'LL SHOW YOU JUST A FEW EXAMPLES OF THE BENEFITS OF THIS FIELD OF STUDY.
THAT IS SO COO--
OW!
W-WHAT WAS THAT!?
S-SOMETHING--
IT...
SOMETHING BIT ME!
IT...IT BURNS!

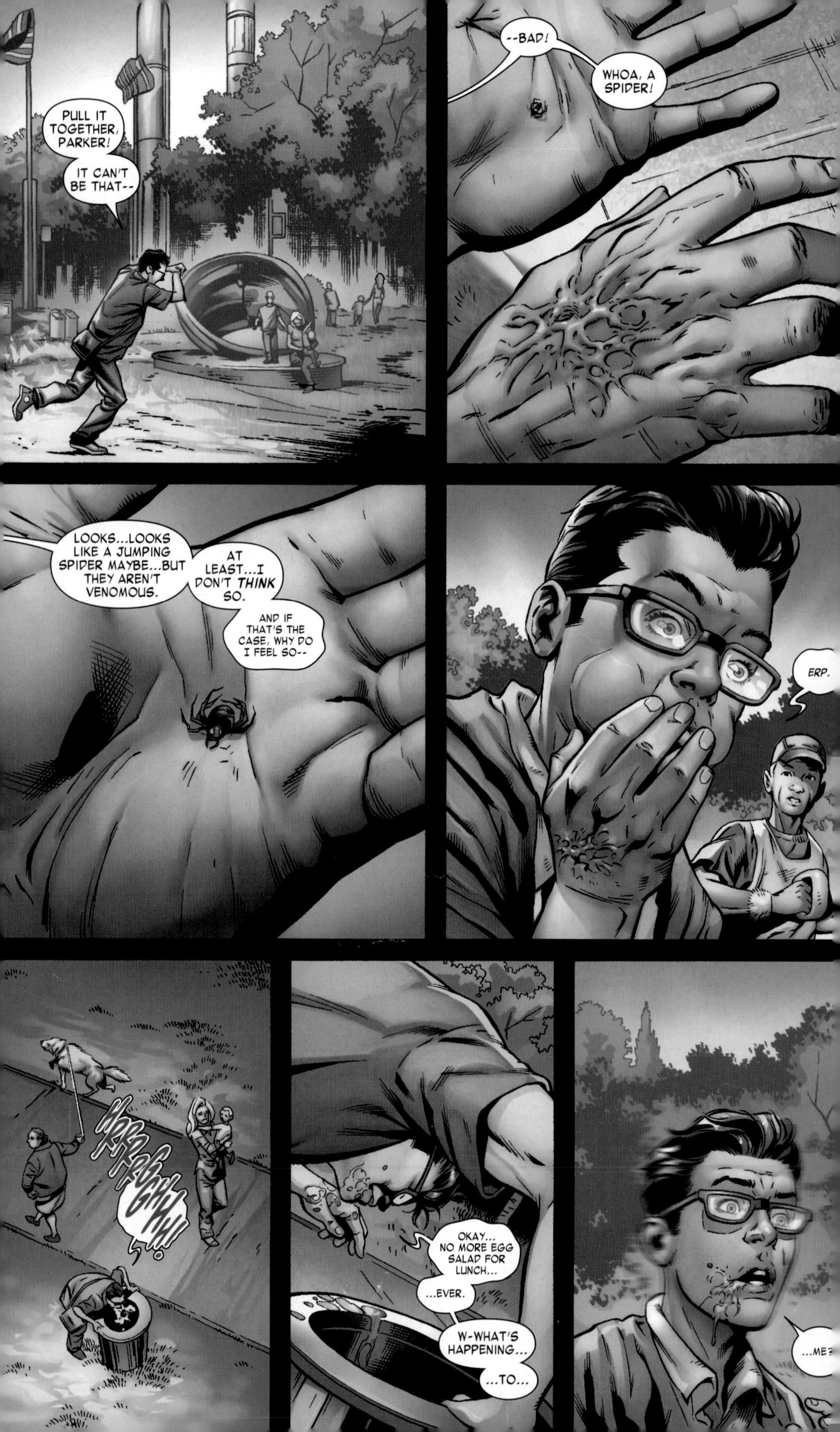
PULL IT TOGETHER, PARKER!
IT CAN'T BE THAT--
--BAD!
WHOA, A SPIDER!
LOOKS...LOOKS LIKE A JUMPING SPIDER MAYBE...BUT THEY AREN'T VENOMOUS.
AT LEAST...I DON'T THINK SO.
AND IF THAT'S THE CASE, WHY DO I FEEL SO--
ERP.
HRRRGHHH!!
OKAY... NO MORE EGG SALAD FOR LUNCH...
...EVER.
W-WHAT'S HAPPENING...
...TO...
...ME?

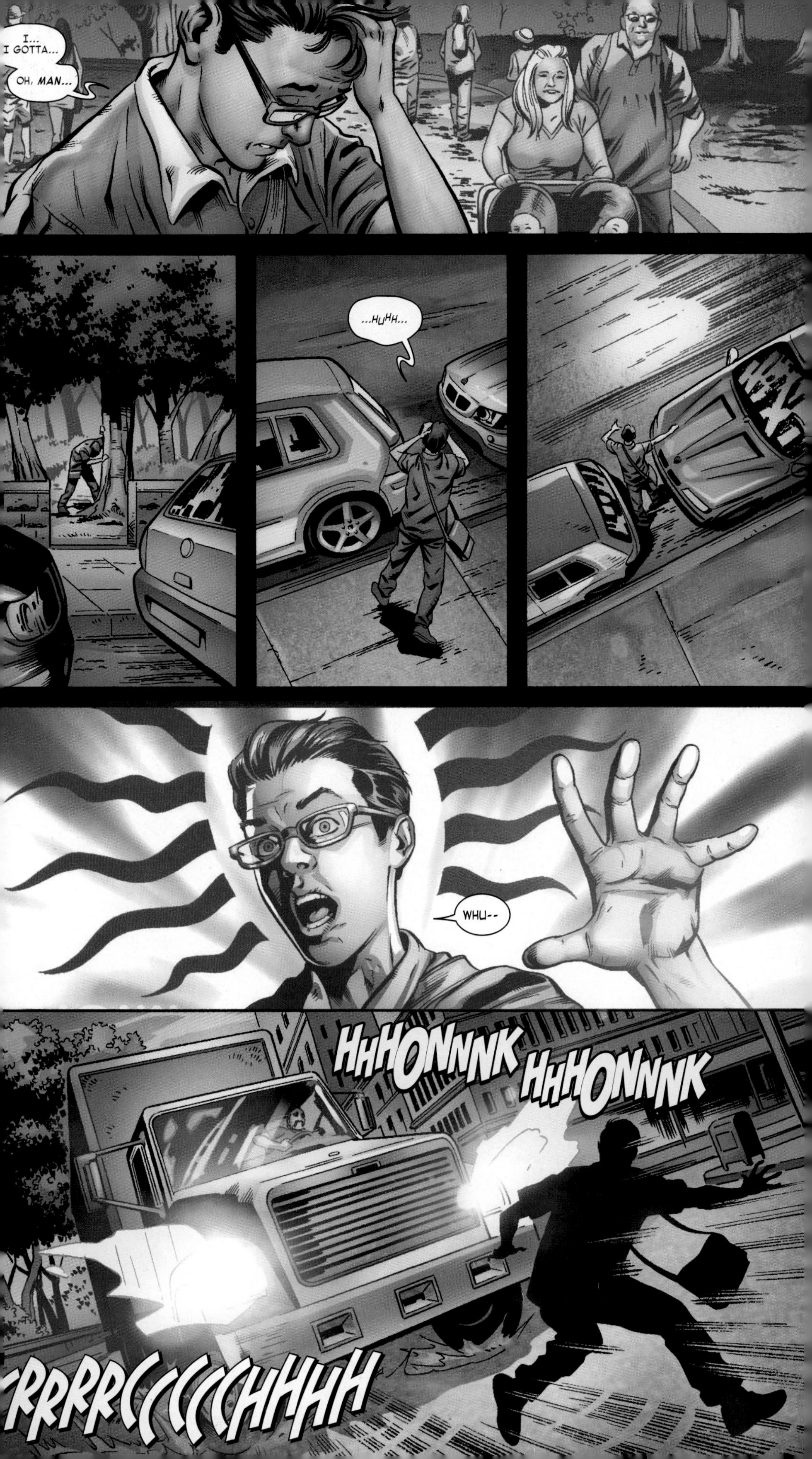
I... I GOTTA...
OH, MAN...
...HUHH...
WHU--
HHHONNNK HHHONNNK
RRRRCCCCCHHHH

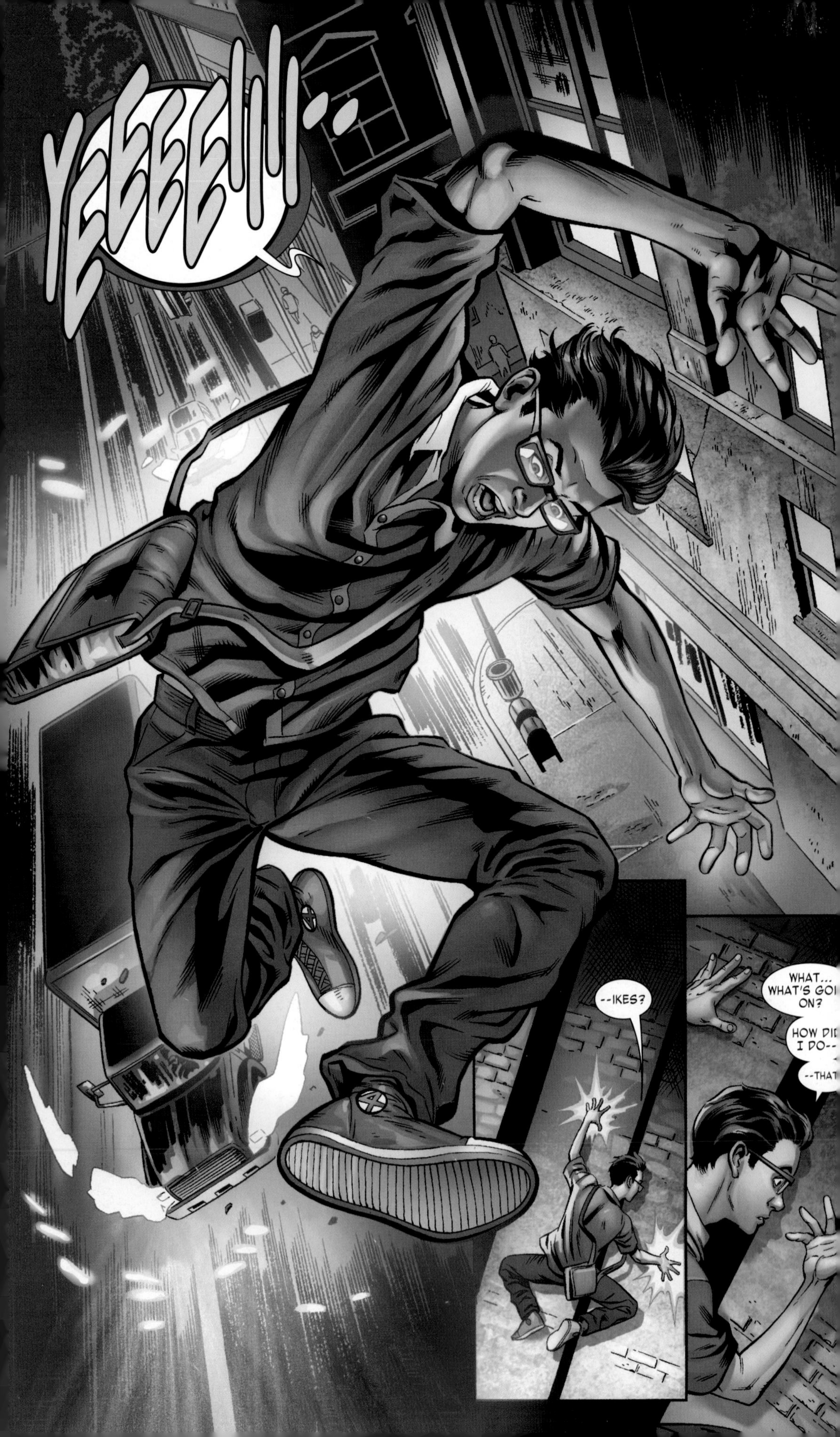
YEEEEIIII--
--IKES?
WHAT... WHAT'S GOI ON?
HOW DID I DO--
--THAT

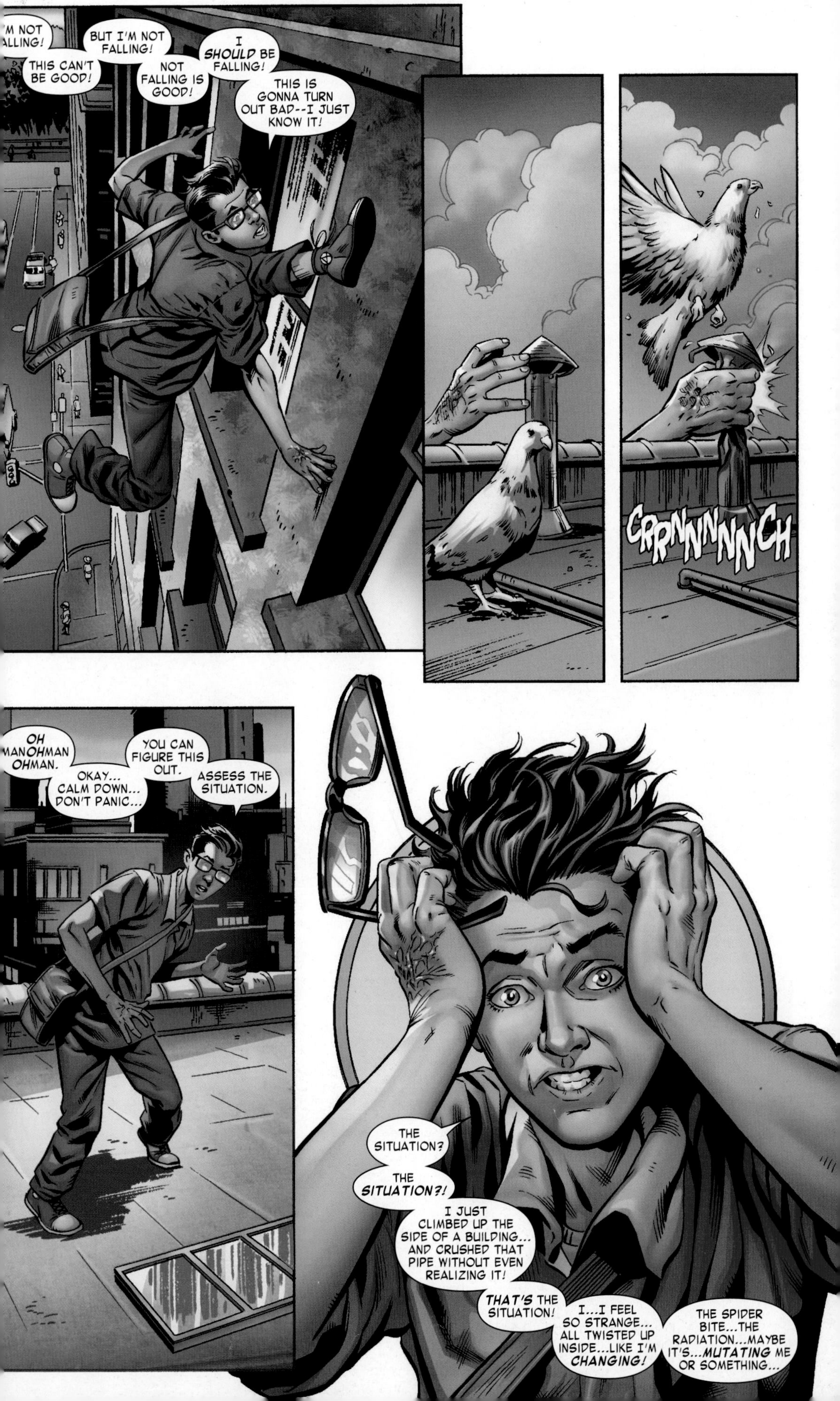

'M NOT
ALLING!
THIS CAN'T BE GOOD!
BUT I'M NOT FALLING!
NOT FALLING IS GOOD!
I *SHOULD* BE FALLING!
THIS IS GONNA TURN OUT BAD--I JUST KNOW IT!
CRRNNNNNCH
OH MAN*OH*MAN *OH*MAN.
OKAY... CALM DOWN... DON'T PANIC...
YOU CAN FIGURE THIS OUT.
ASSESS THE SITUATION.
THE SITUATION?
THE *SITUATION?!*
I JUST CLIMBED UP THE SIDE OF A BUILDING... AND CRUSHED THAT PIPE WITHOUT EVEN REALIZING IT!
THAT'S THE SITUATION!
I...I FEEL SO STRANGE... ALL TWISTED UP INSIDE...LIKE I'M *CHANGING!*
THE SPIDER BITE...THE RADIATION...MAYBE IT'S...*MUTATING* ME OR SOMETHING...

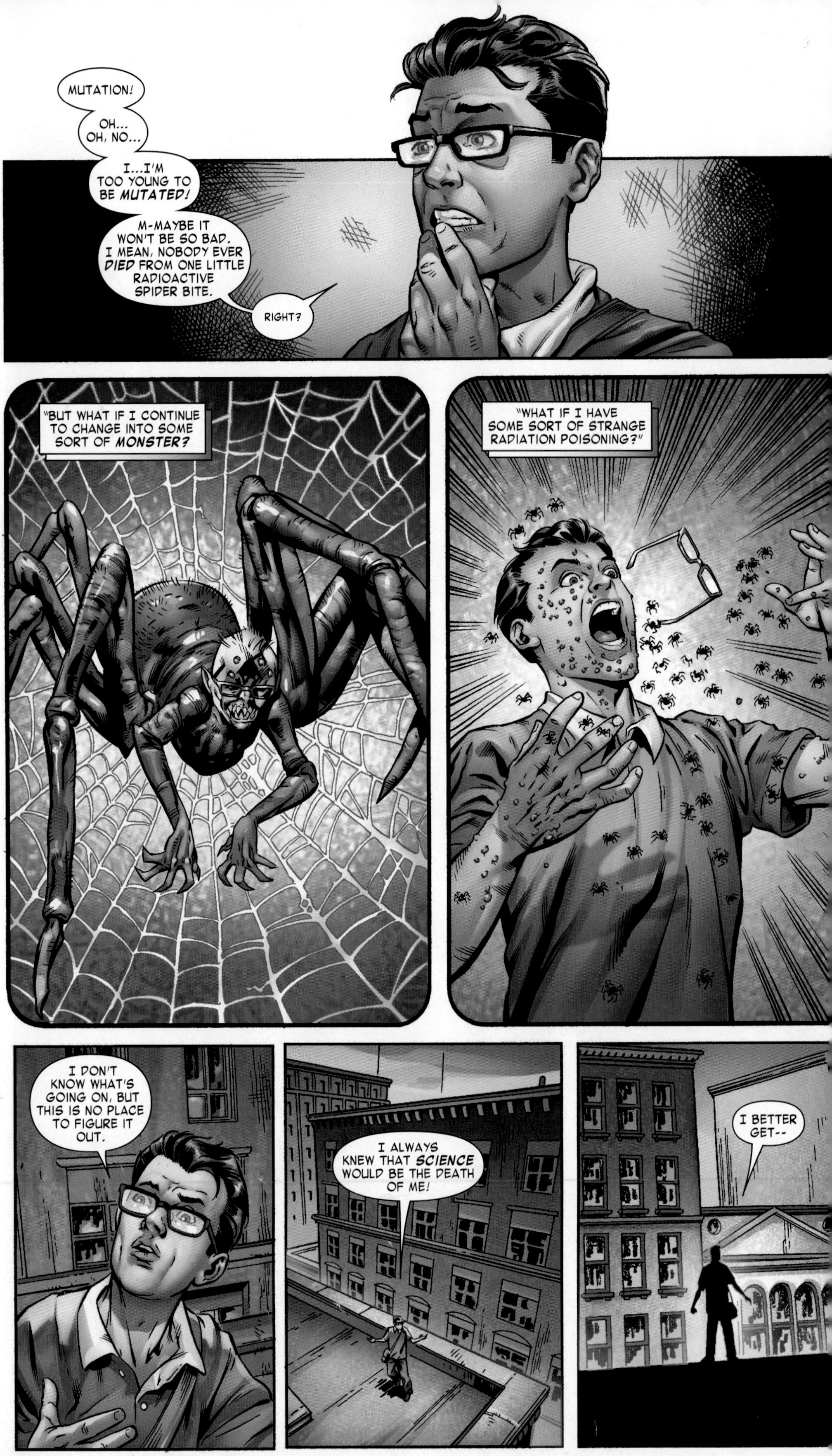
MUTATION!
OH... OH, NO...
I...I'M TOO YOUNG TO BE MUTATED!
M-MAYBE IT WON'T BE SO BAD. I MEAN, NOBODY EVER DIED FROM ONE LITTLE RADIOACTIVE SPIDER BITE.
RIGHT?
"BUT WHAT IF I CONTINUE TO CHANGE INTO SOME SORT OF MONSTER?
"WHAT IF I HAVE SOME SORT OF STRANGE RADIATION POISONING?"
I DON'T KNOW WHAT'S GOING ON, BUT THIS IS NO PLACE TO FIGURE IT OUT.
I ALWAYS KNEW THAT SCIENCE WOULD BE THE DEATH OF ME!
I BETTER GET--

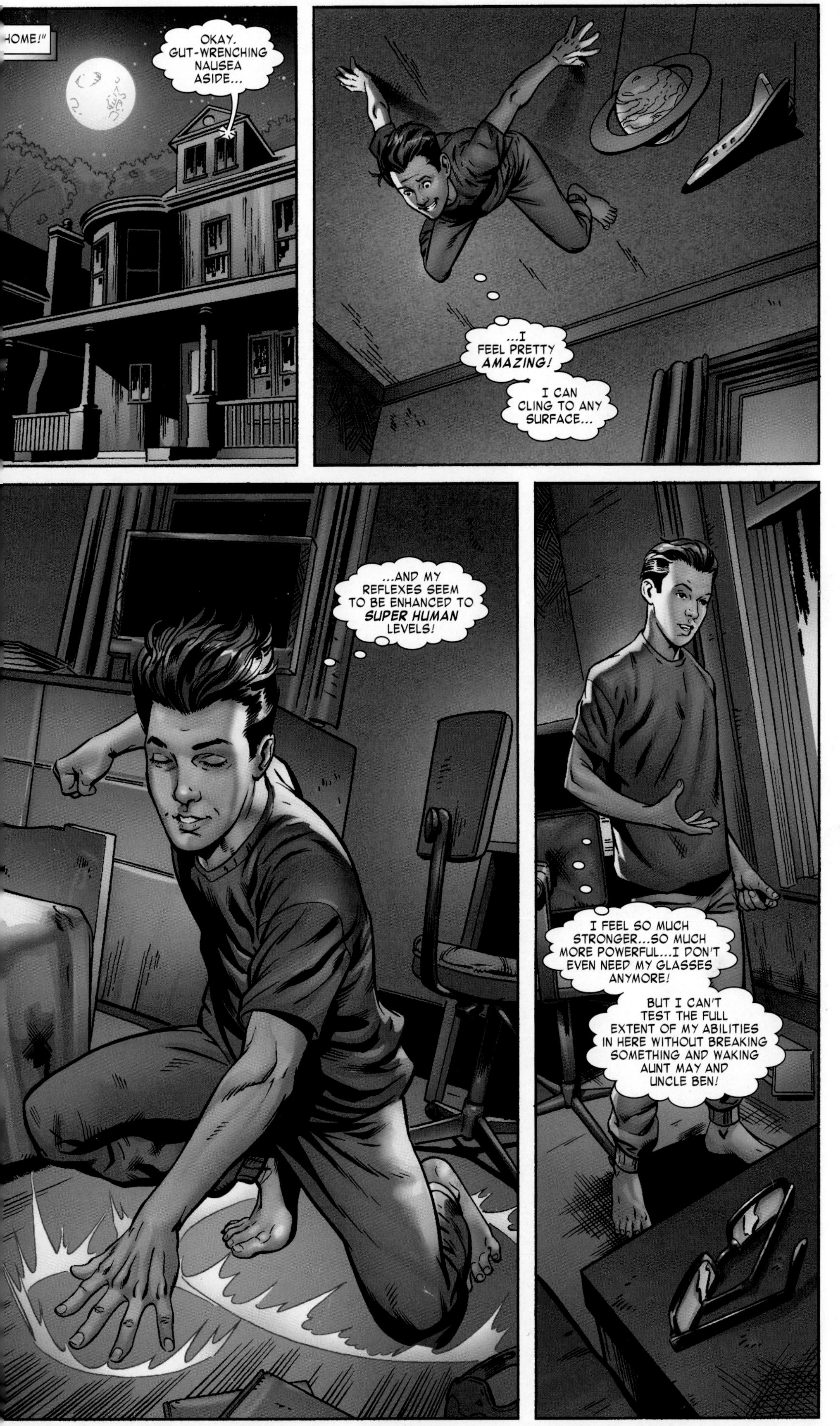
HOME!"
OKAY. GUT-WRENCHING NAUSEA ASIDE...
...I FEEL PRETTY AMAZING!
I CAN CLING TO ANY SURFACE...
...AND MY REFLEXES SEEM TO BE ENHANCED TO SUPER HUMAN LEVELS!
I FEEL SO MUCH STRONGER...SO MUCH MORE POWERFUL...I DON'T EVEN NEED MY GLASSES ANYMORE!
BUT I CAN'T TEST THE FULL EXTENT OF MY ABILITIES IN HERE WITHOUT BREAKING SOMETHING AND WAKING AUNT MAY AND UNCLE BEN!

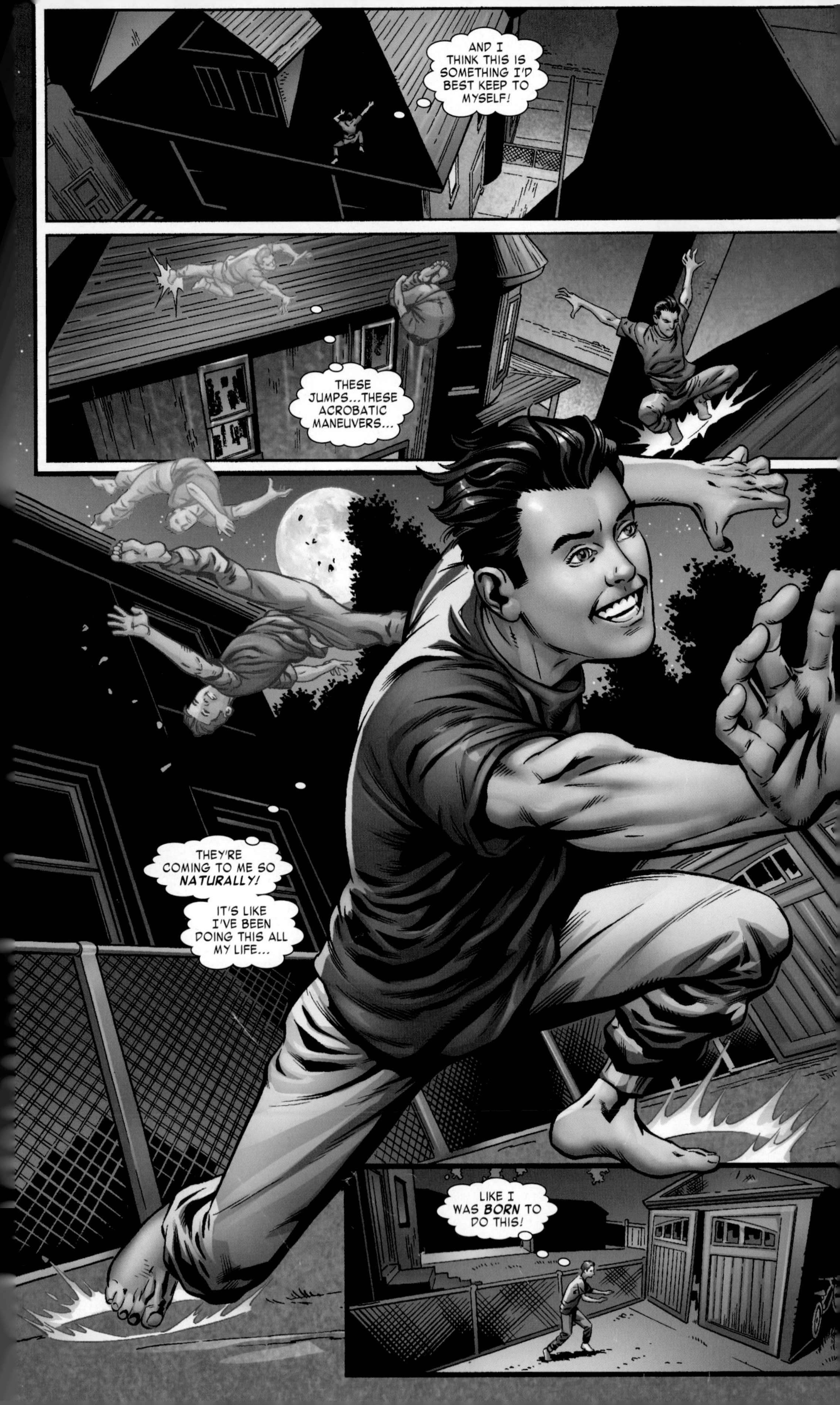
AND I THINK THIS IS SOMETHING I'D BEST KEEP TO MYSELF!
THESE JUMPS...THESE ACROBATIC MANEUVERS...
THEY'RE COMING TO ME SO **NATURALLY!**
IT'S LIKE I'VE BEEN DOING THIS ALL MY LIFE...
LIKE I WAS **BORN** TO DO THIS!

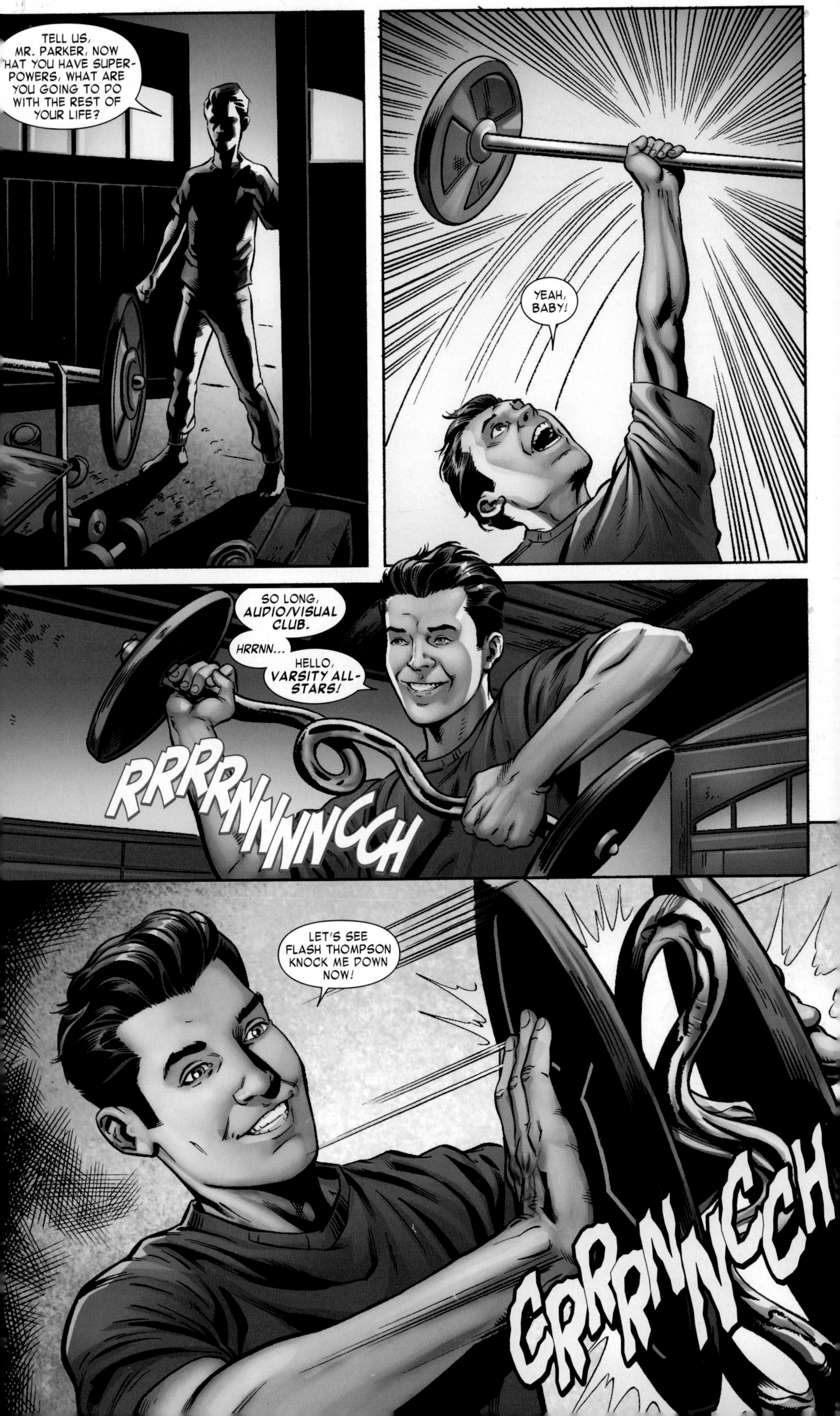

TELL US, MR. PARKER, NOW HAT YOU HAVE SUPER-POWERS, WHAT ARE YOU GOING TO DO WITH THE REST OF YOUR LIFE?
YEAH, BABY!
SO LONG, AUDIO/VISUAL CLUB.
HRRNN...
HELLO, VARSITY ALL-STARS!
RRRRNNNNNCCH
LET'S SEE FLASH THOMPSON KNOCK ME DOWN NOW!
CRRRNNCCH

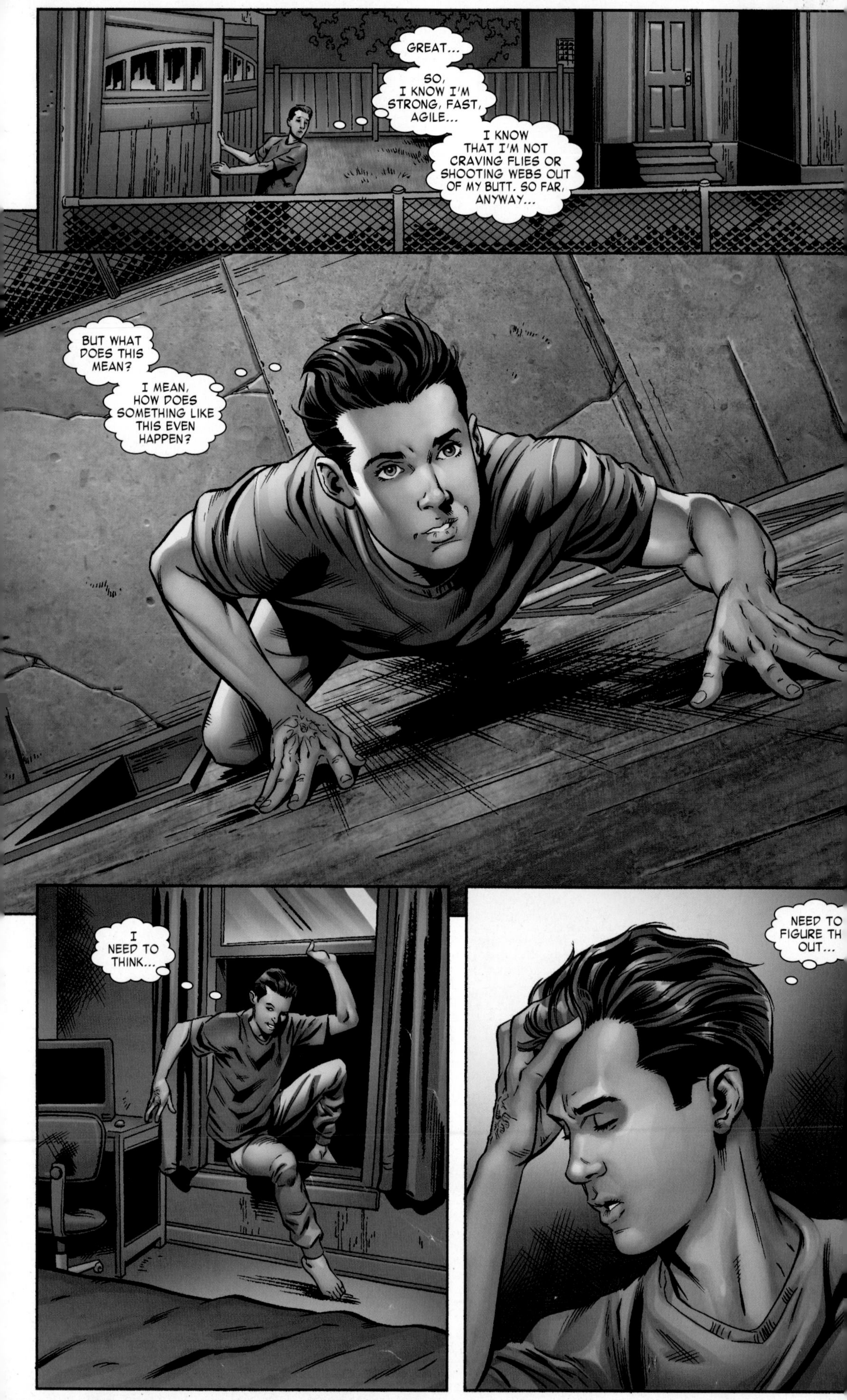
GREAT...
SO, I KNOW I'M STRONG, FAST, AGILE...
I KNOW THAT I'M NOT CRAVING FLIES OR SHOOTING WEBS OUT OF MY BUTT. SO FAR, ANYWAY...
BUT WHAT DOES THIS MEAN?
I MEAN, HOW DOES SOMETHING LIKE THIS EVEN HAPPEN?
I NEED TO THINK...

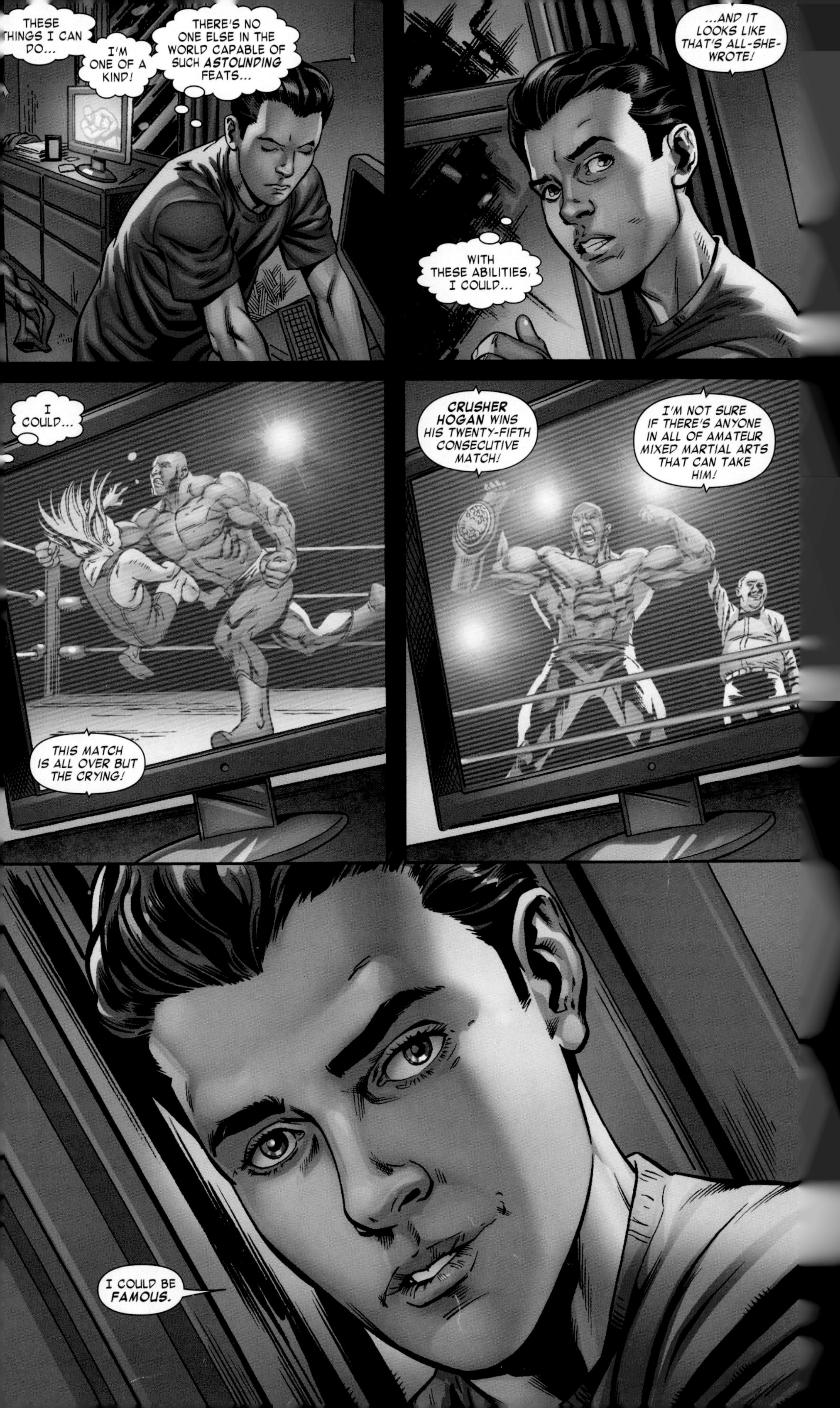
THESE THINGS I CAN DO...
I'M ONE OF A KIND!
THERE'S NO ONE ELSE IN THE WORLD CAPABLE OF SUCH ASTOUNDING FEATS...
...AND IT LOOKS LIKE THAT'S ALL-SHE-WROTE!
WITH THESE ABILITIES, I COULD...
I COULD...
THIS MATCH IS ALL OVER BUT THE CRYING!
CRUSHER HOGAN WINS HIS TWENTY-FIFTH CONSECUTIVE MATCH!
I'M NOT SURE IF THERE'S ANYONE IN ALL OF AMATEUR MIXED MARTIAL ARTS THAT CAN TAKE HIM!
I COULD BE FAMOUS.

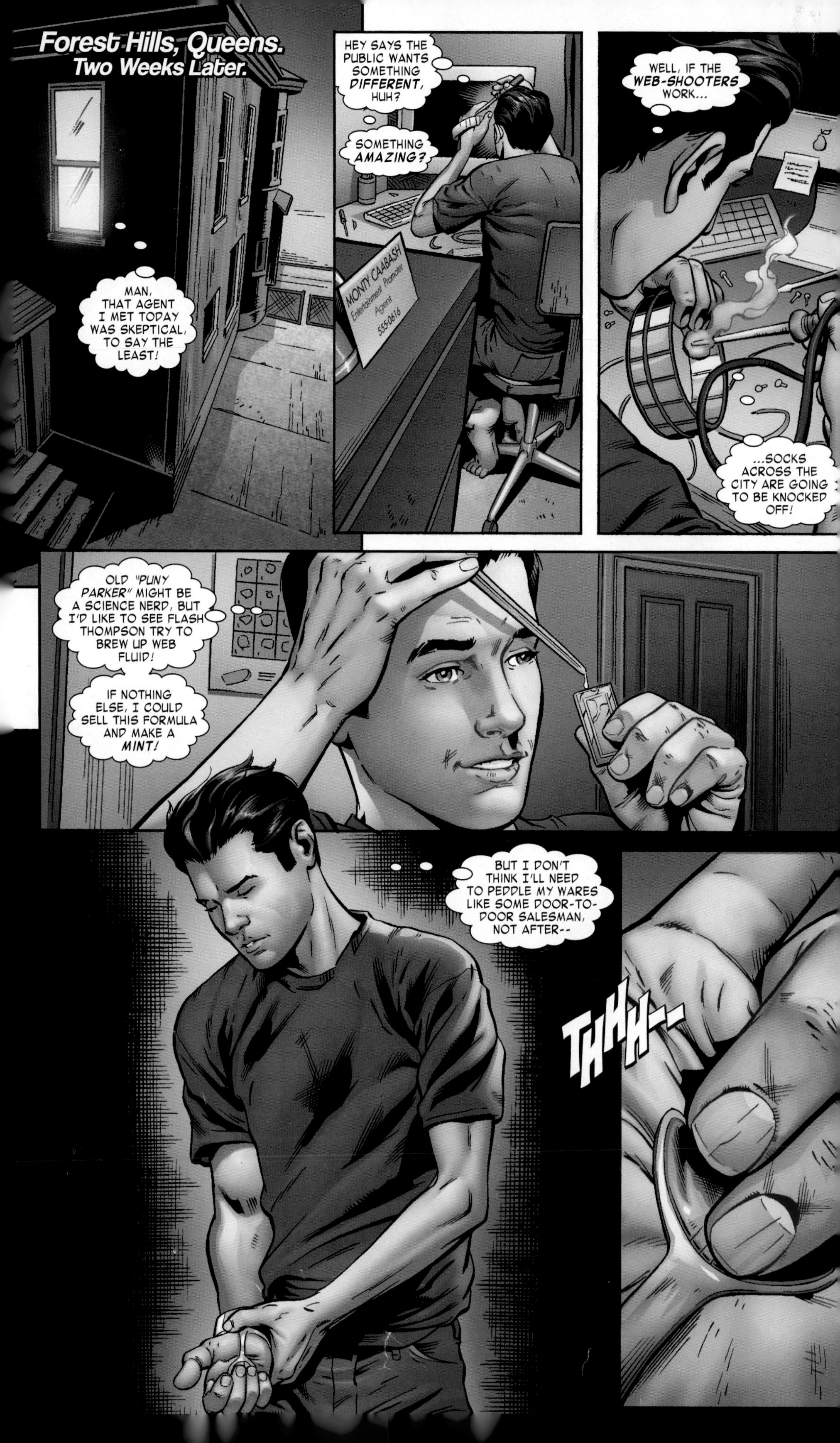
Forest Hills, Queens. Two Weeks Later.
MAN, THAT AGENT I MET TODAY WAS SKEPTICAL, TO SAY THE LEAST!
HEY SAYS THE PUBLIC WANTS SOMETHING DIFFERENT, HUH?
SOMETHING AMAZING?
MONTY CAABASH
Entertainment Promoter
Agent
555-0616
WELL, IF THE WEB-SHOOTERS WORK...
...SOCKS ACROSS THE CITY ARE GOING TO BE KNOCKED OFF!
OLD "PUNY PARKER" MIGHT BE A SCIENCE NERD, BUT I'D LIKE TO SEE FLASH THOMPSON TRY TO BREW UP WEB FLUID!
IF NOTHING ELSE, I COULD SELL THIS FORMULA AND MAKE A MINT!
BUT I DON'T THINK I'LL NEED TO PEDDLE MY WARES LIKE SOME DOOR-TO-DOOR SALESMAN, NOT AFTER--
THHH--

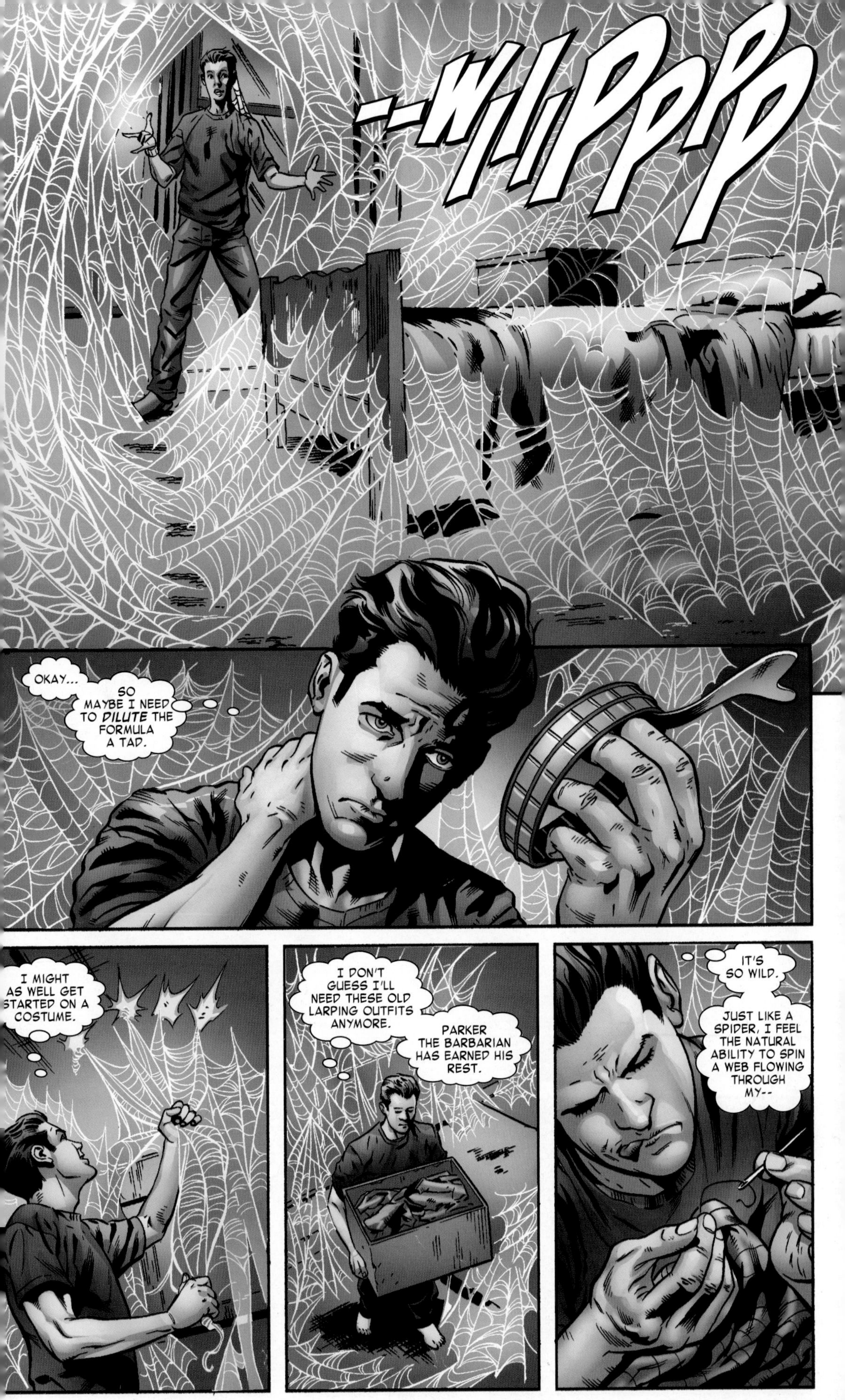
--WHIPPPP
OKAY...
SO MAYBE I NEED TO *DILUTE* THE FORMULA A TAD.
I MIGHT AS WELL GET STARTED ON A COSTUME.
I DON'T GUESS I'LL NEED THESE OLD LARPING OUTFITS ANYMORE.
PARKER THE BARBARIAN HAS EARNED HIS REST.
IT'S SO WILD.
JUST LIKE A SPIDER, I FEEL THE NATURAL ABILITY TO SPIN A WEB FLOWING THROUGH MY--

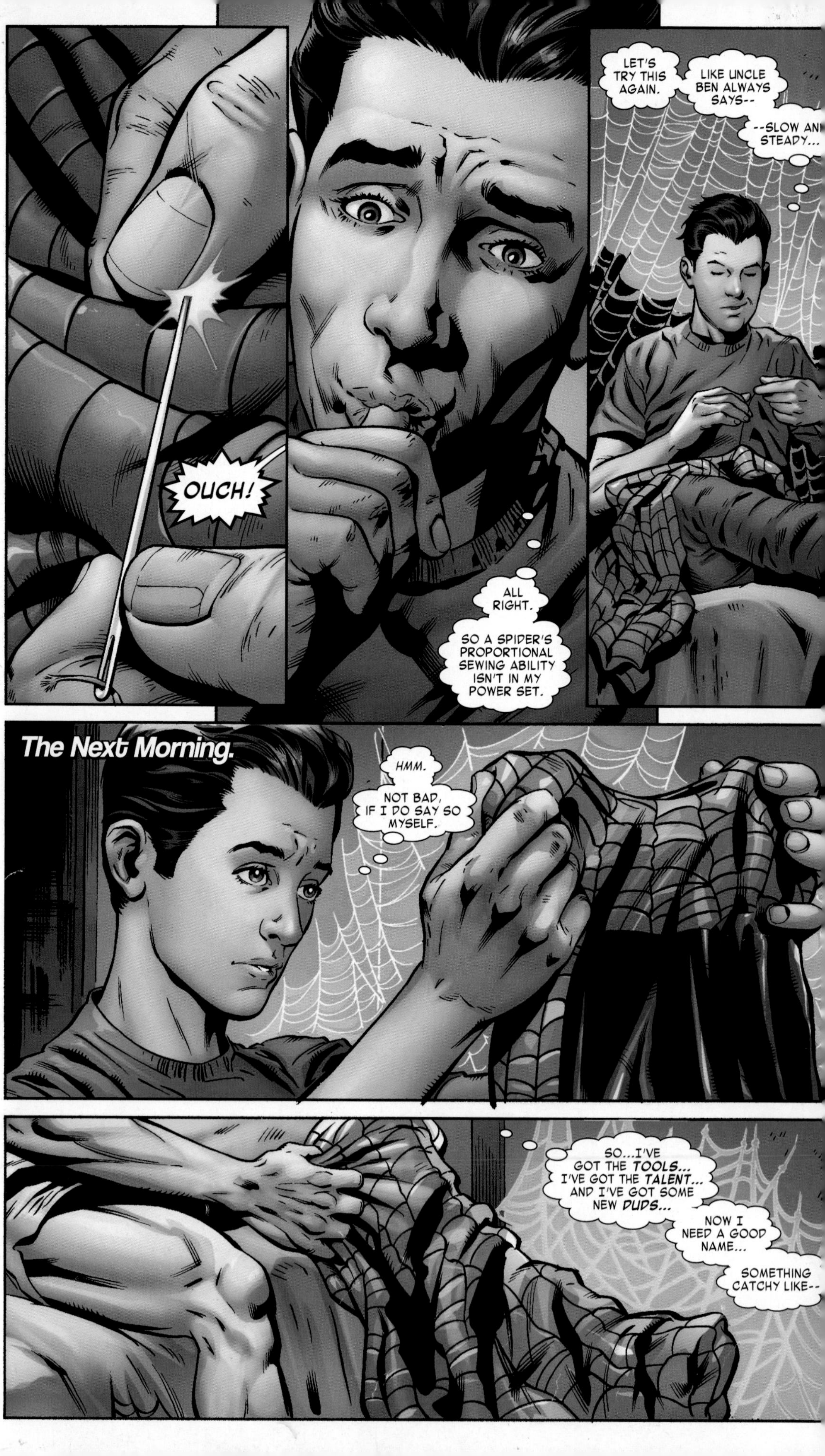
OUCH!
ALL RIGHT.
SO A SPIDER'S PROPORTIONAL SEWING ABILITY ISN'T IN MY POWER SET.
LET'S TRY THIS AGAIN.
LIKE UNCLE BEN ALWAYS SAYS--
--SLOW AN STEADY...
The Next Morning.
HMM.
NOT BAD, IF I DO SAY SO MYSELF.
SO...I'VE GOT THE TOOLS... I'VE GOT THE TALENT... AND I'VE GOT SOME NEW DUDS...
NOW I NEED A GOOD NAME...
SOMETHING CATCHY LIKE--

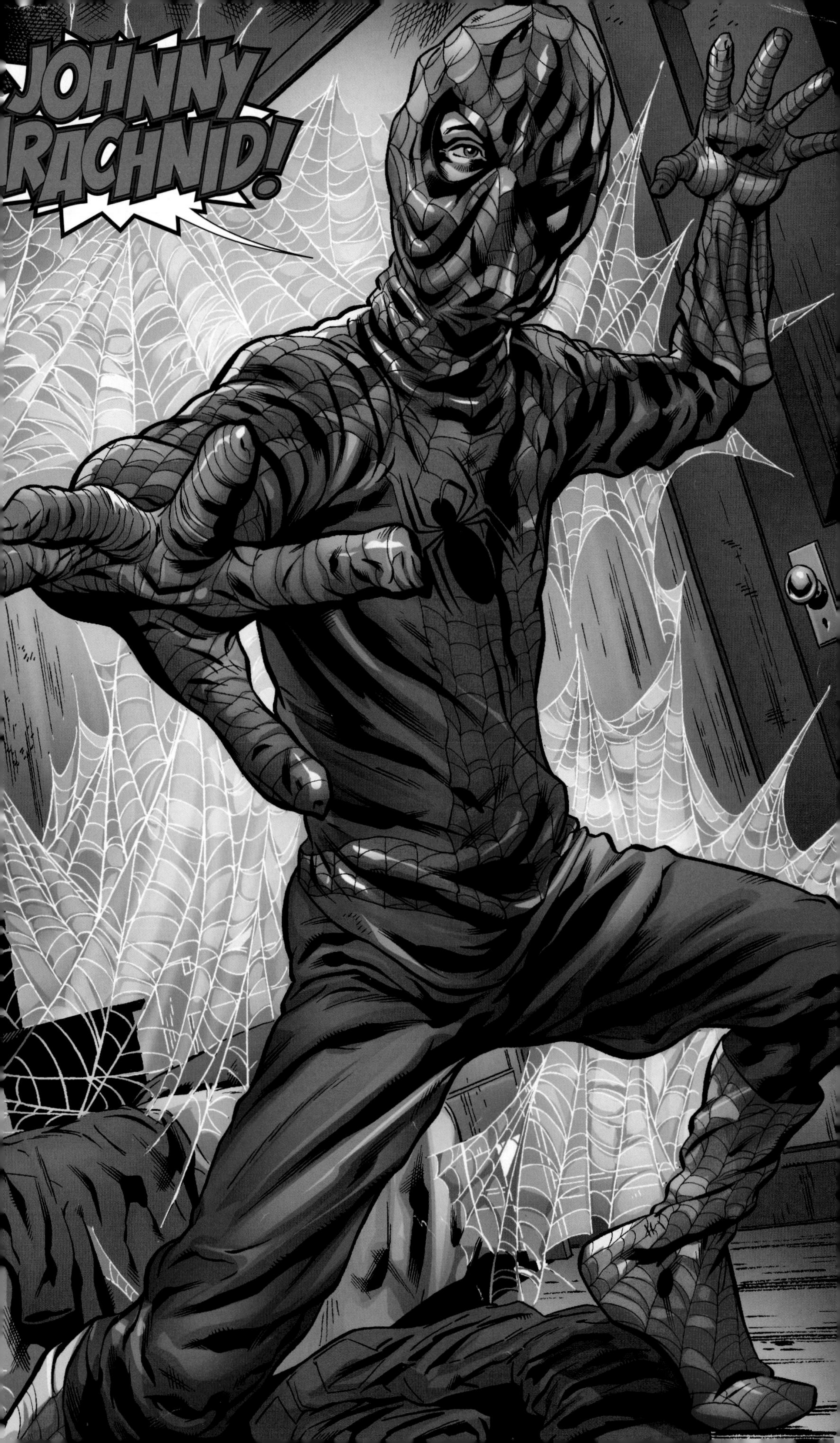
JOHNNY
RACHNID!

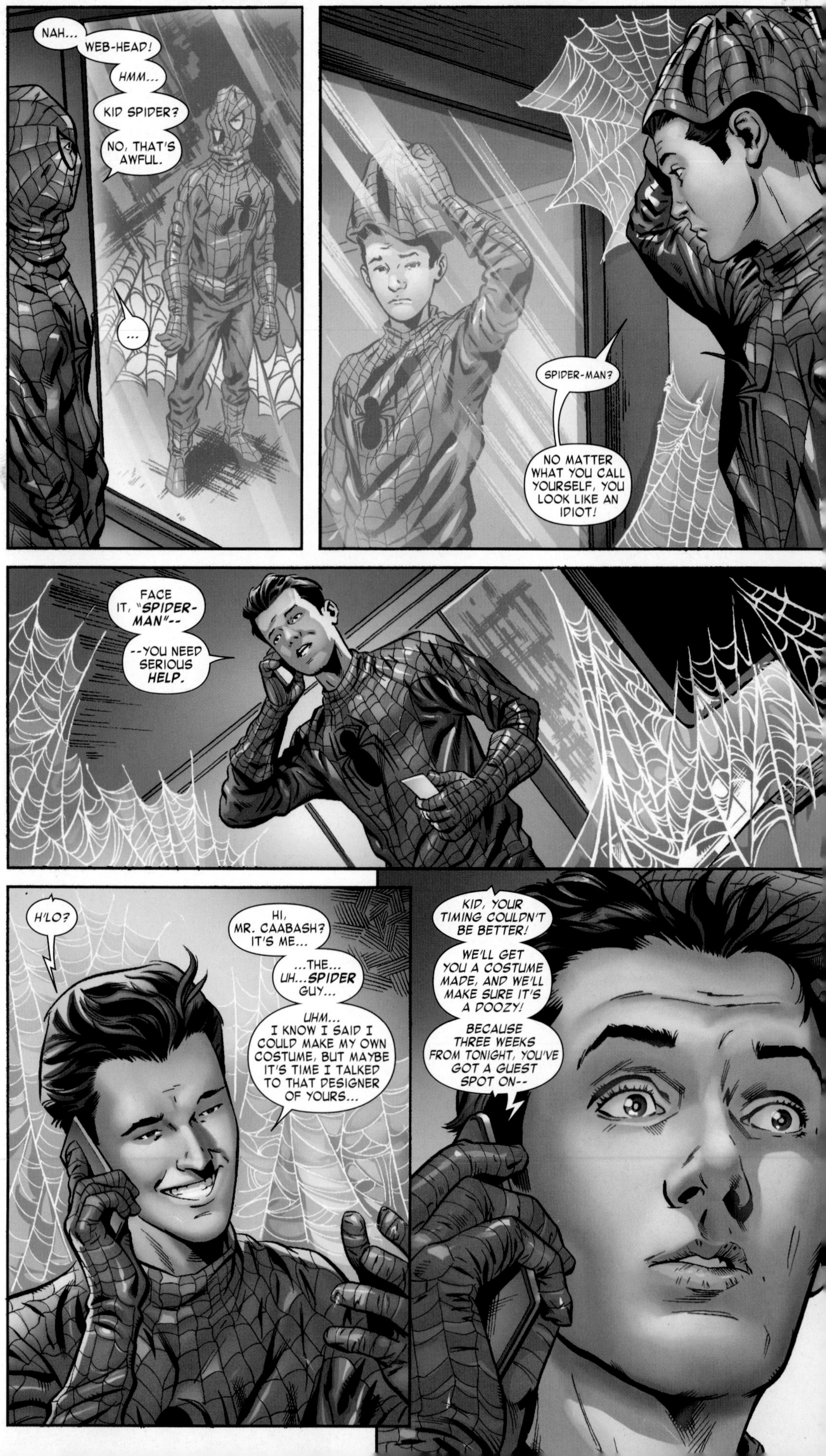
NAH...
WEB-HEAD!
HMM...
KID SPIDER?
NO, THAT'S AWFUL.
...
SPIDER-MAN?
NO MATTER WHAT YOU CALL YOURSELF, YOU LOOK LIKE AN IDIOT!
FACE IT, "SPIDER-MAN"--
--YOU NEED SERIOUS HELP.
H'LO?
HI, MR. CAABASH? IT'S ME...
...THE... UH...SPIDER GUY...
UHM... I KNOW I SAID I COULD MAKE MY OWN COSTUME, BUT MAYBE IT'S TIME I TALKED TO THAT DESIGNER OF YOURS...
KID, YOUR TIMING COULDN'T BE BETTER!
WE'LL GET YOU A COSTUME MADE, AND WE'LL MAKE SURE IT'S A DOOZY!
BECAUSE THREE WEEKS FROM TONIGHT, YOU'VE GOT A GUEST SPOT ON--

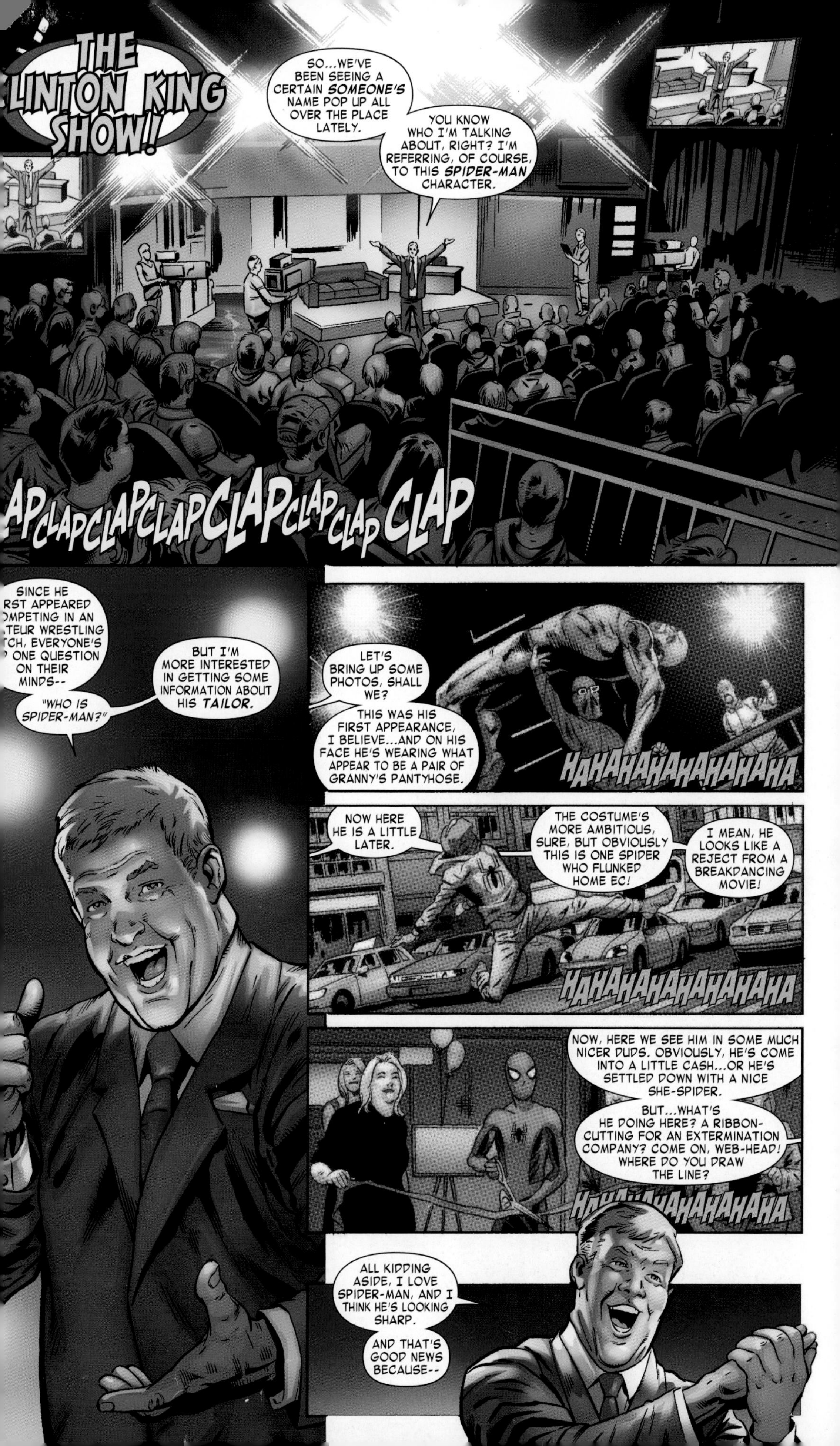
THE LINTON KING SHOW!!
SO...WE'VE BEEN SEEING A CERTAIN SOMEONE'S NAME POP UP ALL OVER THE PLACE LATELY.
YOU KNOW WHO I'M TALKING ABOUT, RIGHT? I'M REFERRING, OF COURSE, TO THIS SPIDER-MAN CHARACTER.
AP CLAP CLAP CLAP CLAP CLAP CLAP CLAP
SINCE HE RST APPEARED OMPETING IN AN TEUR WRESTLING TCH, EVERYONE'S ONE QUESTION ON THEIR MINDS--
"WHO IS SPIDER-MAN?"
BUT I'M MORE INTERESTED IN GETTING SOME INFORMATION ABOUT HIS TAILOR.
LET'S BRING UP SOME PHOTOS, SHALL WE?
THIS WAS HIS FIRST APPEARANCE, I BELIEVE...AND ON HIS FACE HE'S WEARING WHAT APPEAR TO BE A PAIR OF GRANNY'S PANTYHOSE.
HAHAHAHAHAHAHAHAHA
NOW HERE HE IS A LITTLE LATER.
THE COSTUME'S MORE AMBITIOUS, SURE, BUT OBVIOUSLY THIS IS ONE SPIDER WHO FLUNKED HOME EC!
I MEAN, HE LOOKS LIKE A REJECT FROM A BREAKDANCING MOVIE!
HAHAHAHAHAHAHAHAHA
NOW, HERE WE SEE HIM IN SOME MUCH NICER DUDS. OBVIOUSLY, HE'S COME INTO A LITTLE CASH...OR HE'S SETTLED DOWN WITH A NICE SHE-SPIDER.
BUT...WHAT'S HE DOING HERE? A RIBBON-CUTTING FOR AN EXTERMINATION COMPANY? COME ON, WEB-HEAD! WHERE DO YOU DRAW THE LINE?
HAHAHAHAHAHAHAHA
ALL KIDDING ASIDE, I LOVE SPIDER-MAN, AND I THINK HE'S LOOKING SHARP.
AND THAT'S GOOD NEWS BECAUSE--

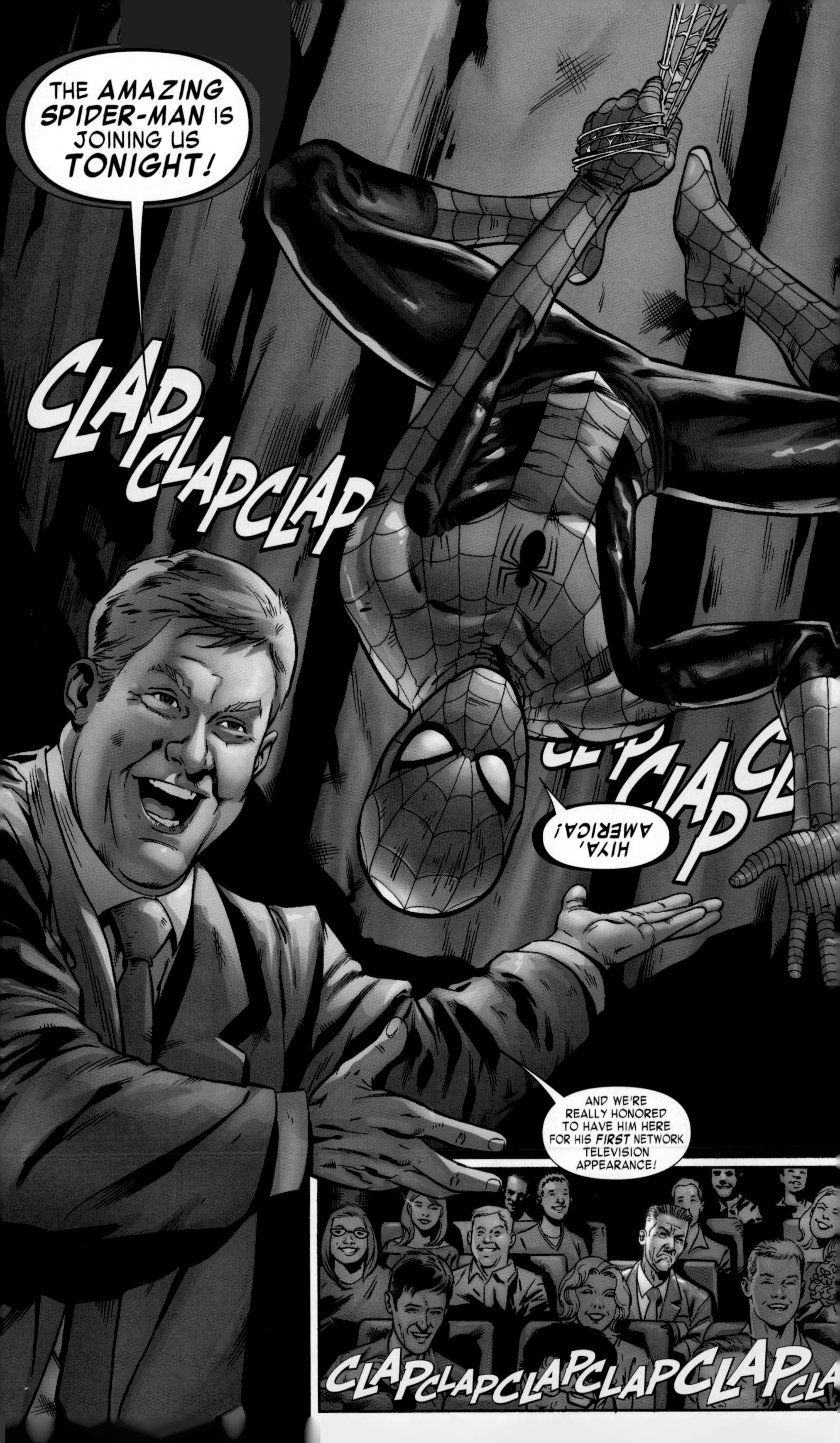
THE AMAZING SPIDER-MAN IS JOINING US TONIGHT!
CLAPCLAPCLAPCLAP
CLAPCLAP
HIYA, AMERICA!
AND WE'RE REALLY HONORED TO HAVE HIM HERE FOR HIS FIRST NETWORK TELEVISION APPEARANCE!
CLAPCLAPCLAPCLAPCLAP

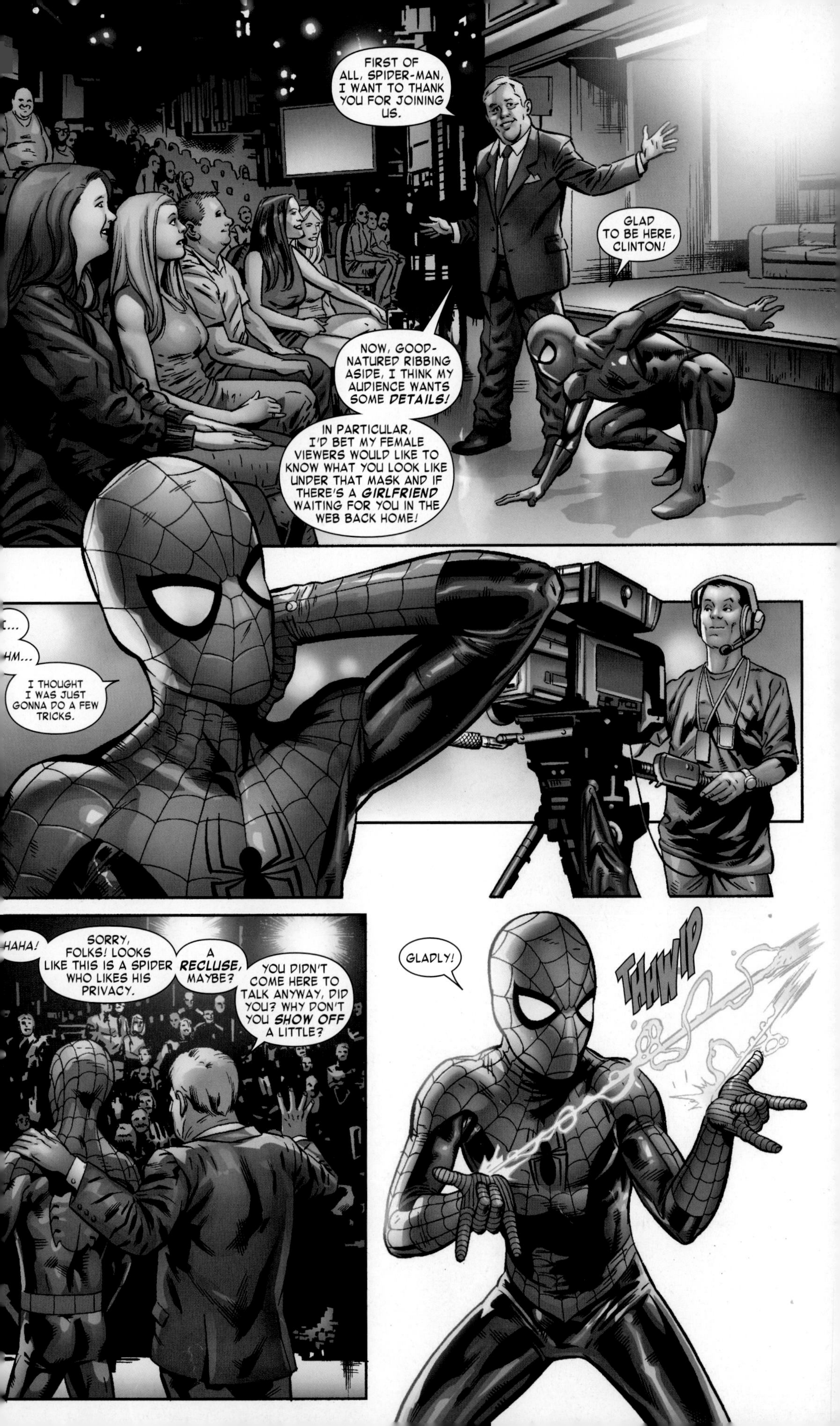
FIRST OF ALL, SPIDER-MAN, I WANT TO THANK YOU FOR JOINING US.
GLAD TO BE HERE, CLINTON!
NOW, GOOD-NATURED RIBBING ASIDE, I THINK MY AUDIENCE WANTS SOME *DETAILS!*
IN PARTICULAR, I'D BET MY FEMALE VIEWERS WOULD LIKE TO KNOW WHAT YOU LOOK LIKE UNDER THAT MASK AND IF THERE'S A *GIRLFRIEND* WAITING FOR YOU IN THE WEB BACK HOME!
HM...
I THOUGHT I WAS JUST GONNA DO A FEW TRICKS.
HAHA!
SORRY, FOLKS! LOOKS LIKE THIS IS A SPIDER WHO LIKES HIS PRIVACY.
A *RECLUSE,* MAYBE?
YOU DIDN'T COME HERE TO TALK ANYWAY, DID YOU? WHY DON'T YOU *SHOW OFF* A LITTLE?
GLADLY!
THWIP

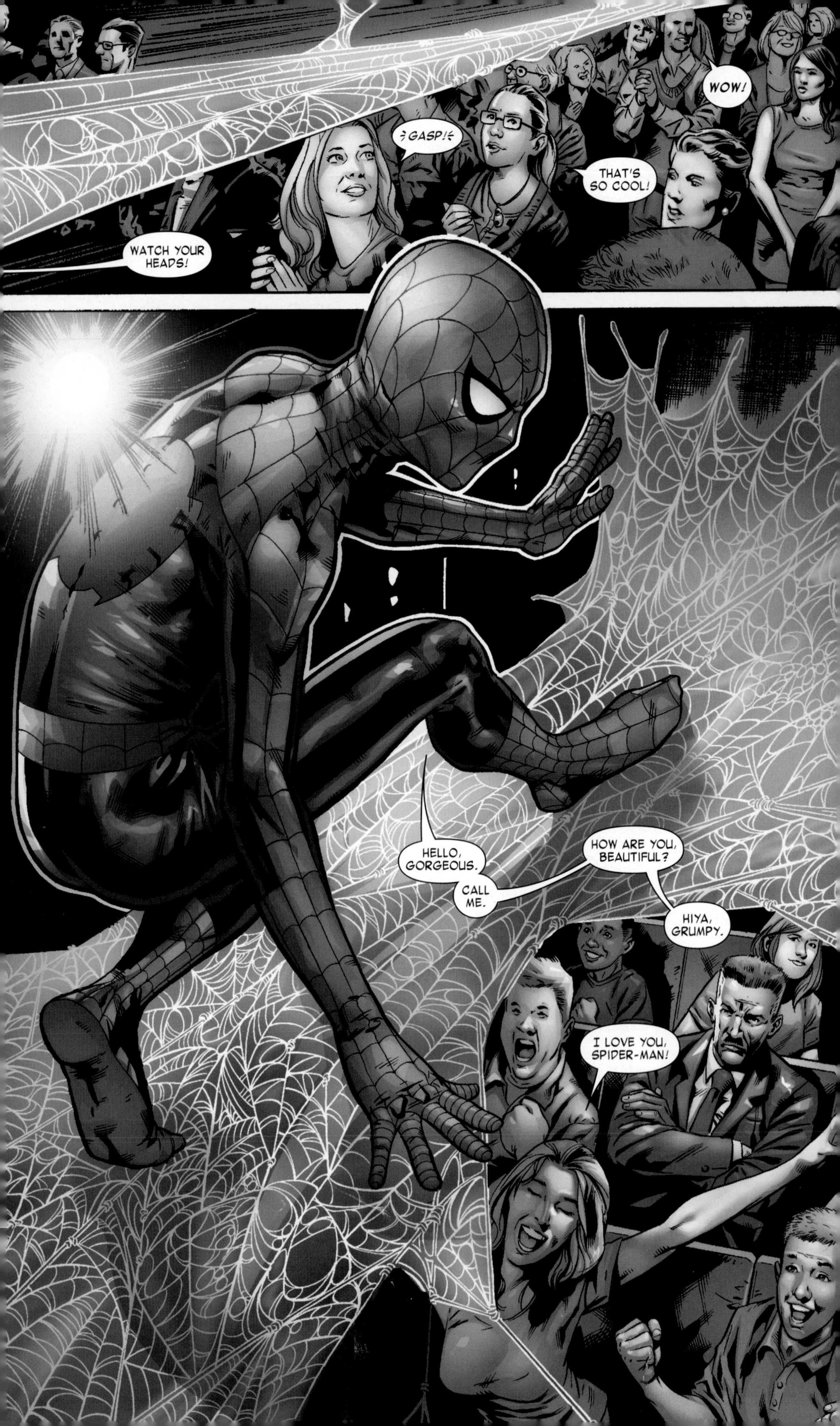
WATCH YOUR HEADS!
GASP!
THAT'S SO COOL!
WOW!
HELLO, GORGEOUS.
CALL ME.
HOW ARE YOU, BEAUTIFUL?
HIYA, GRUMPY.
I LOVE YOU, SPIDER-MAN!

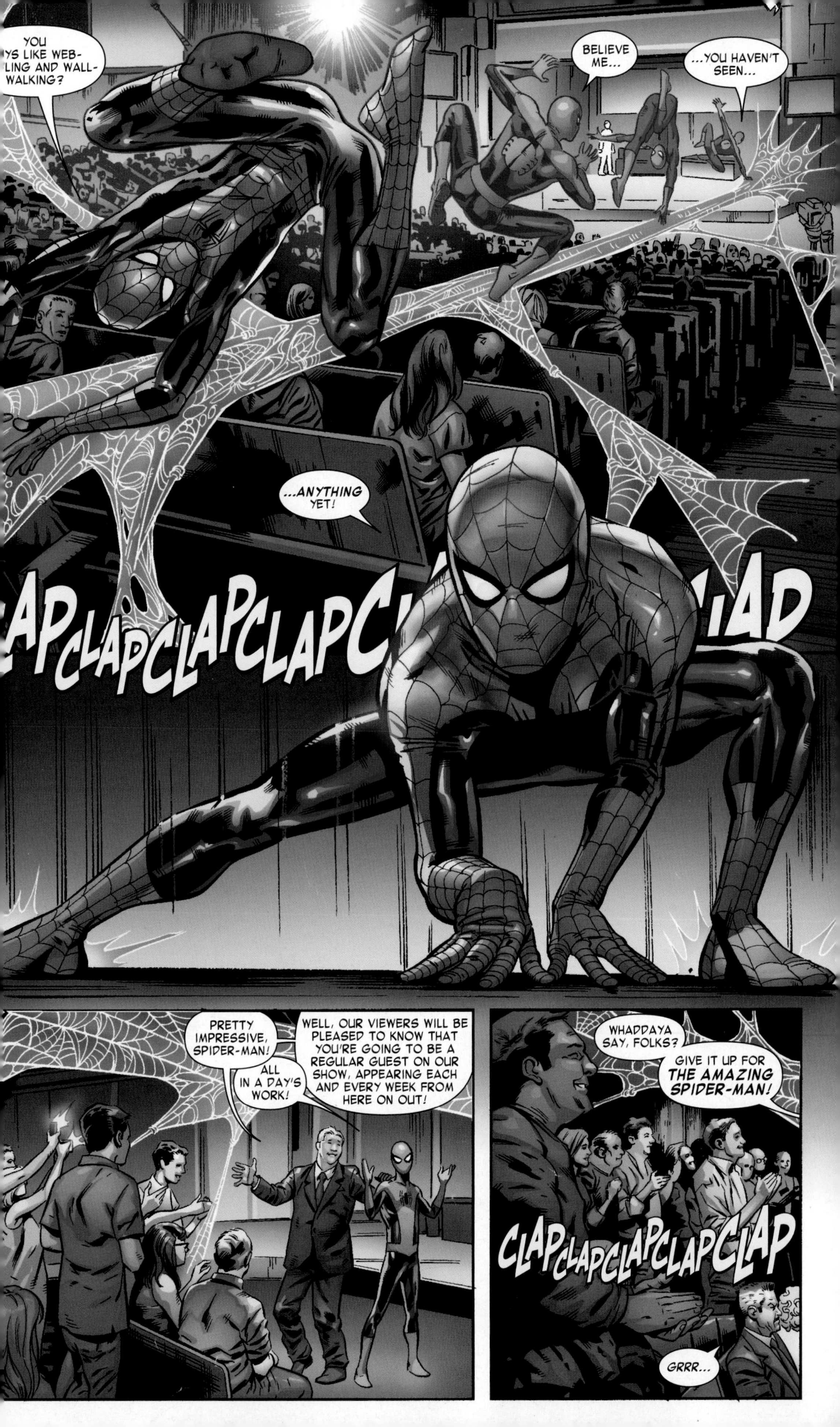
YOU
YS LIKE WEB-
LING AND WALL-
WALKING?
BELIEVE
ME...
...YOU HAVEN'T
SEEN...
...ANYTHING
YET!
CLAPCLAPCLAPCLAPCLAP
PRETTY
IMPRESSIVE,
SPIDER-MAN!
ALL
IN A DAY'S
WORK!
WELL, OUR VIEWERS WILL BE
PLEASED TO KNOW THAT
YOU'RE GOING TO BE A
REGULAR GUEST ON OUR
SHOW, APPEARING EACH
AND EVERY WEEK FROM
HERE ON OUT!
WHADDAYA
SAY, FOLKS?
GIVE IT UP FOR
THE AMAZING
SPIDER-MAN!
CLAPCLAPCLAPCLAPCLAP
GRRR...

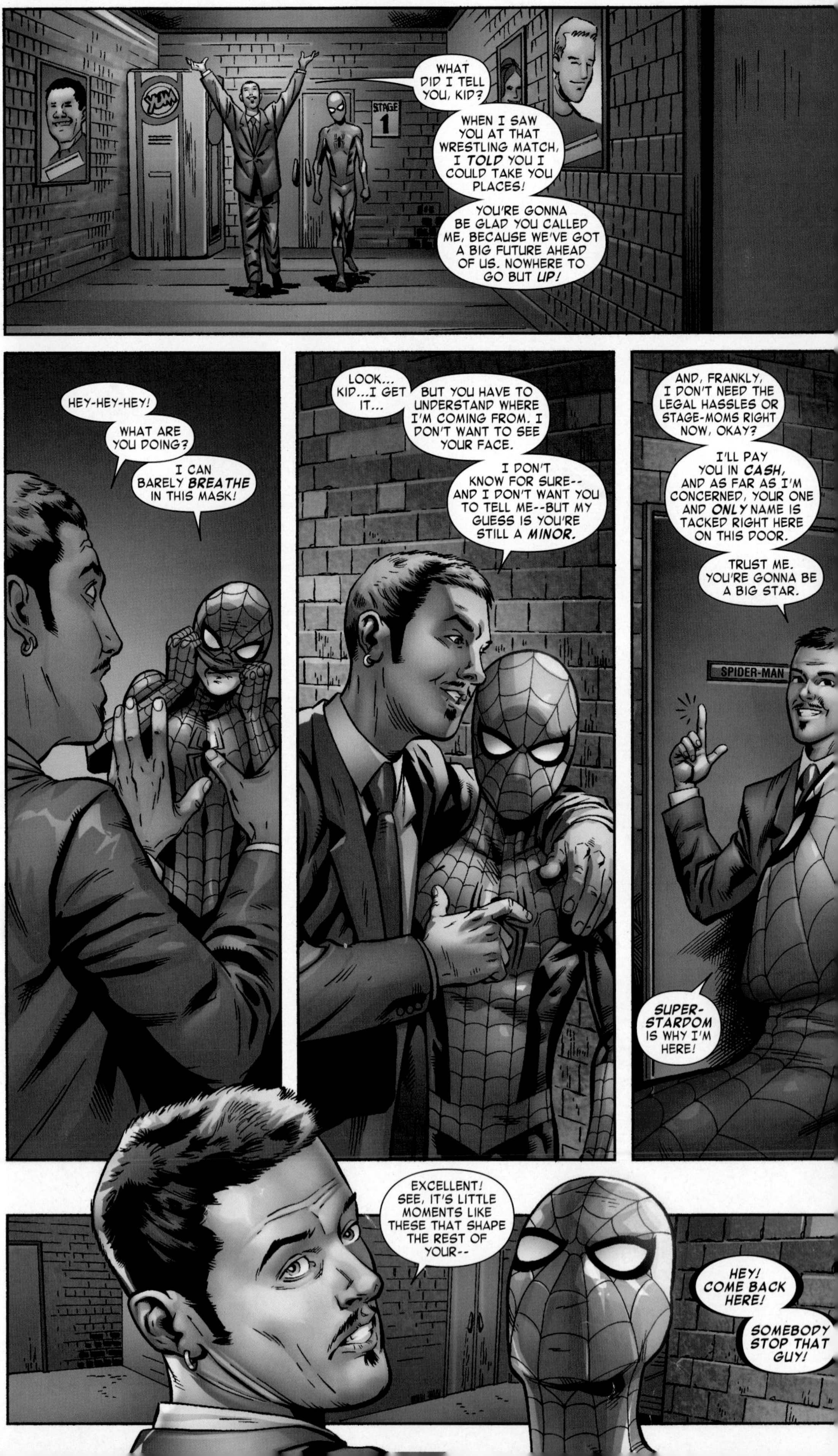

STAGE 1
WHAT DID I TELL YOU, KID?
WHEN I SAW YOU AT THAT WRESTLING MATCH, I *TOLD* YOU I COULD TAKE YOU PLACES!
YOU'RE GONNA BE GLAD YOU CALLED ME, BECAUSE WE'VE GOT A BIG FUTURE AHEAD OF US. NOWHERE TO GO BUT *UP!*
HEY-HEY-HEY!
WHAT ARE YOU DOING?
I CAN BARELY *BREATHE* IN THIS MASK!
LOOK... KID...I GET IT...
BUT YOU HAVE TO UNDERSTAND WHERE I'M COMING FROM. I DON'T WANT TO SEE YOUR FACE.
I DON'T KNOW FOR SURE--AND I DON'T WANT YOU TO TELL ME--BUT MY GUESS IS YOU'RE STILL A *MINOR.*
AND, FRANKLY, I DON'T NEED THE LEGAL HASSLES OR STAGE-MOMS RIGHT NOW, OKAY?
I'LL PAY YOU IN *CASH,* AND AS FAR AS I'M CONCERNED, YOUR ONE AND *ONLY* NAME IS TACKED RIGHT HERE ON THIS DOOR.
TRUST ME. YOU'RE GONNA BE A BIG STAR.
SPIDER-MAN
SUPER-STARDOM IS WHY I'M HERE!
EXCELLENT! SEE, IT'S LITTLE MOMENTS LIKE THESE THAT SHAPE THE REST OF YOUR--
HEY! COME BACK HERE!
SOMEBODY STOP THAT GUY!

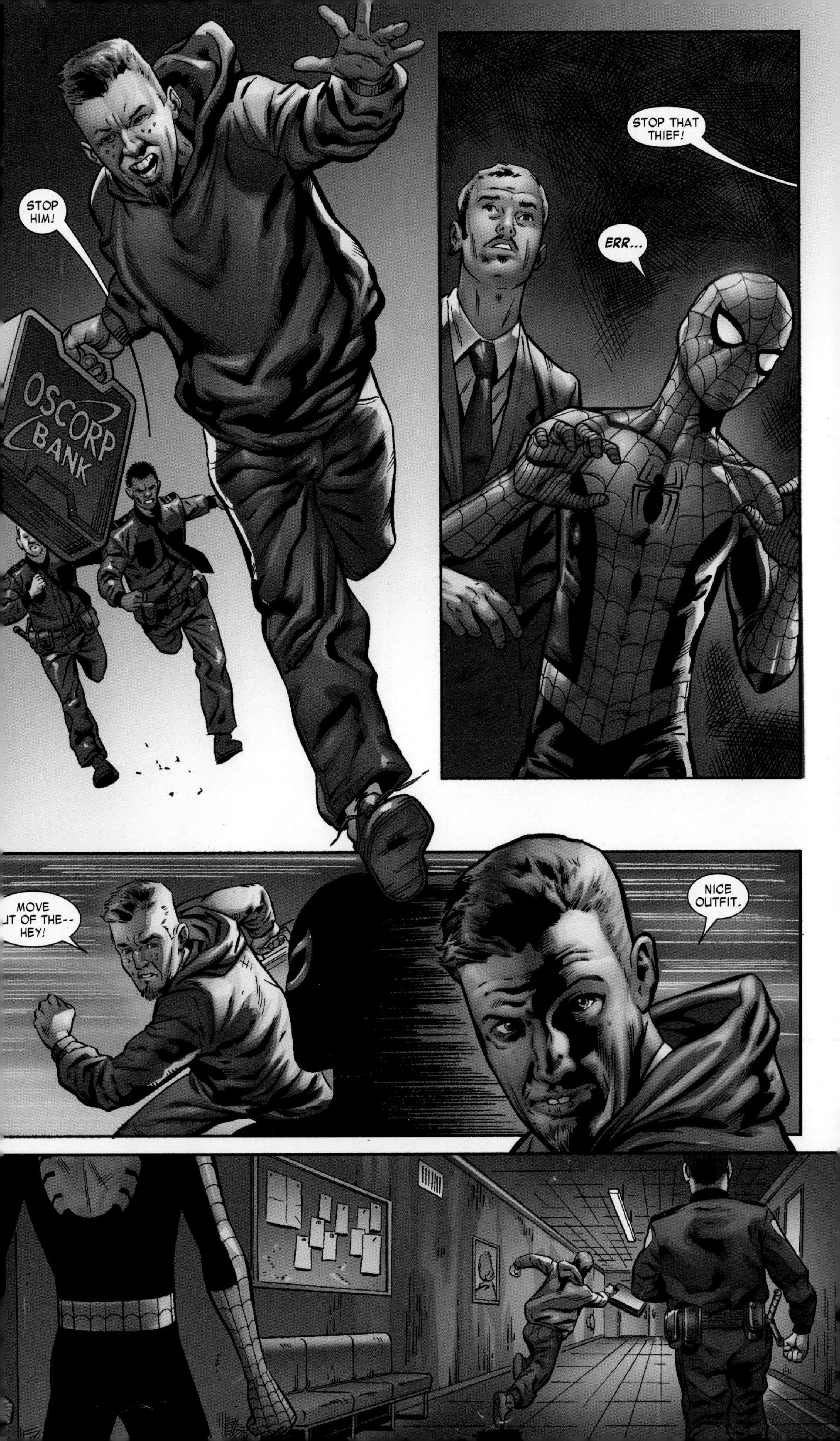
STOP HIM!
STOP THAT THIEF!
ERR...
OSCORP BANK
MOVE
IT OF THE--
HEY!
NICE OUTFIT.

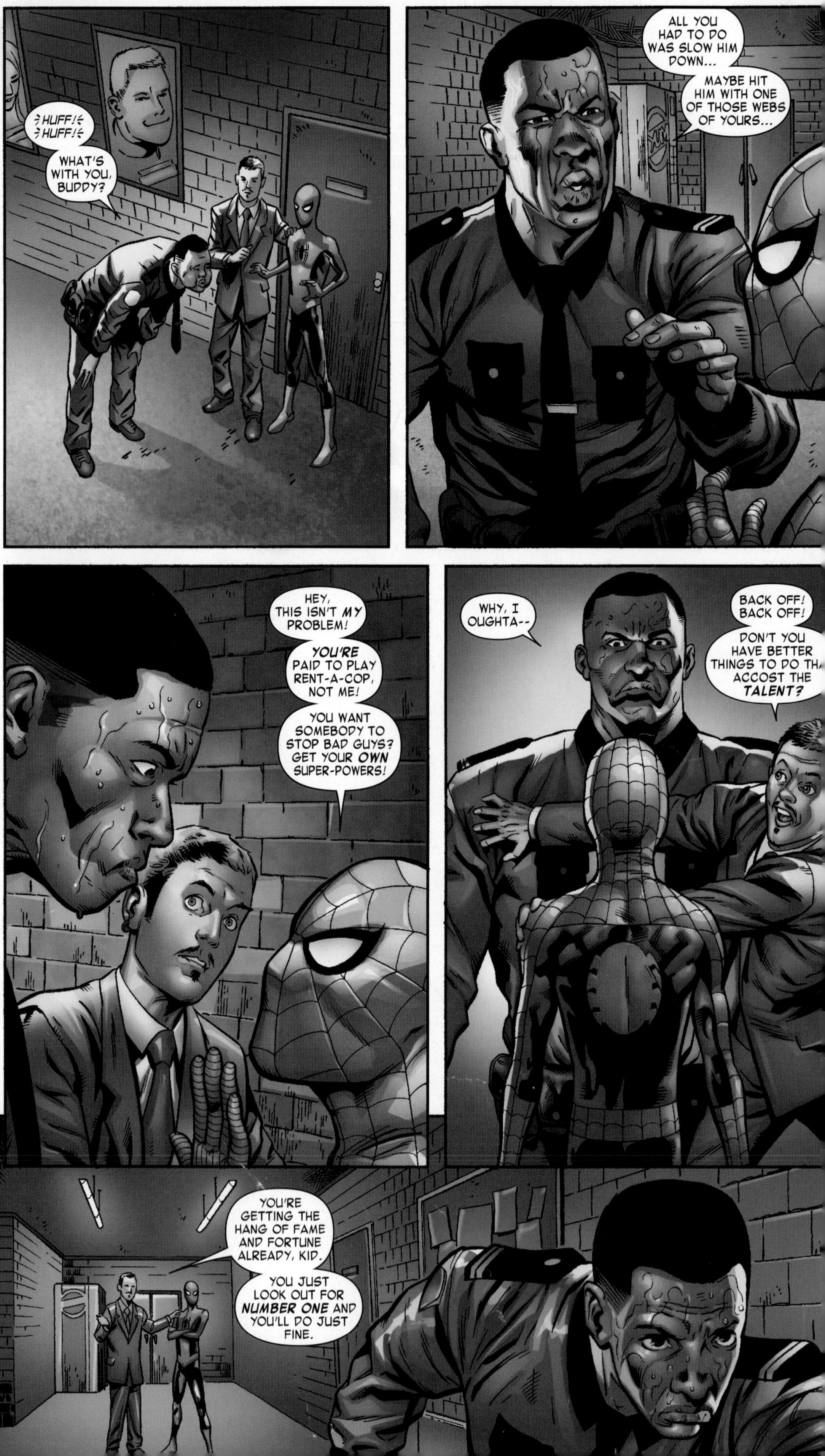
HUFF! HUFF!
WHAT'S WITH YOU, BUDDY?
ALL YOU HAD TO DO WAS SLOW HIM DOWN...
MAYBE HIT HIM WITH ONE OF THOSE WEBS OF YOURS...
HEY, THIS ISN'T MY PROBLEM!
YOU'RE PAID TO PLAY RENT-A-COP, NOT ME!
YOU WANT SOMEBODY TO STOP BAD GUYS? GET YOUR OWN SUPER-POWERS!
WHY, I OUGHTA--
BACK OFF! BACK OFF!
DON'T YOU HAVE BETTER THINGS TO DO TH ACCOST THE TALENT?
YOU'RE GETTING THE HANG OF FAME AND FORTUNE ALREADY, KID.
YOU JUST LOOK OUT FOR NUMBER ONE AND YOU'LL DO JUST FINE.

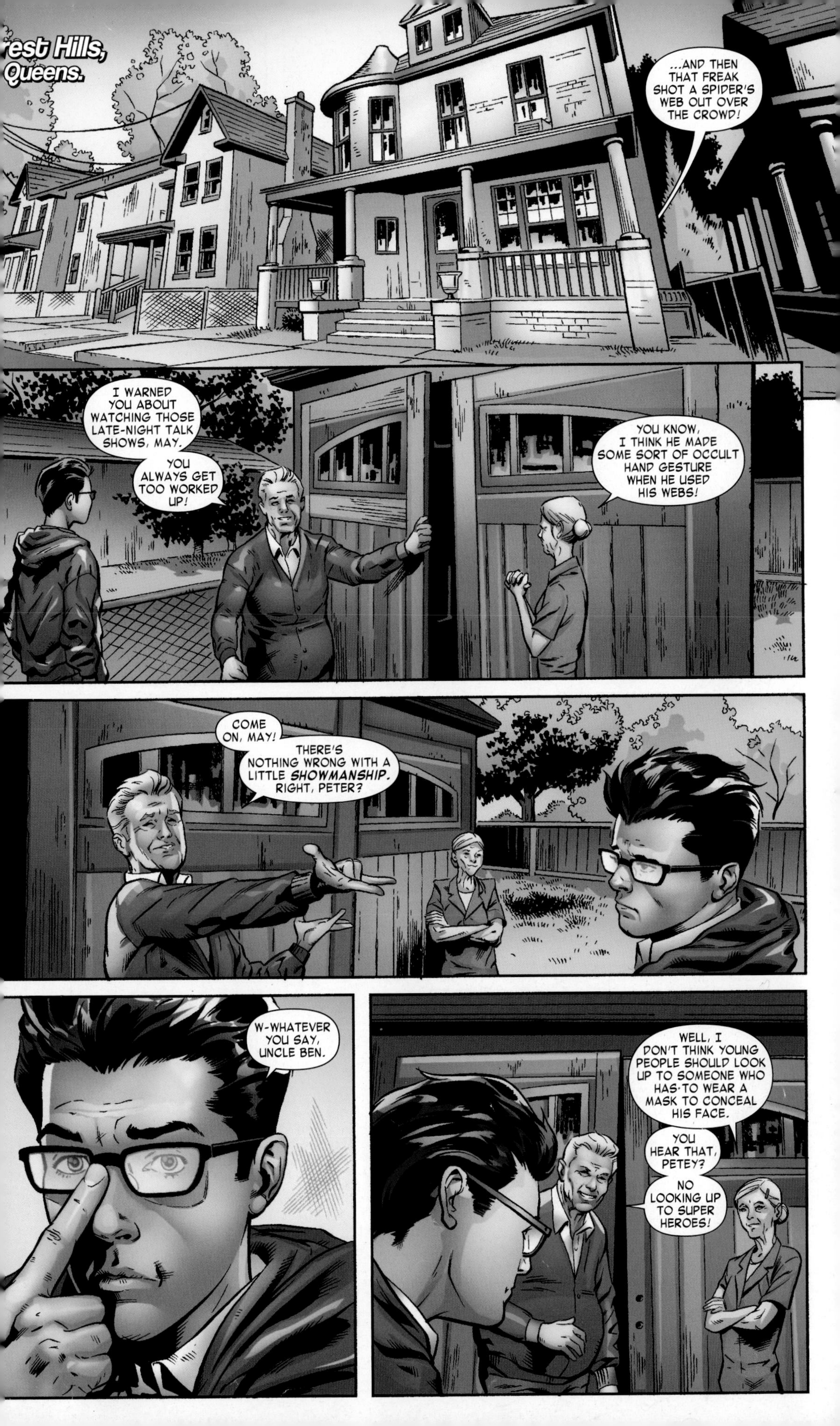
rest Hills, Queens.
...AND THEN THAT FREAK SHOT A SPIDER'S WEB OUT OVER THE CROWD!
I WARNED YOU ABOUT WATCHING THOSE LATE-NIGHT TALK SHOWS, MAY.
YOU ALWAYS GET TOO WORKED UP!
YOU KNOW, I THINK HE MADE SOME SORT OF OCCULT HAND GESTURE WHEN HE USED HIS WEBS!
COME ON, MAY!
THERE'S NOTHING WRONG WITH A LITTLE SHOWMANSHIP. RIGHT, PETER?
W-WHATEVER YOU SAY, UNCLE BEN.
WELL, I DON'T THINK YOUNG PEOPLE SHOULD LOOK UP TO SOMEONE WHO HAS TO WEAR A MASK TO CONCEAL HIS FACE.
YOU HEAR THAT, PETEY?
NO LOOKING UP TO SUPER HEROES!

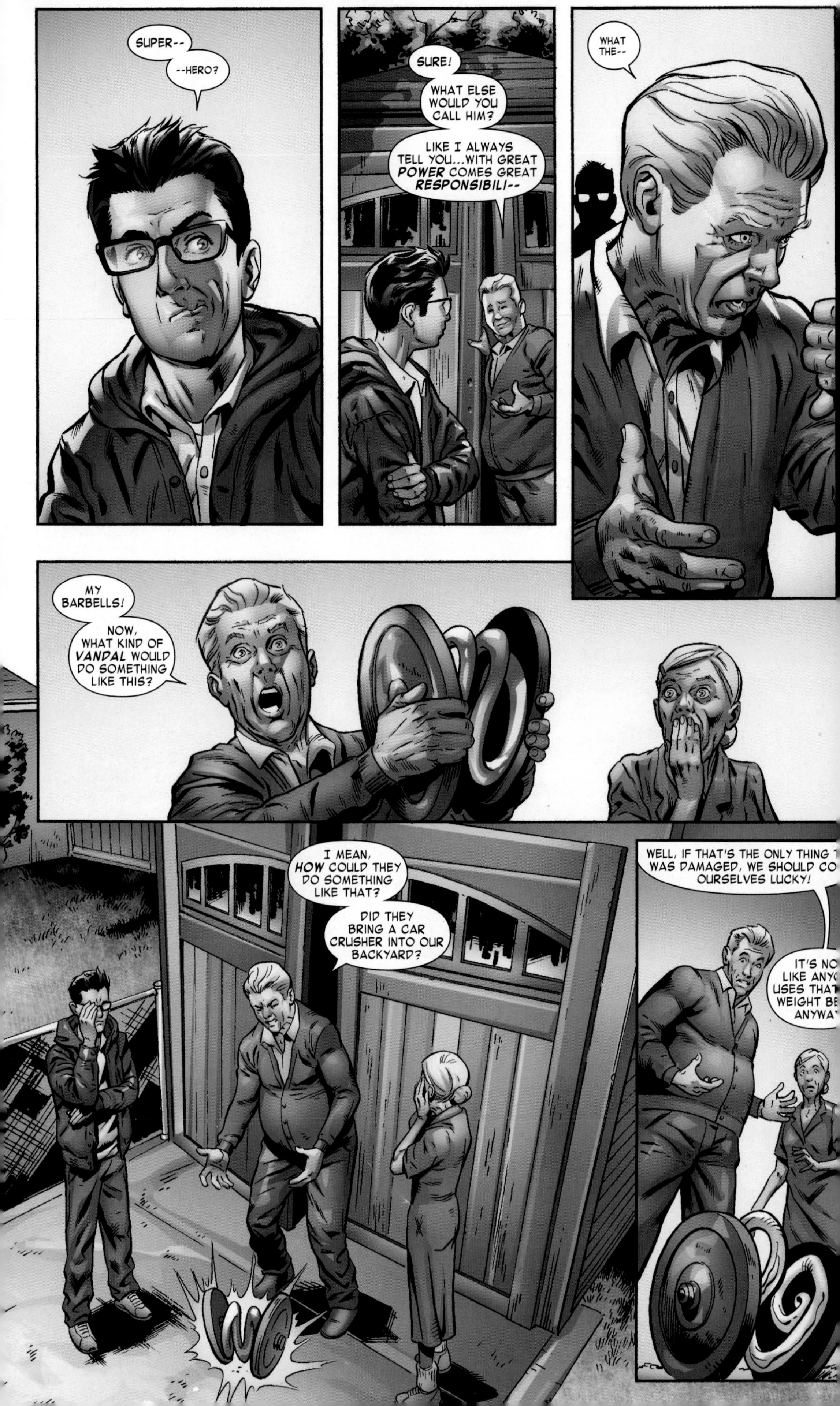
SUPER--
--HERO?
SURE!
WHAT ELSE WOULD YOU CALL HIM?
LIKE I ALWAYS TELL YOU...WITH GREAT POWER COMES GREAT RESPONSIBILI--
WHAT THE--
MY BARBELLS!
NOW, WHAT KIND OF VANDAL WOULD DO SOMETHING LIKE THIS?
I MEAN, HOW COULD THEY DO SOMETHING LIKE THAT?
DID THEY BRING A CAR CRUSHER INTO OUR BACKYARD?
WELL, IF THAT'S THE ONLY THING T WAS DAMAGED, WE SHOULD CO OURSELVES LUCKY!
IT'S NO LIKE ANYO USES THAT WEIGHT BE ANYWA

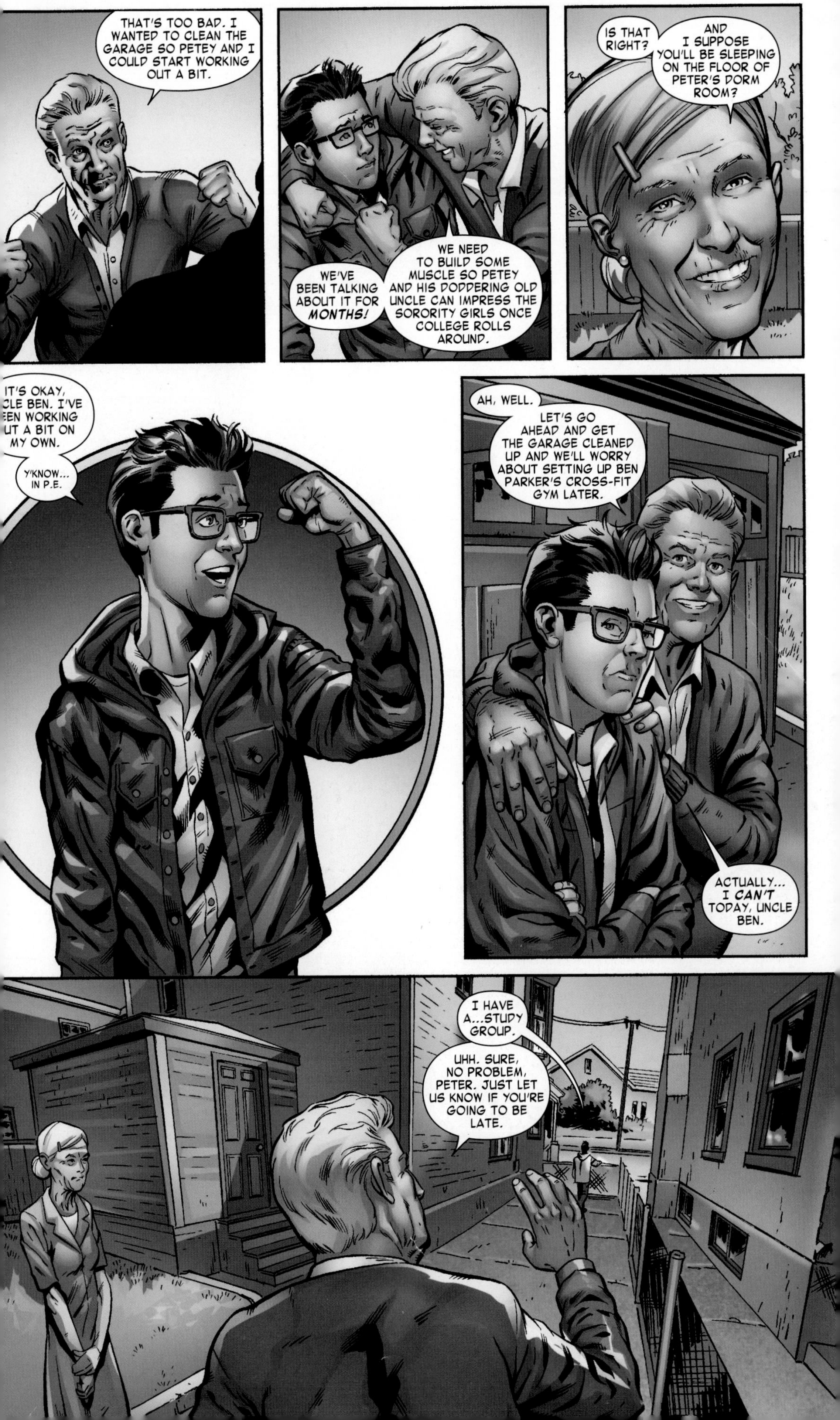
THAT'S TOO BAD. I WANTED TO CLEAN THE GARAGE SO PETEY AND I COULD START WORKING OUT A BIT.
WE'VE BEEN TALKING ABOUT IT FOR MONTHS!
WE NEED TO BUILD SOME MUSCLE SO PETEY AND HIS DODDERING OLD UNCLE CAN IMPRESS THE SORORITY GIRLS ONCE COLLEGE ROLLS AROUND.
IS THAT RIGHT?
AND I SUPPOSE YOU'LL BE SLEEPING ON THE FLOOR OF PETER'S DORM ROOM?
IT'S OKAY, CLE BEN. I'VE EEN WORKING UT A BIT ON MY OWN.
Y'KNOW... IN P.E.
AH, WELL.
LET'S GO AHEAD AND GET THE GARAGE CLEANED UP AND WE'LL WORRY ABOUT SETTING UP BEN PARKER'S CROSS-FIT GYM LATER.
ACTUALLY... I CAN'T TODAY, UNCLE BEN.
I HAVE A...STUDY GROUP.
UHH. SURE, NO PROBLEM, PETER. JUST LET US KNOW IF YOU'RE GOING TO BE LATE.

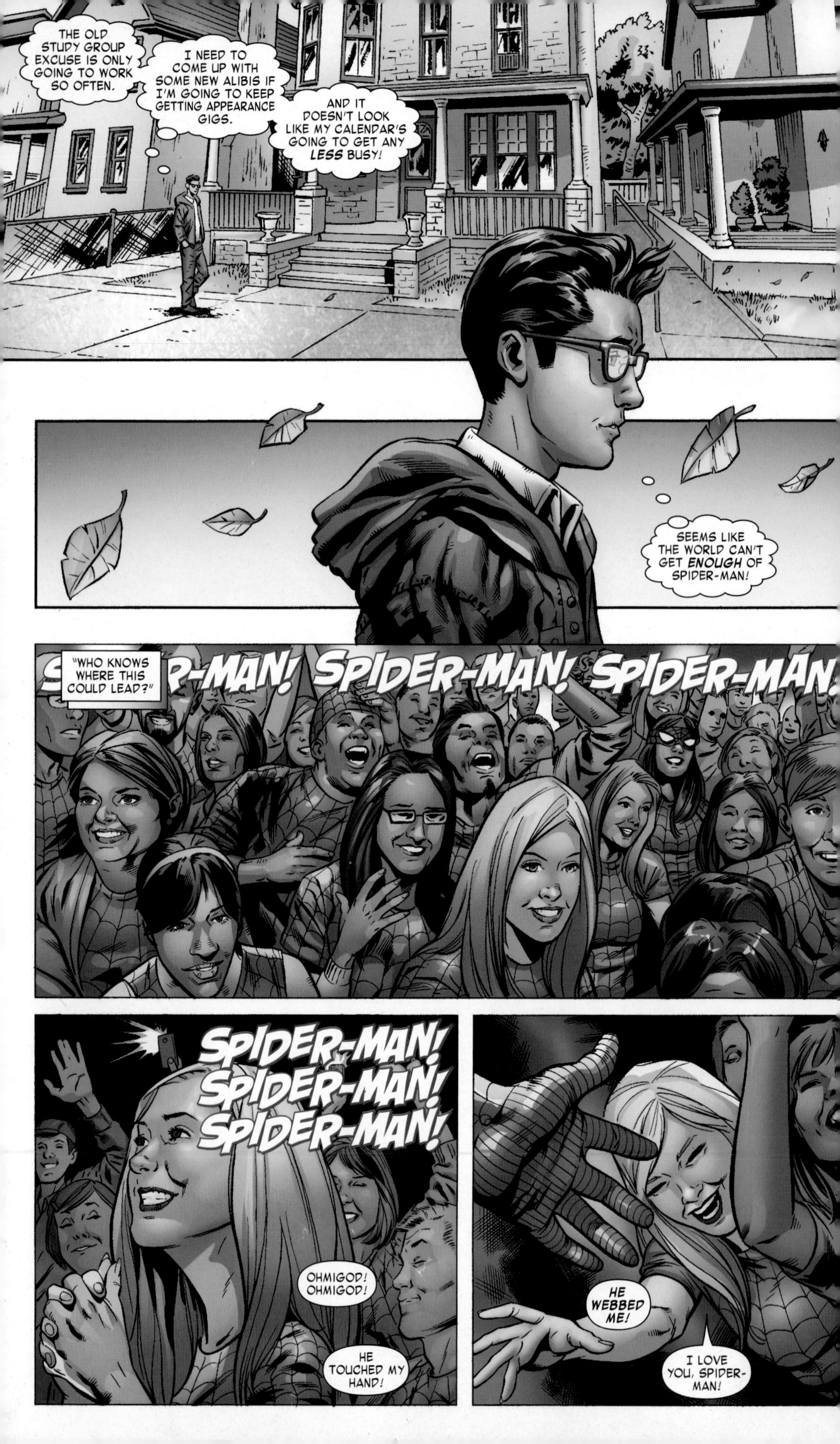
THE OLD STUDY GROUP EXCUSE IS ONLY GOING TO WORK SO OFTEN.
I NEED TO COME UP WITH SOME NEW ALIBIS IF I'M GOING TO KEEP GETTING APPEARANCE GIGS.
AND IT DOESN'T LOOK LIKE MY CALENDAR'S GOING TO GET ANY LESS BUSY!
SEEMS LIKE THE WORLD CAN'T GET ENOUGH OF SPIDER-MAN!
"WHO KNOWS WHERE THIS COULD LEAD?"
-MAN! SPIDER-MAN! SPIDER-MAN!
SPIDER-MAN! SPIDER-MAN! SPIDER-MAN!
OHMIGOD! OHMIGOD!
HE TOUCHED MY HAND!
HE WEBBED ME!
I LOVE YOU, SPIDER-MAN!

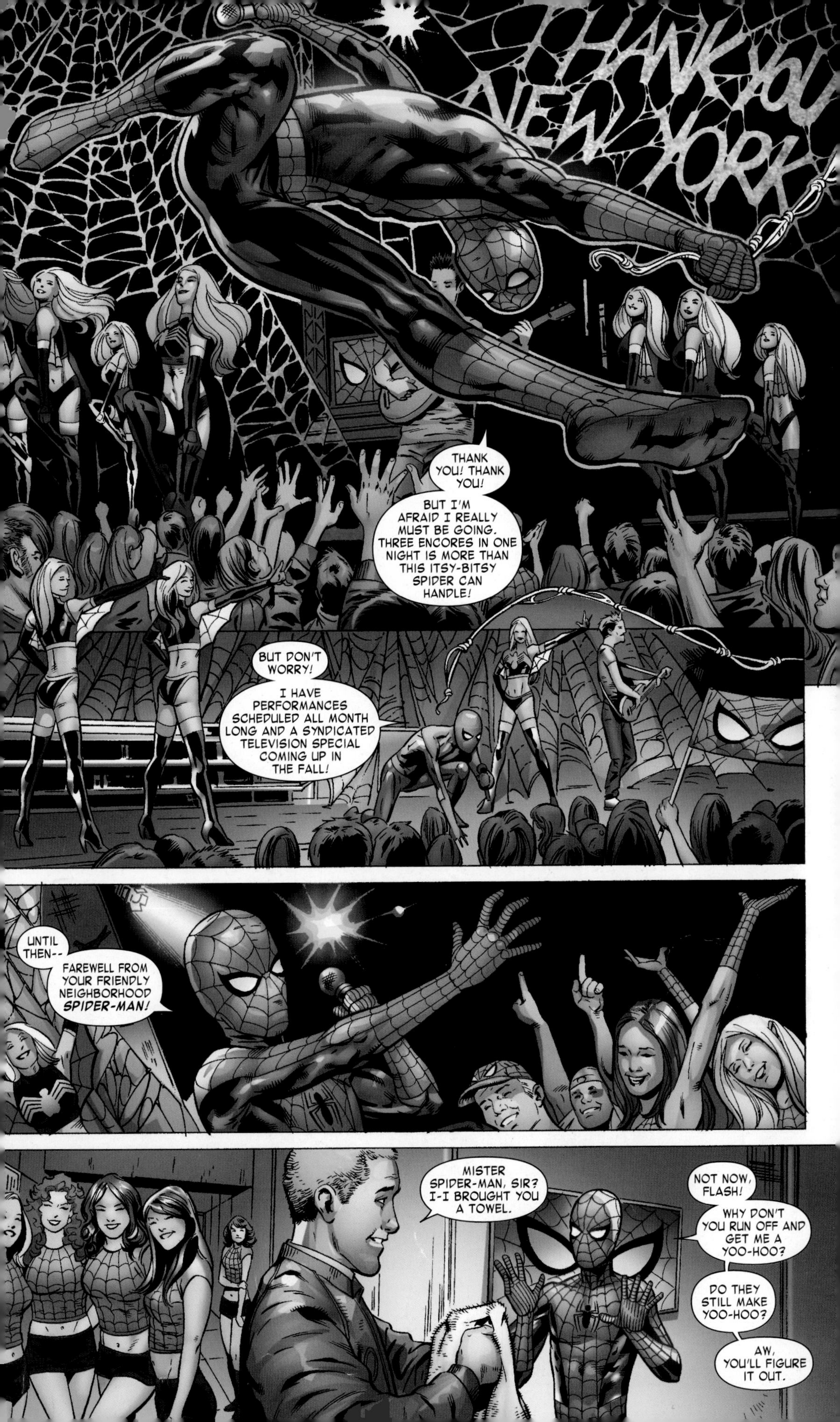
THANK YOU NEW YORK
THANK YOU! THANK YOU!
BUT I'M AFRAID I REALLY MUST BE GOING. THREE ENCORES IN ONE NIGHT IS MORE THAN THIS ITSY-BITSY SPIDER CAN HANDLE!
BUT DON'T WORRY!
I HAVE PERFORMANCES SCHEDULED ALL MONTH LONG AND A SYNDICATED TELEVISION SPECIAL COMING UP IN THE FALL!
UNTIL THEN--
FAREWELL FROM YOUR FRIENDLY NEIGHBORHOOD *SPIDER-MAN!*
MISTER SPIDER-MAN, SIR? I-I BROUGHT YOU A TOWEL.
NOT NOW, FLASH!
WHY DON'T YOU RUN OFF AND GET ME A YOO-HOO?
DO THEY STILL MAKE YOO-HOO?
AW, YOU'LL FIGURE IT OUT.

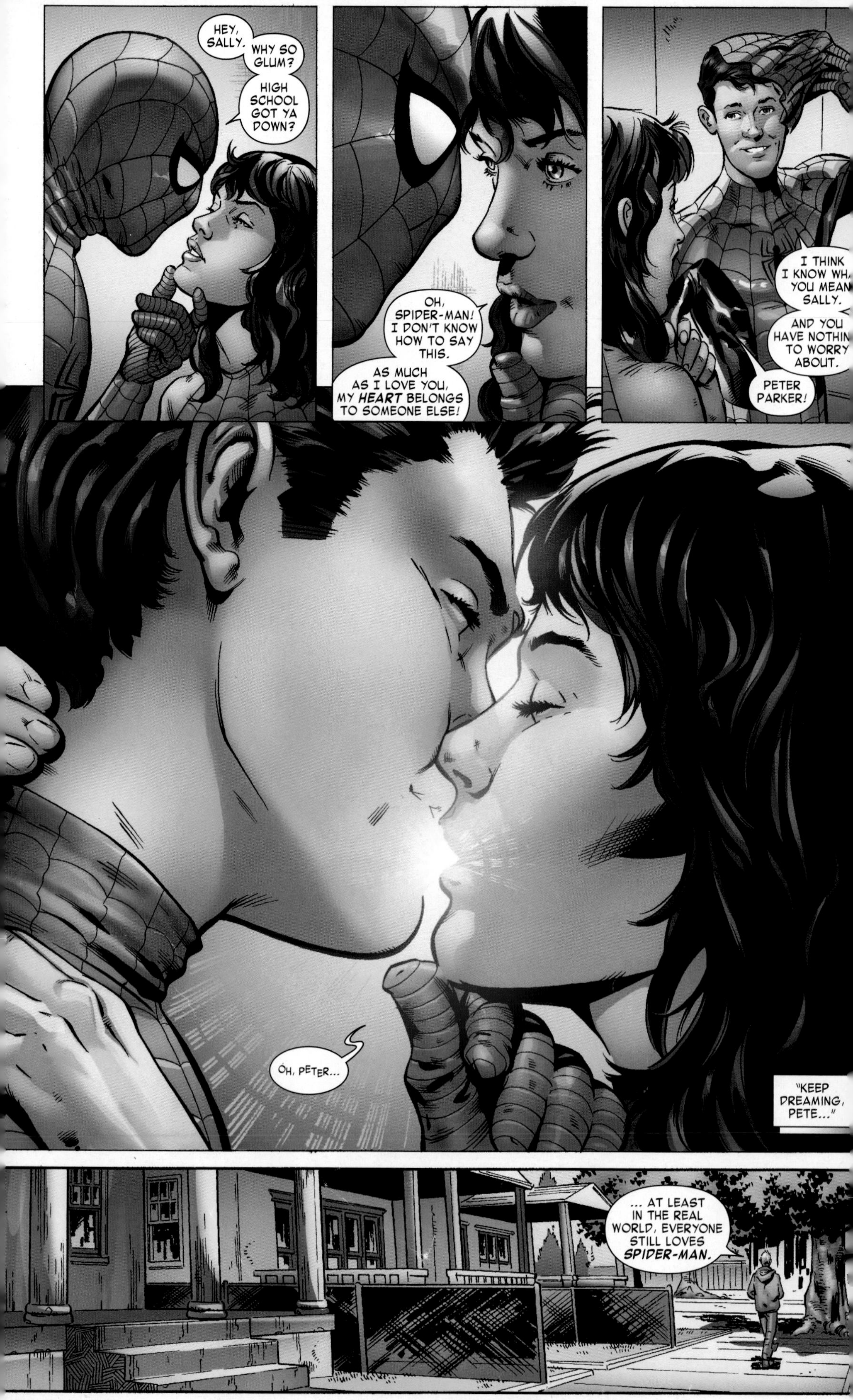
HEY, SALLY.
WHY SO GLUM?
HIGH SCHOOL GOT YA DOWN?
OH, SPIDER-MAN! I DON'T KNOW HOW TO SAY THIS.
AS MUCH AS I LOVE YOU, MY HEART BELONGS TO SOMEONE ELSE!
I THINK I KNOW WHA YOU MEAN SALLY.
AND YOU HAVE NOTHIN TO WORRY ABOUT.
PETER PARKER!
OH, PETER...
"KEEP DREAMING, PETE..."
... AT LEAST IN THE REAL WORLD, EVERYONE STILL LOVES SPIDER-MAN.

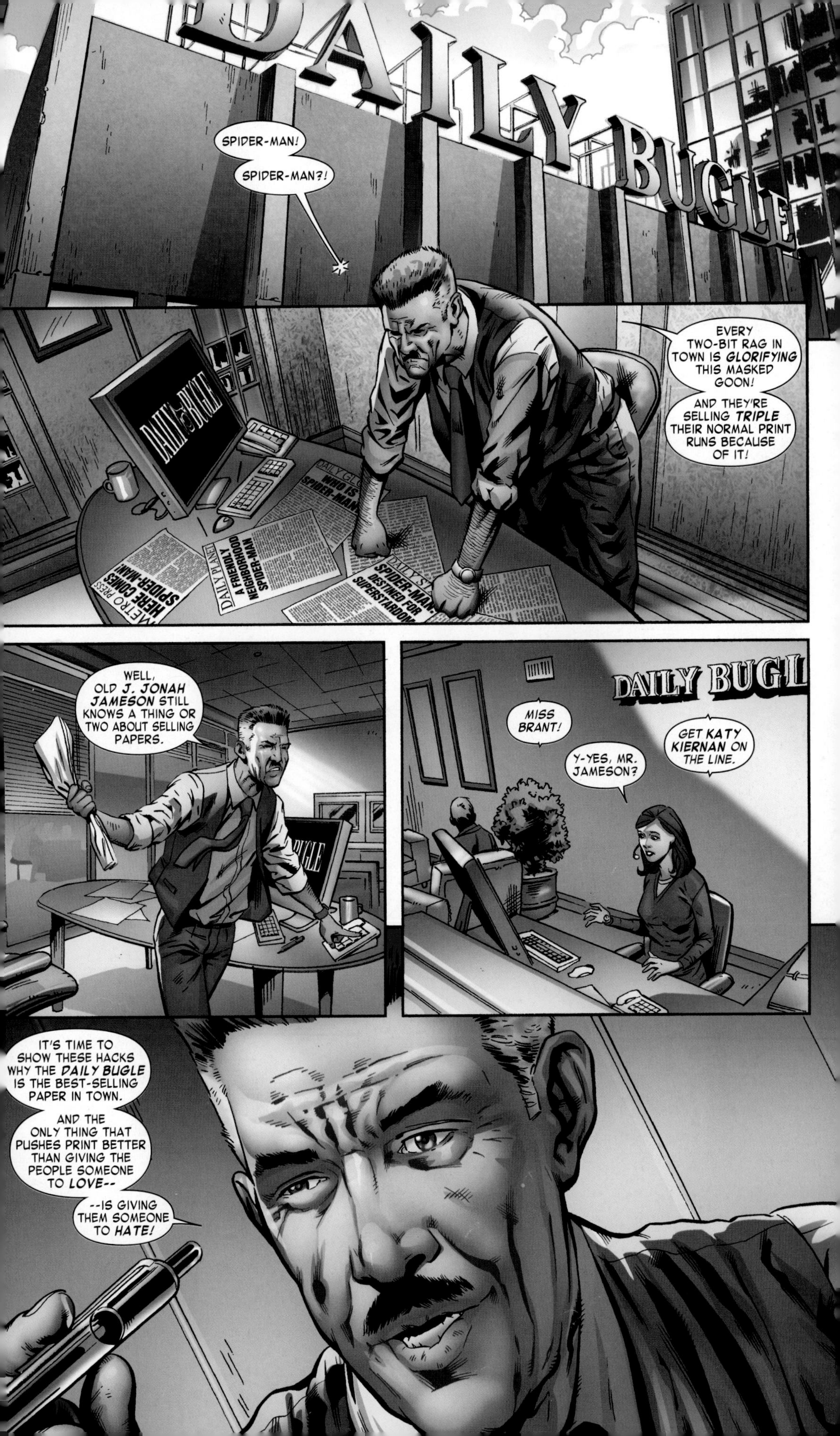
DAILY BUGLE
SPIDER-MAN!
SPIDER-MAN?!
EVERY TWO-BIT RAG IN TOWN IS GLORIFYING THIS MASKED GOON!
AND THEY'RE SELLING TRIPLE THEIR NORMAL PRINT RUNS BECAUSE OF IT!
WHO IS SPIDER-MAN
METRO PRESS HERE COMES SPIDER-MAN!
DAILY PLANET A FRIENDLY NEIGHBORHOOD SPIDER-MAN
SPIDER-MAN: DESTINED FOR SUPERSTARDOM
WELL, OLD J. JONAH JAMESON STILL KNOWS A THING OR TWO ABOUT SELLING PAPERS.
MISS BRANT!
Y-YES, MR. JAMESON?
GET KATY KIERNAN ON THE LINE.
IT'S TIME TO SHOW THESE HACKS WHY THE DAILY BUGLE IS THE BEST-SELLING PAPER IN TOWN.
AND THE ONLY THING THAT PUSHES PRINT BETTER THAN GIVING THE PEOPLE SOMEONE TO LOVE--
--IS GIVING THEM SOMEONE TO HATE!

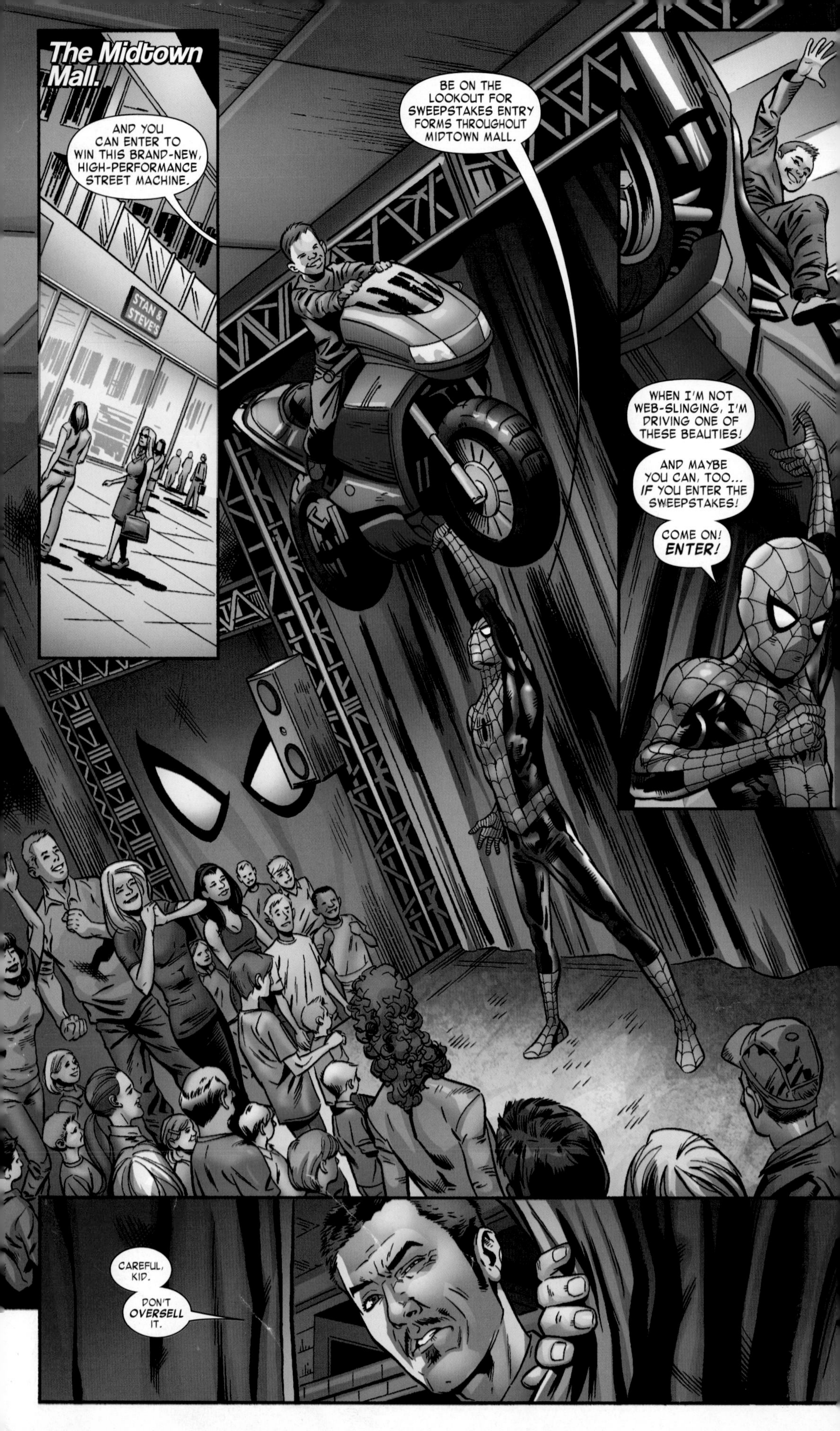

The Midtown Mall.
AND YOU CAN ENTER TO WIN THIS BRAND-NEW, HIGH-PERFORMANCE STREET MACHINE.
STAN & STEVE'S
BE ON THE LOOKOUT FOR SWEEPSTAKES ENTRY FORMS THROUGHOUT MIDTOWN MALL.
WHEN I'M NOT WEB-SLINGING, I'M DRIVING ONE OF THESE BEAUTIES!
AND MAYBE YOU CAN, TOO... *IF* YOU ENTER THE SWEEPSTAKES!
COME ON! **ENTER!**
CAREFUL, KID.
DON'T **OVERSELL** IT.

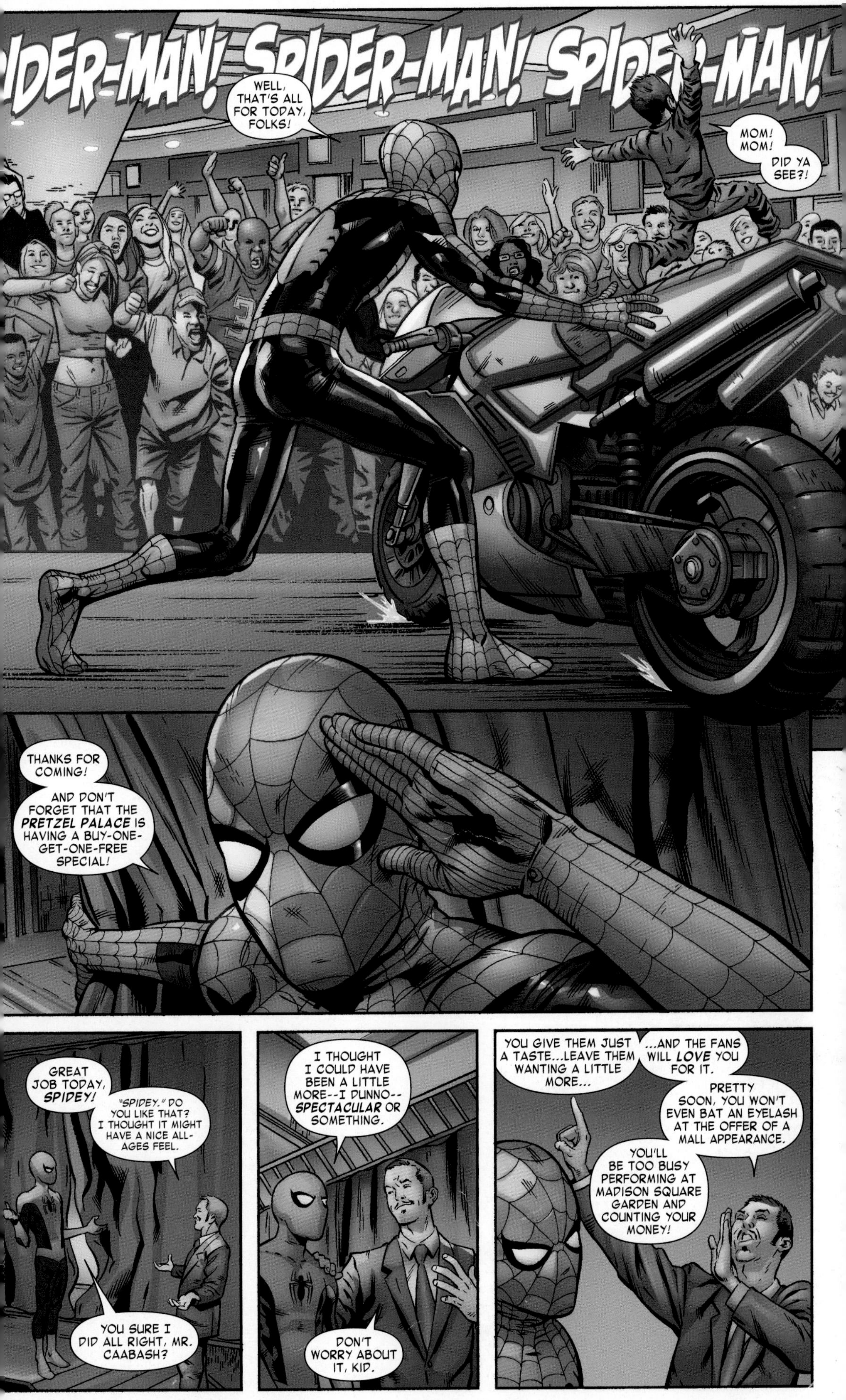
IDER-MAN! SPIDER-MAN! SPIDER-MAN!
WELL, THAT'S ALL FOR TODAY, FOLKS!
MOM! MOM!
DID YA SEE?!
THANKS FOR COMING!
AND DON'T FORGET THAT THE PRETZEL PALACE IS HAVING A BUY-ONE-GET-ONE-FREE SPECIAL!
GREAT JOB TODAY, SPIDEY!
"SPIDEY." DO YOU LIKE THAT? I THOUGHT IT MIGHT HAVE A NICE ALL-AGES FEEL.
YOU SURE I DID ALL RIGHT, MR. CAABASH?
I THOUGHT I COULD HAVE BEEN A LITTLE MORE--I DUNNO--SPECTACULAR OR SOMETHING.
DON'T WORRY ABOUT IT, KID.
YOU GIVE THEM JUST A TASTE...LEAVE THEM WANTING A LITTLE MORE...
...AND THE FANS WILL LOVE YOU FOR IT.
PRETTY SOON, YOU WON'T EVEN BAT AN EYELASH AT THE OFFER OF A MALL APPEARANCE.
YOU'LL BE TOO BUSY PERFORMING AT MADISON SQUARE GARDEN AND COUNTING YOUR MONEY!

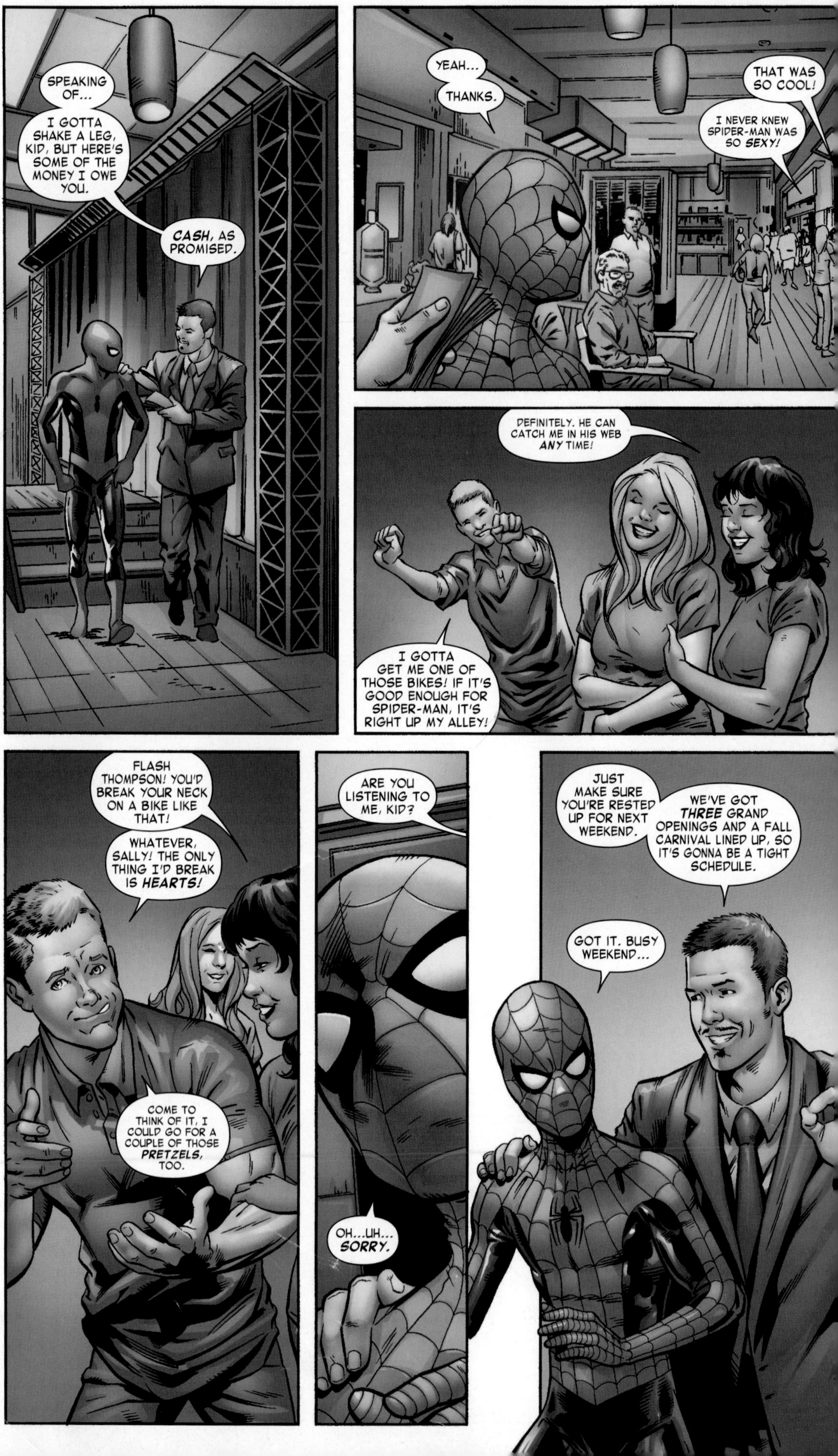
SPEAKING OF...
I GOTTA SHAKE A LEG, KID, BUT HERE'S SOME OF THE MONEY I OWE YOU.
CASH, AS PROMISED.
YEAH...
THANKS.
THAT WAS SO COOL!
I NEVER KNEW SPIDER-MAN WAS SO SEXY!
DEFINITELY. HE CAN CATCH ME IN HIS WEB ANY TIME!
I GOTTA GET ME ONE OF THOSE BIKES! IF IT'S GOOD ENOUGH FOR SPIDER-MAN, IT'S RIGHT UP MY ALLEY!
FLASH THOMPSON! YOU'D BREAK YOUR NECK ON A BIKE LIKE THAT!
WHATEVER, SALLY! THE ONLY THING I'D BREAK IS HEARTS!
COME TO THINK OF IT, I COULD GO FOR A COUPLE OF THOSE PRETZELS, TOO.
ARE YOU LISTENING TO ME, KID?
OH...UH... SORRY.
JUST MAKE SURE YOU'RE RESTED UP FOR NEXT WEEKEND.
WE'VE GOT THREE GRAND OPENINGS AND A FALL CARNIVAL LINED UP, SO IT'S GONNA BE A TIGHT SCHEDULE.
GOT IT. BUSY WEEKEND...

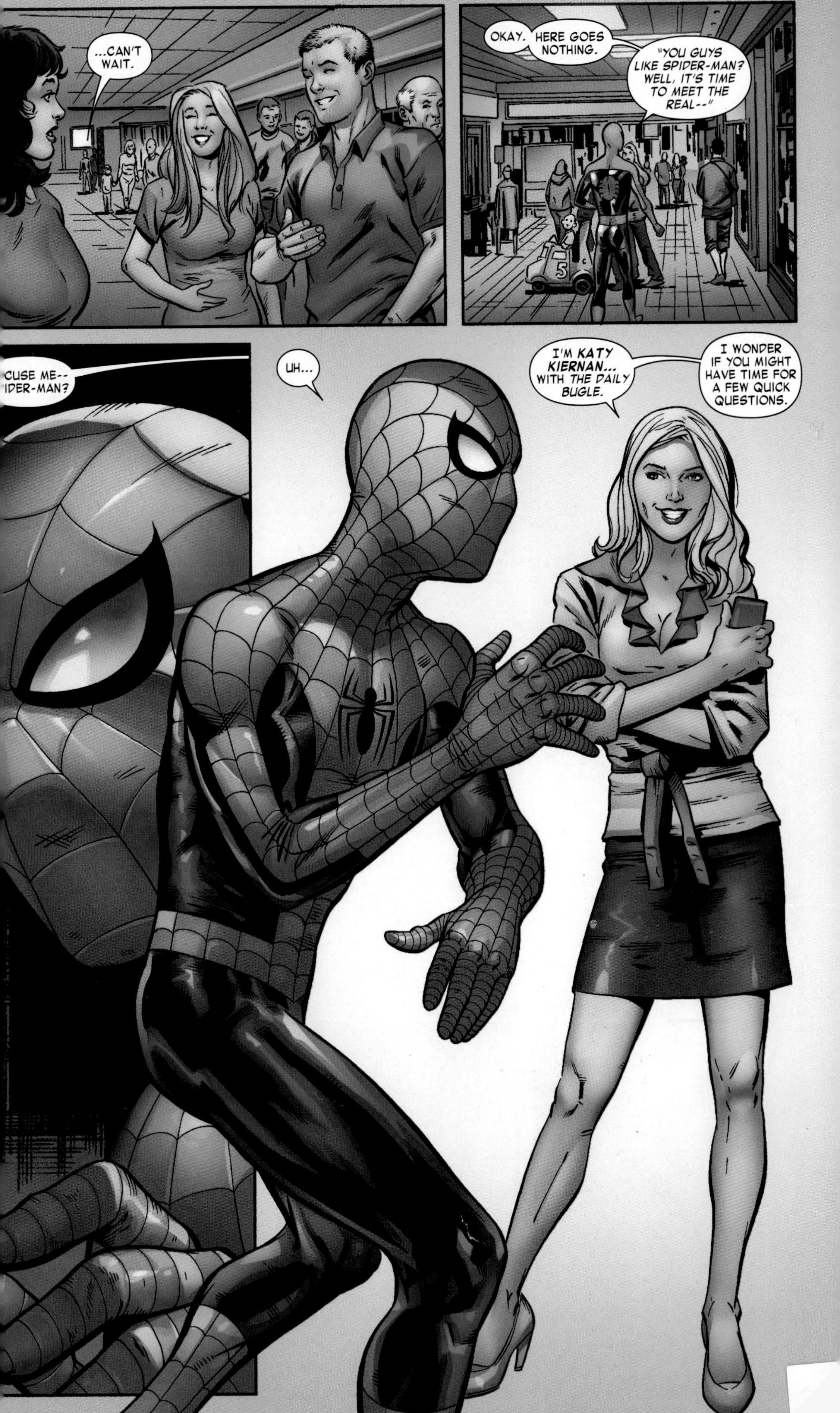

...CAN'T WAIT.
OKAY.
HERE GOES NOTHING.
"YOU GUYS LIKE SPIDER-MAN? WELL, IT'S TIME TO MEET THE REAL--"
CUSE ME-- IDER-MAN?
UH...
I'M KATY KIERNAN... WITH THE DAILY BUGLE.
I WONDER IF YOU MIGHT HAVE TIME FOR A FEW QUICK QUESTIONS.

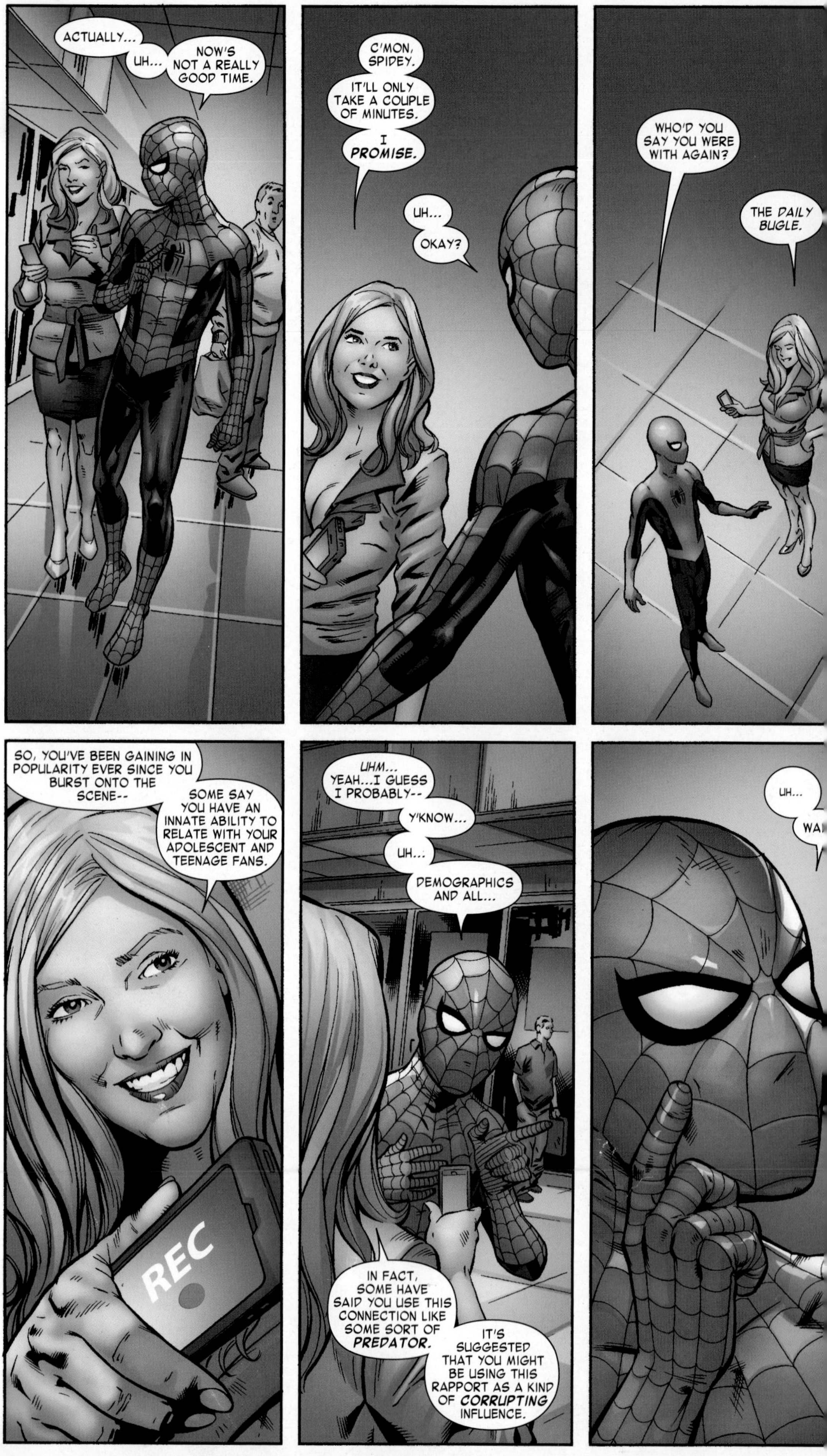

ACTUALLY...
UH...
NOW'S NOT A REALLY GOOD TIME.
C'MON, SPIDEY.
IT'LL ONLY TAKE A COUPLE OF MINUTES.
I *PROMISE.*
UH...
OKAY?
WHO'D YOU SAY YOU WERE WITH AGAIN?
THE *DAILY BUGLE.*
SO, YOU'VE BEEN GAINING IN POPULARITY EVER SINCE YOU BURST ONTO THE SCENE--
SOME SAY YOU HAVE AN INNATE ABILITY TO RELATE WITH YOUR ADOLESCENT AND TEENAGE FANS.
REC
UHM... YEAH...I GUESS I PROBABLY--
Y'KNOW...
UH...
DEMOGRAPHICS AND ALL...
IN FACT, SOME HAVE SAID YOU USE THIS CONNECTION LIKE SOME SORT OF *PREDATOR.*
IT'S SUGGESTED THAT YOU MIGHT BE USING THIS RAPPORT AS A KIND OF *CORRUPTING* INFLUENCE.
UH...

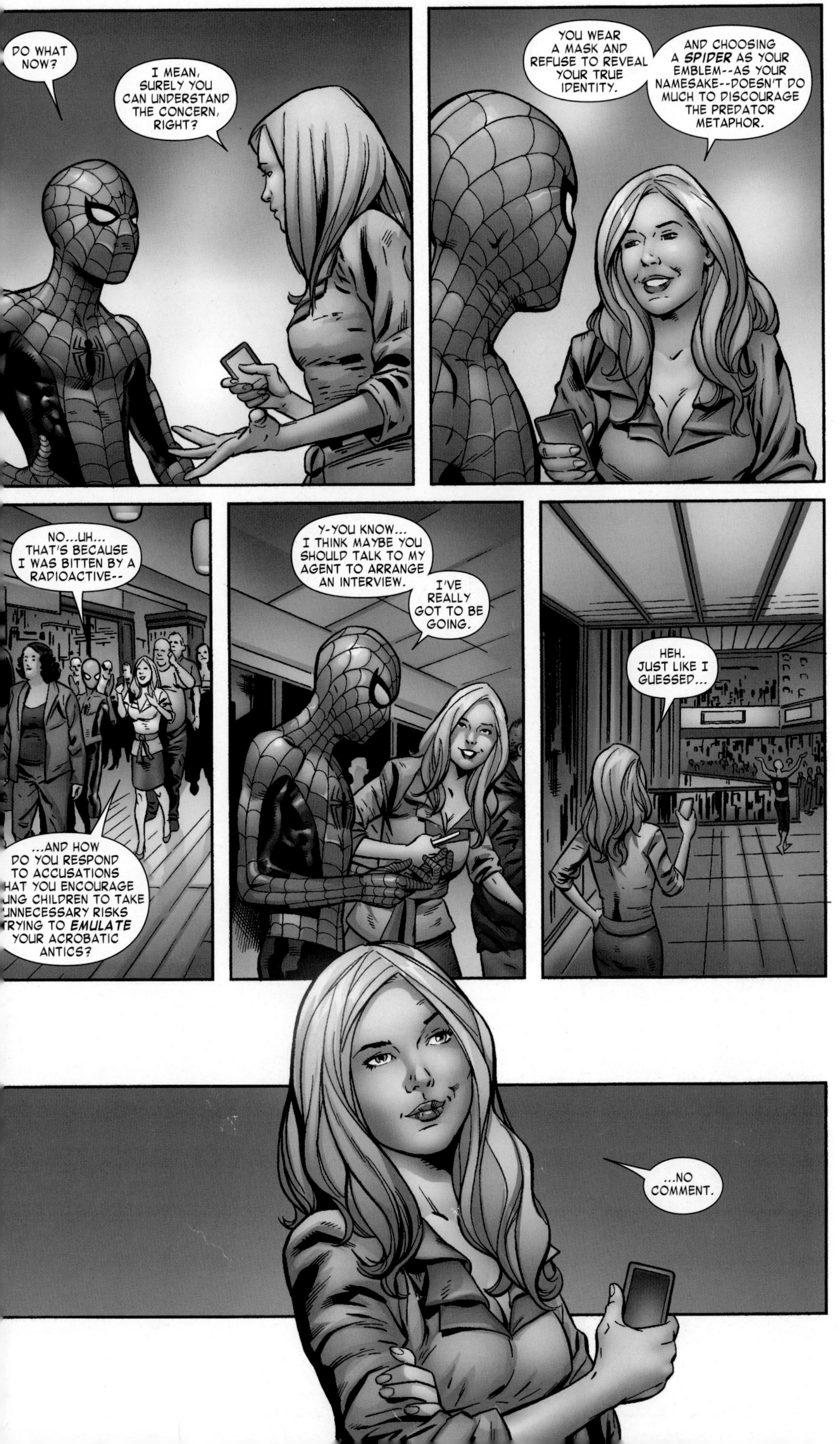
DO WHAT NOW?
I MEAN, SURELY YOU CAN UNDERSTAND THE CONCERN, RIGHT?
YOU WEAR A MASK AND REFUSE TO REVEAL YOUR TRUE IDENTITY.
AND CHOOSING A **SPIDER** AS YOUR EMBLEM--AS YOUR NAMESAKE--DOESN'T DO MUCH TO DISCOURAGE THE PREDATOR METAPHOR.
NO...UH... THAT'S BECAUSE I WAS BITTEN BY A RADIOACTIVE--
...AND HOW DO YOU RESPOND TO ACCUSATIONS HAT YOU ENCOURAGE UNG CHILDREN TO TAKE UNNECESSARY RISKS RYING TO **EMULATE** YOUR ACROBATIC ANTICS?
Y-YOU KNOW... I THINK MAYBE YOU SHOULD TALK TO MY AGENT TO ARRANGE AN INTERVIEW.
I'VE REALLY GOT TO BE GOING.
HEH. JUST LIKE I GUESSED...
...NO COMMENT.

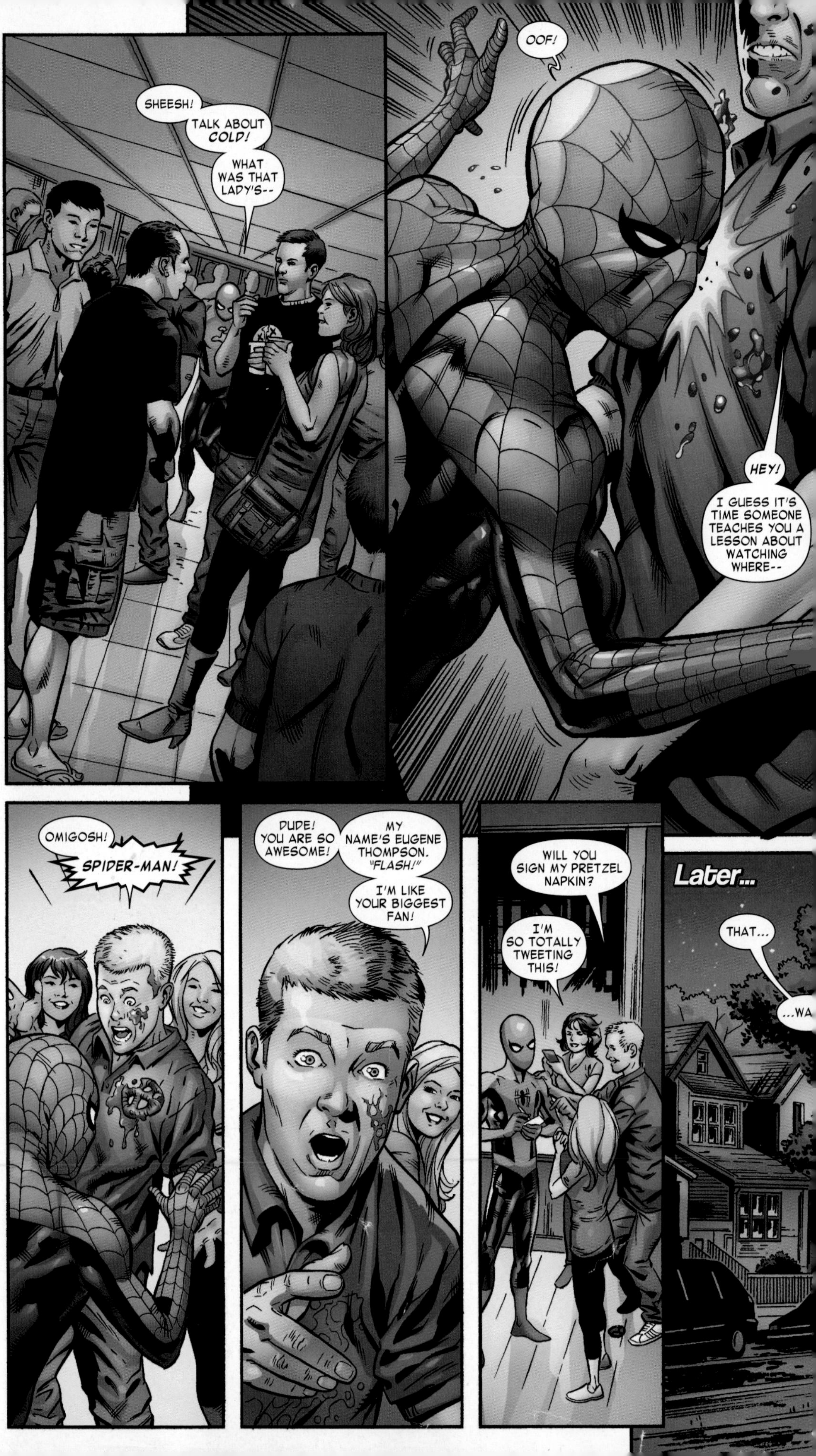
SHEESH!
TALK ABOUT COLD!
WHAT WAS THAT LADY'S--
OOF!
HEY!
I GUESS IT'S TIME SOMEONE TEACHES YOU A LESSON ABOUT WATCHING WHERE--
OMIGOSH!
SPIDER-MAN!
DUDE! YOU ARE SO AWESOME!
MY NAME'S EUGENE THOMPSON. "FLASH!"
I'M LIKE YOUR BIGGEST FAN!
WILL YOU SIGN MY PRETZEL NAPKIN?
I'M SO TOTALLY TWEETING THIS!
Later...
THAT...
...WA

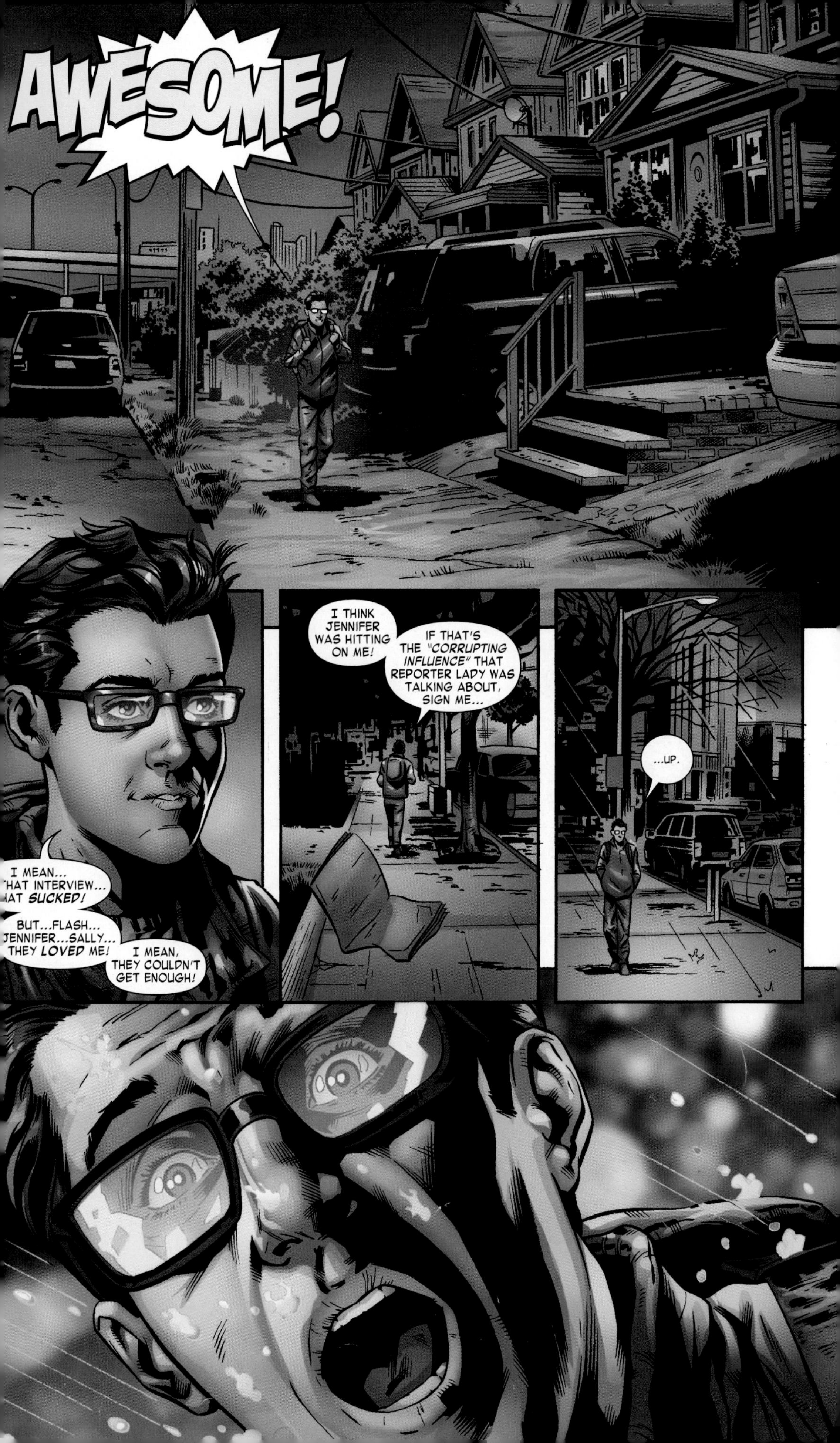
AWESOME!
I MEAN... THAT INTERVIEW... HAT SUCKED!
BUT...FLASH... JENNIFER...SALLY... THEY LOVED ME!
I MEAN, THEY COULDN'T GET ENOUGH!
I THINK JENNIFER WAS HITTING ON ME!
IF THAT'S THE "CORRUPTING INFLUENCE" THAT REPORTER LADY WAS TALKING ABOUT, SIGN ME...
...UP.

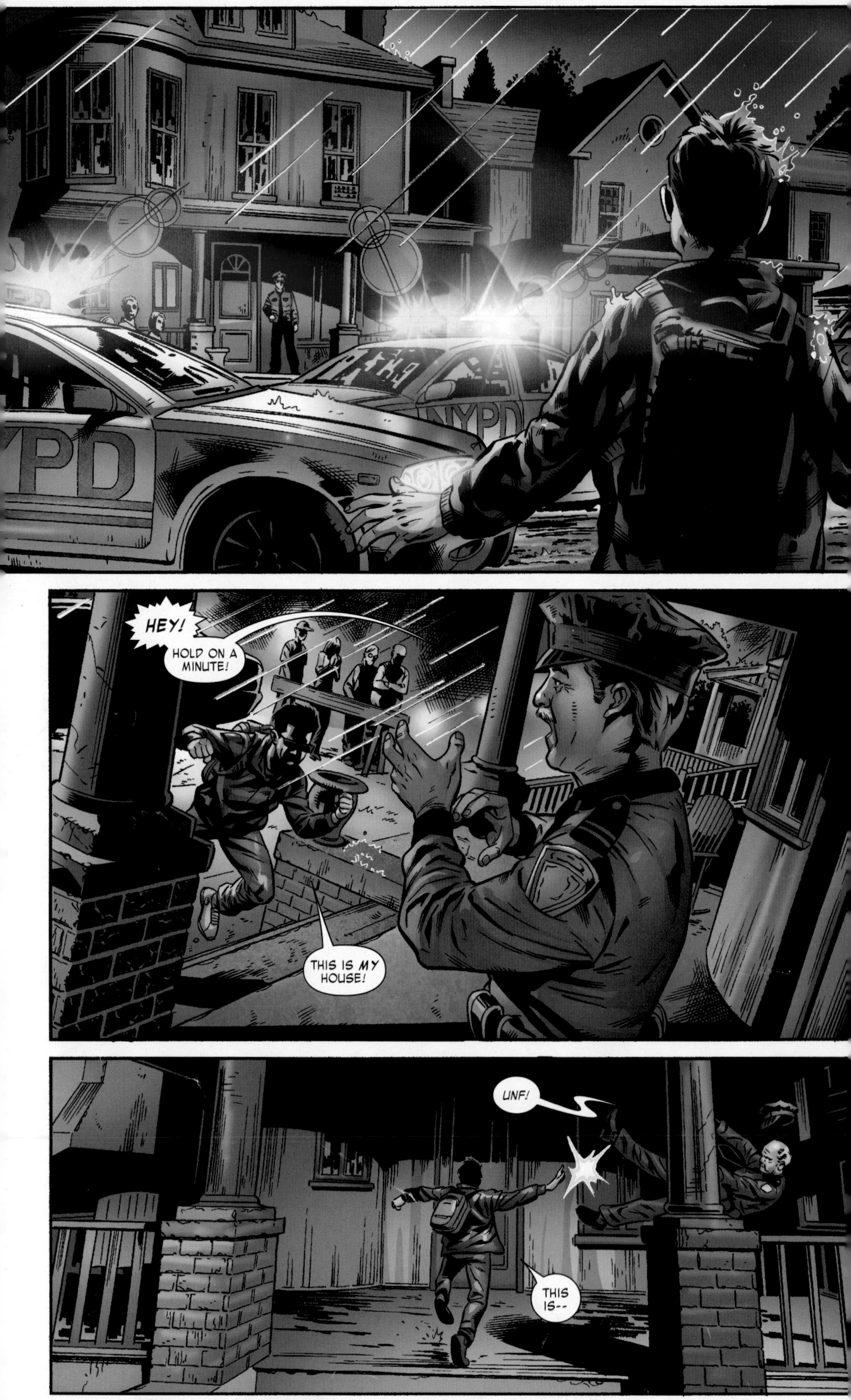
NYPD
NYPD
HEY!
HOLD ON A MINUTE!
THIS IS MY HOUSE!
UNF!
THIS IS--

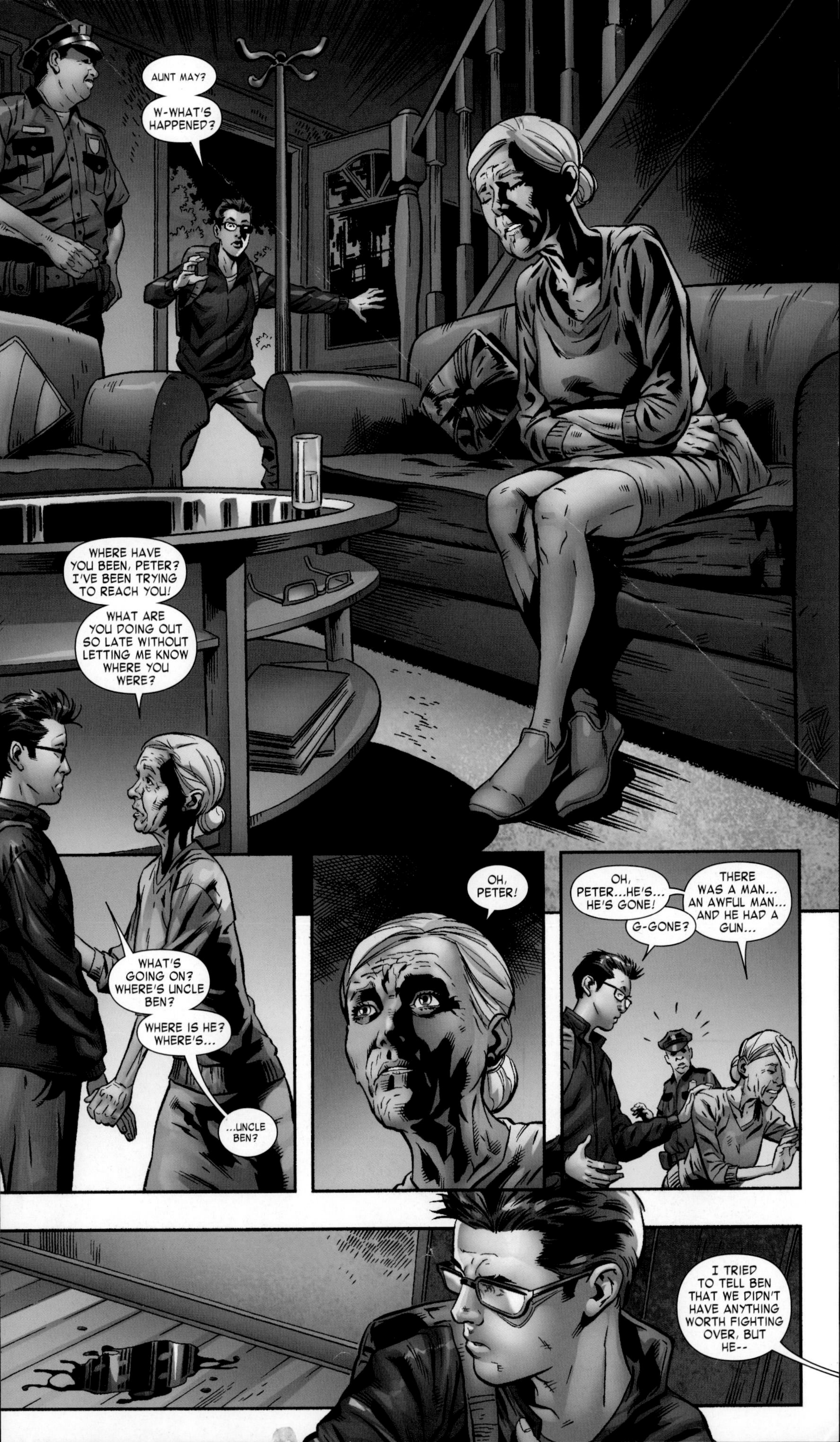
AUNT MAY?
W-WHAT'S HAPPENED?
WHERE HAVE YOU BEEN, PETER? I'VE BEEN TRYING TO REACH YOU!
WHAT ARE YOU DOING OUT SO LATE WITHOUT LETTING ME KNOW WHERE YOU WERE?
WHAT'S GOING ON? WHERE'S UNCLE BEN?
WHERE IS HE? WHERE'S...
...UNCLE BEN?
OH, PETER!
OH, PETER...HE'S... HE'S GONE!
G-GONE?
THERE WAS A MAN... AN AWFUL MAN... AND HE HAD A GUN...
I TRIED TO TELL BEN THAT WE DIDN'T HAVE ANYTHING WORTH FIGHTING OVER, BUT HE--

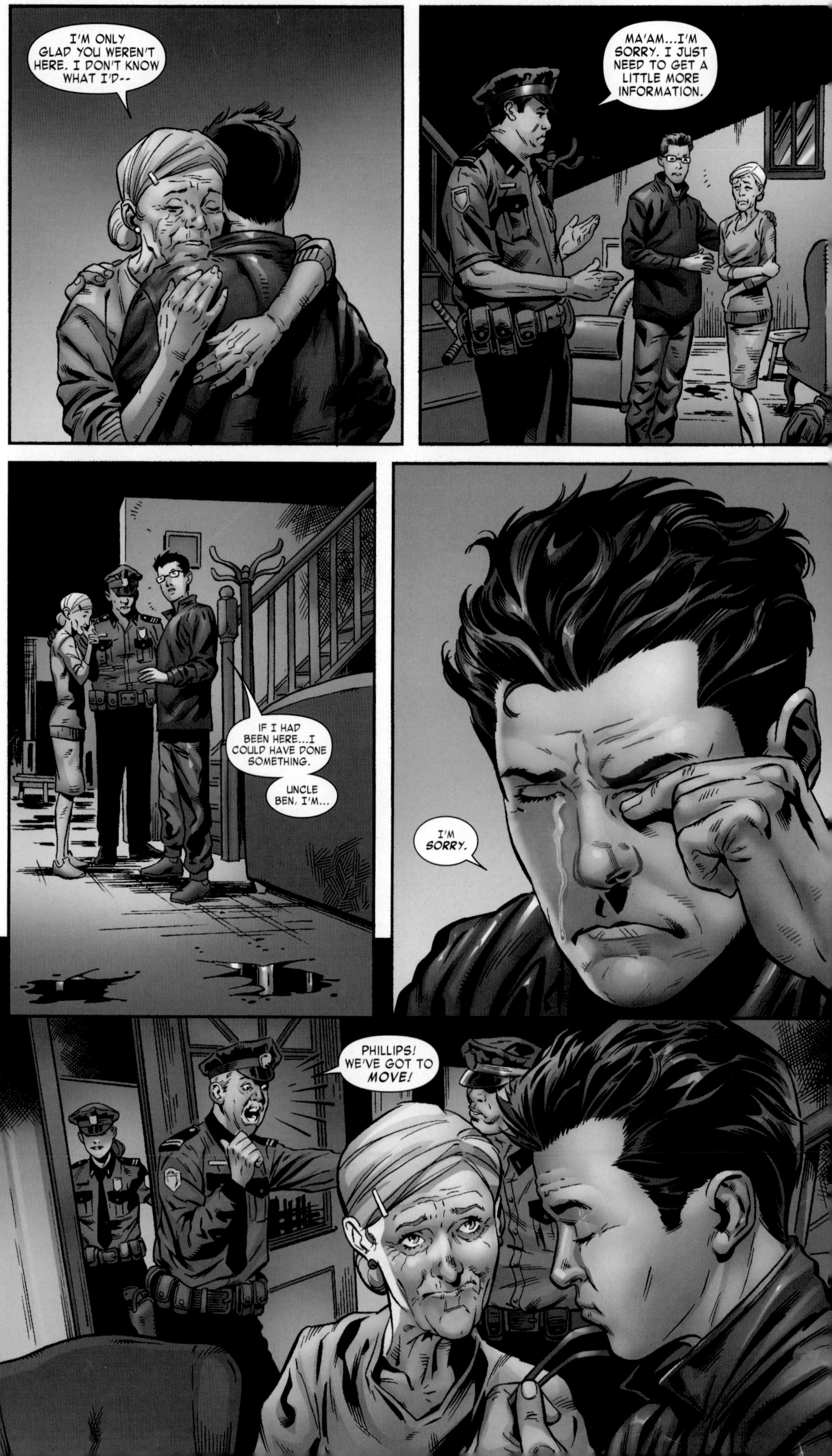
I'M ONLY GLAD YOU WEREN'T HERE. I DON'T KNOW WHAT I'D--
MA'AM...I'M SORRY. I JUST NEED TO GET A LITTLE MORE INFORMATION.
IF I HAD BEEN HERE...I COULD HAVE DONE SOMETHING.
UNCLE BEN, I'M...
I'M SORRY.
PHILLIPS! WE'VE GOT TO MOVE!

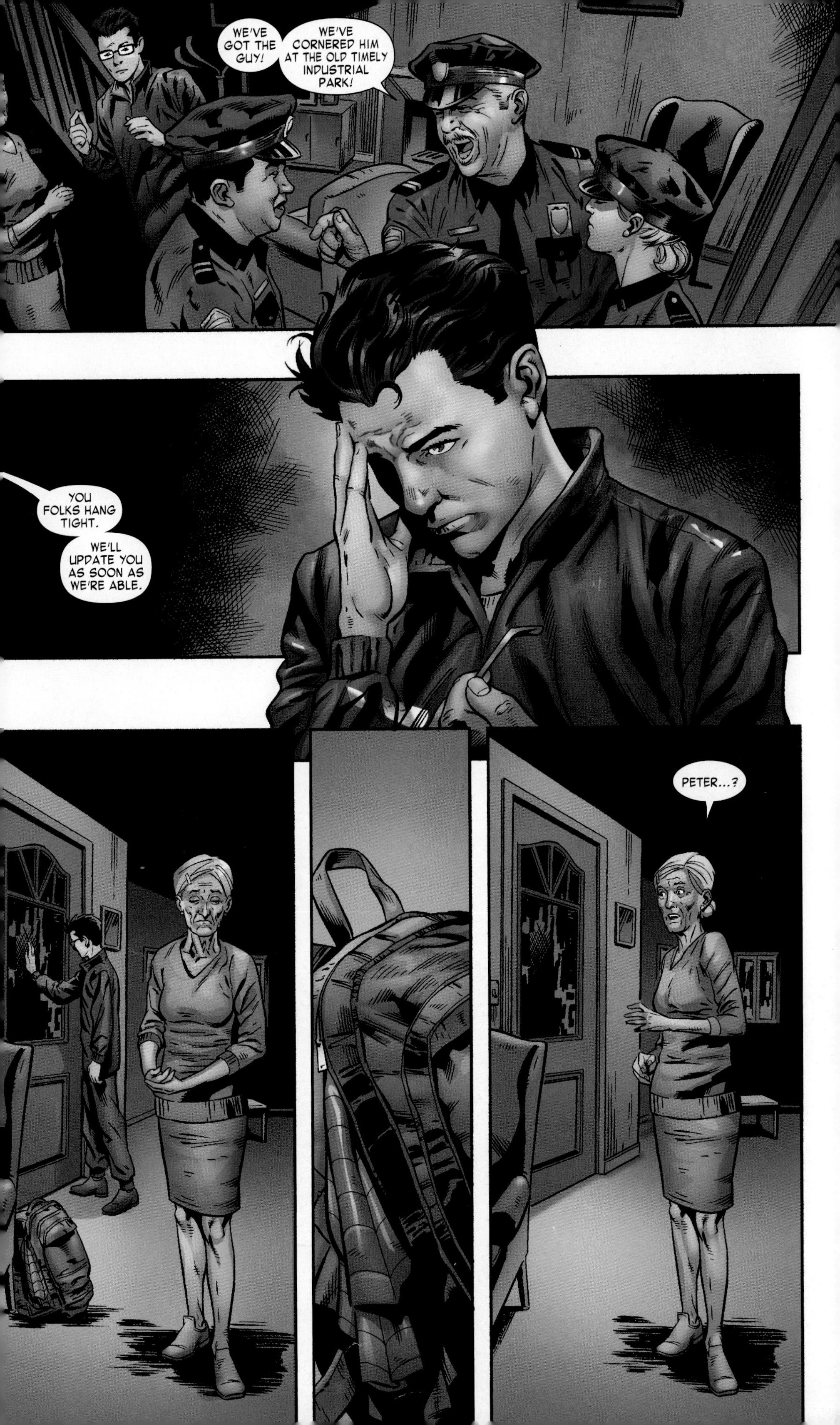
WE'VE GOT THE GUY!
WE'VE CORNERED HIM AT THE OLD TIMELY INDUSTRIAL PARK!
YOU FOLKS HANG TIGHT.
WE'LL UPDATE YOU AS SOON AS WE'RE ABLE.
PETER...?

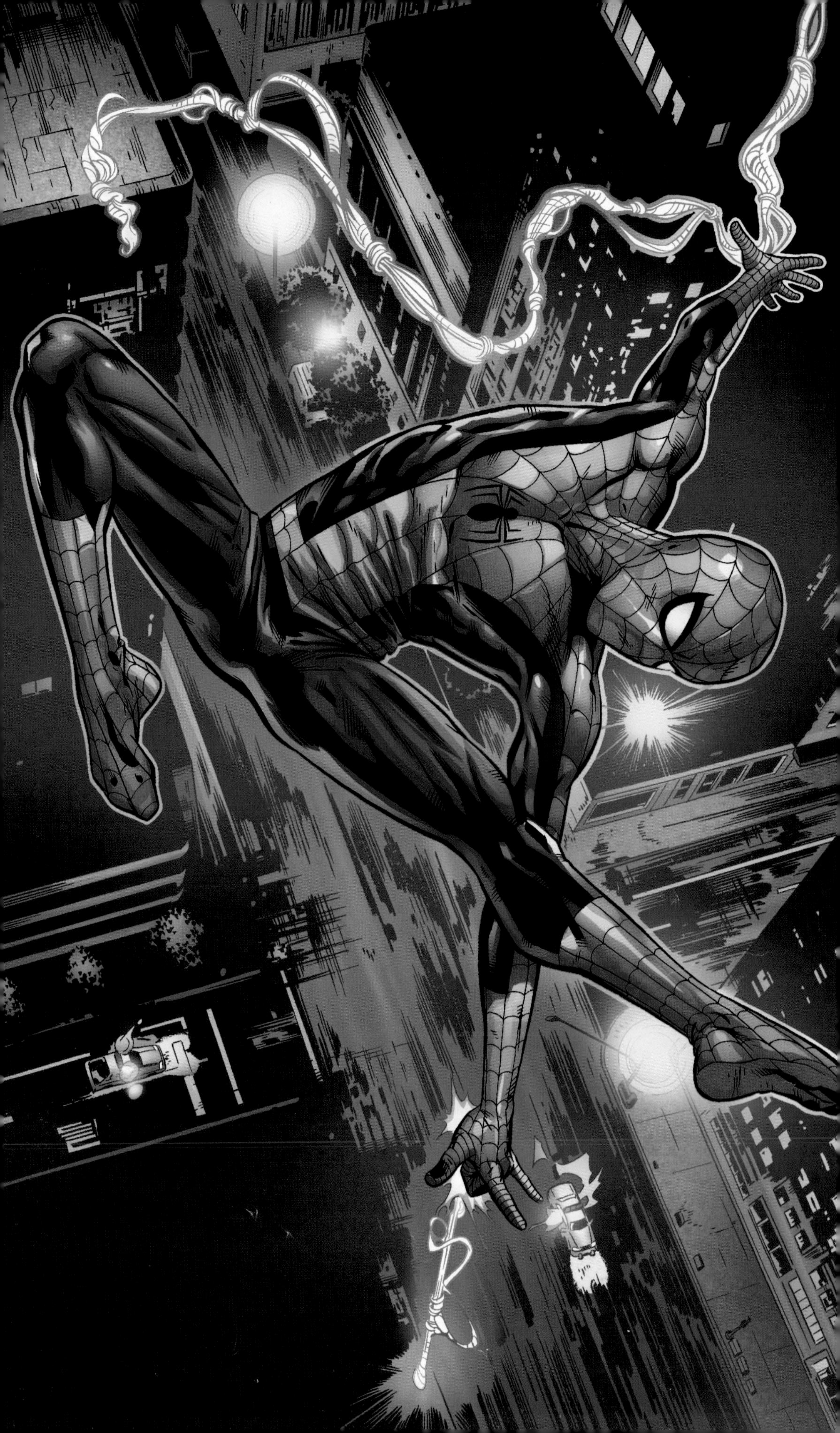

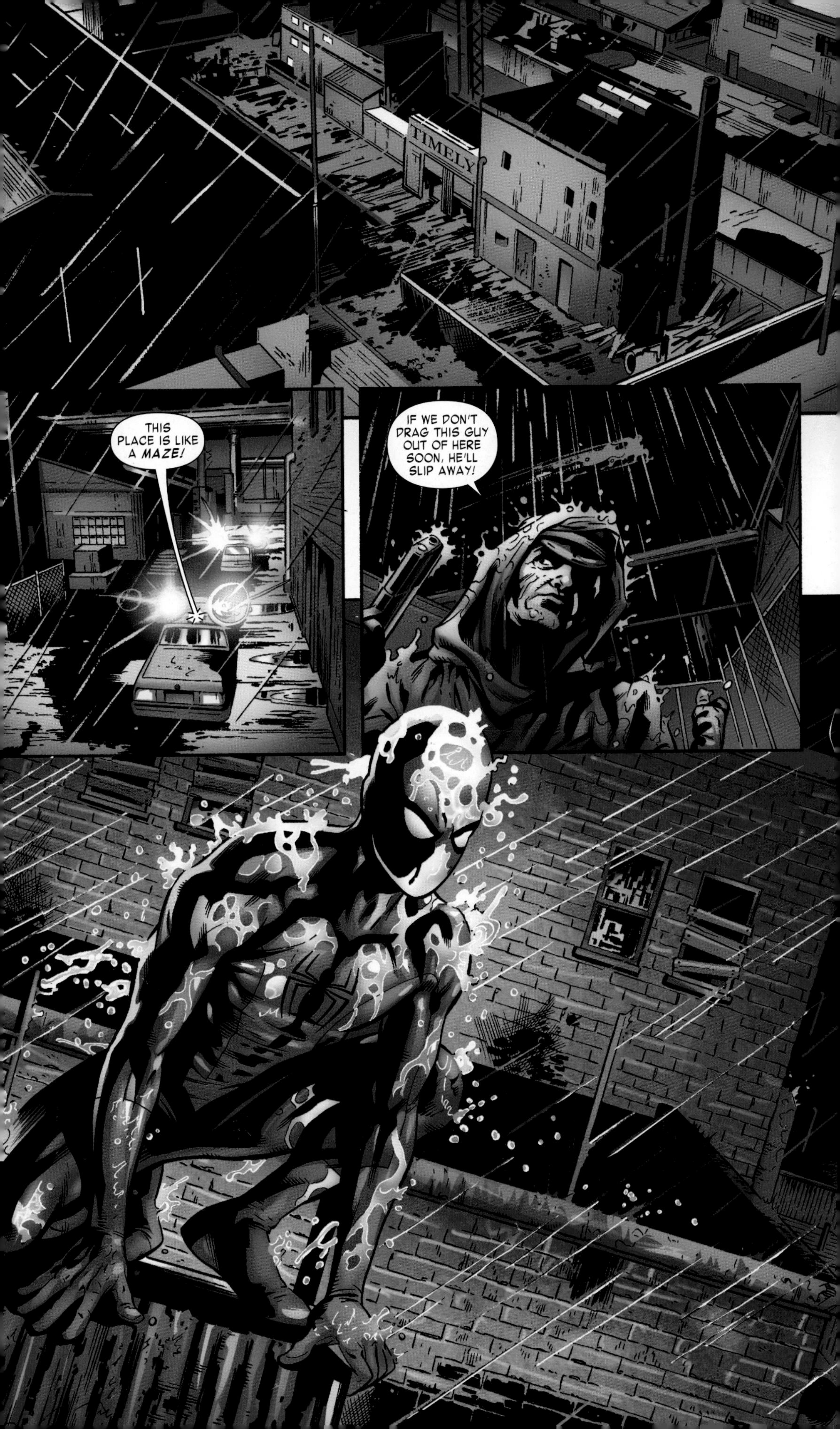
TIMELY
THIS PLACE IS LIKE A MAZE!
IF WE DON'T DRAG THIS GUY OUT OF HERE SOON, HE'LL SLIP AWAY!

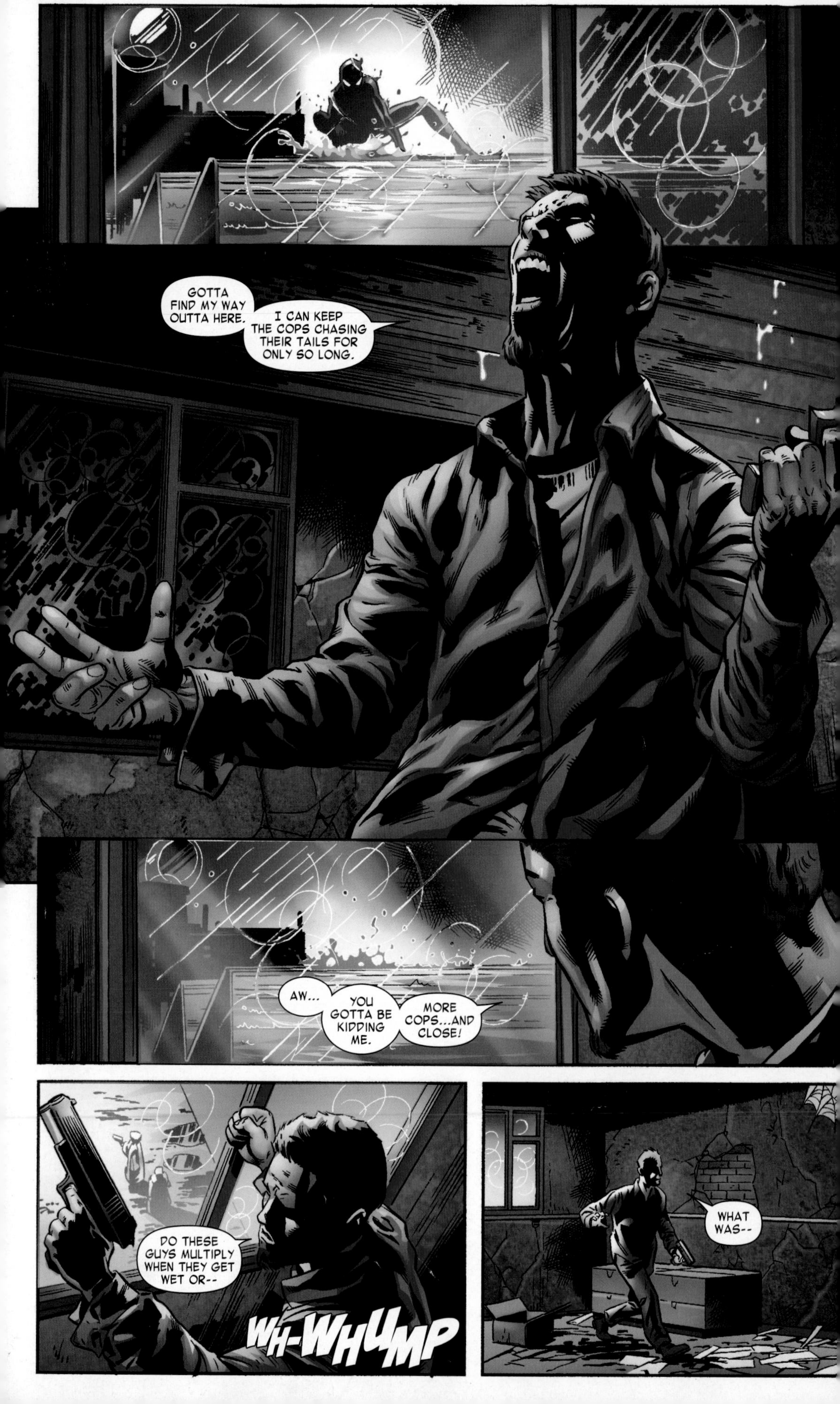
GOTTA FIND MY WAY OUTTA HERE.
I CAN KEEP THE COPS CHASING THEIR TAILS FOR ONLY SO LONG.
AW...
YOU GOTTA BE KIDDING ME.
MORE COPS...AND CLOSE!
DO THESE GUYS MULTIPLY WHEN THEY GET WET OR--
WH-WHUMP
WHAT WAS--

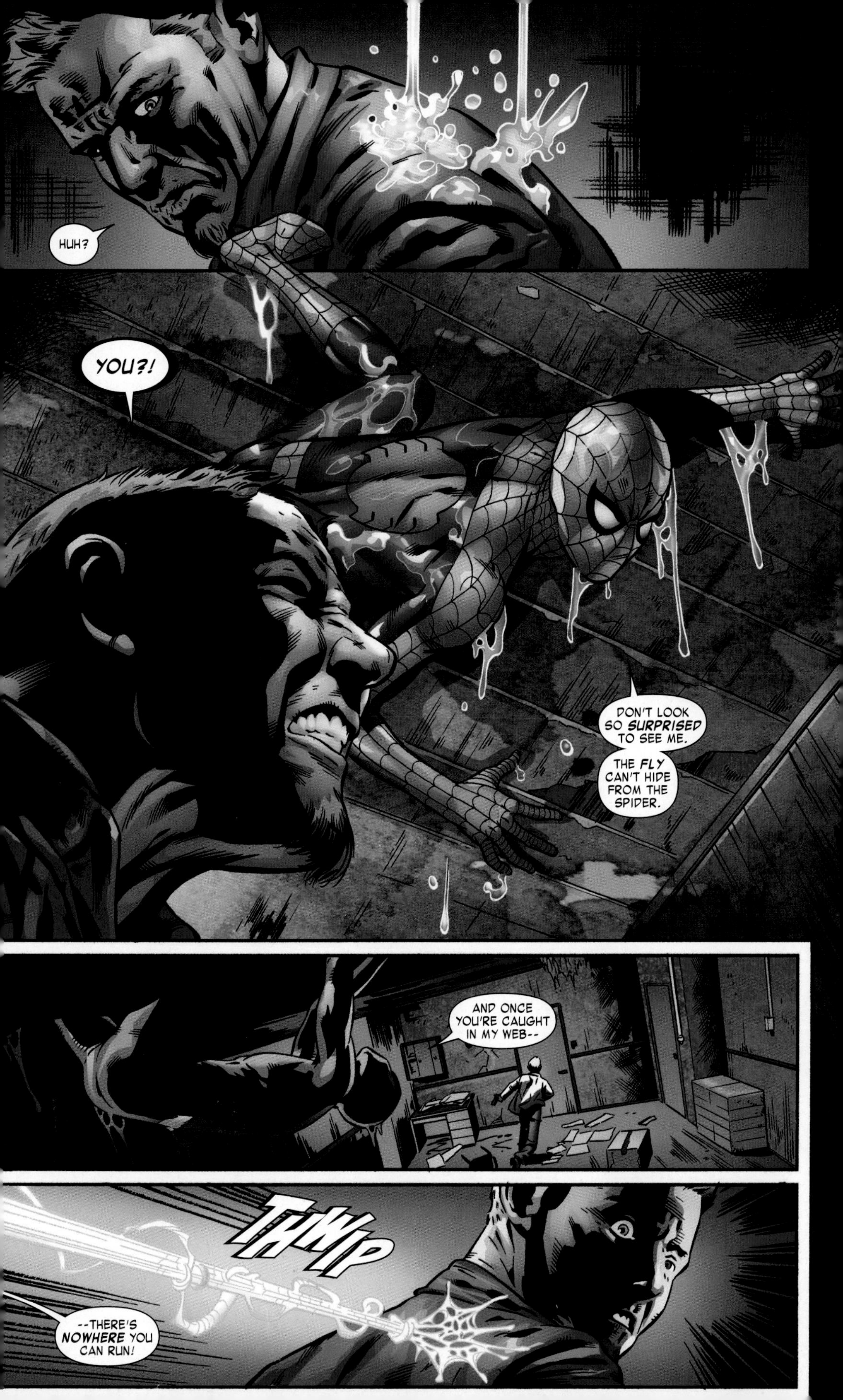
HUH?
YOU?!
DON'T LOOK SO SURPRISED TO SEE ME.
THE FLY CAN'T HIDE FROM THE SPIDER.
AND ONCE YOU'RE CAUGHT IN MY WEB--
THWIP
--THERE'S NOWHERE YOU CAN RUN!

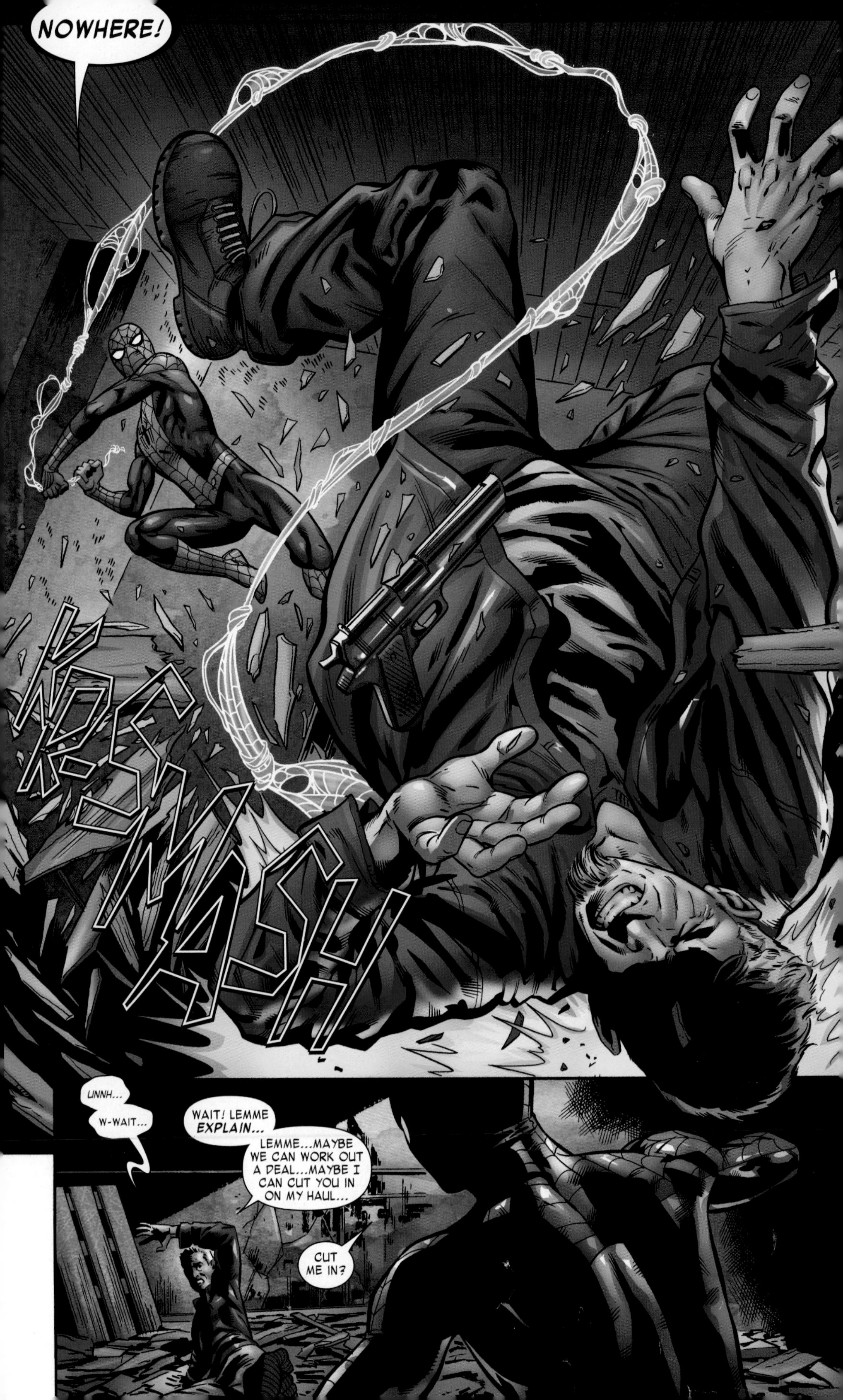
NOWHERE!
KRSSMASH
UNNH...
W-WAIT...
WAIT! LEMME EXPLAIN...
LEMME...MAYBE WE CAN WORK OUT A DEAL...MAYBE I CAN CUT YOU IN ON MY HAUL...
CUT ME IN?

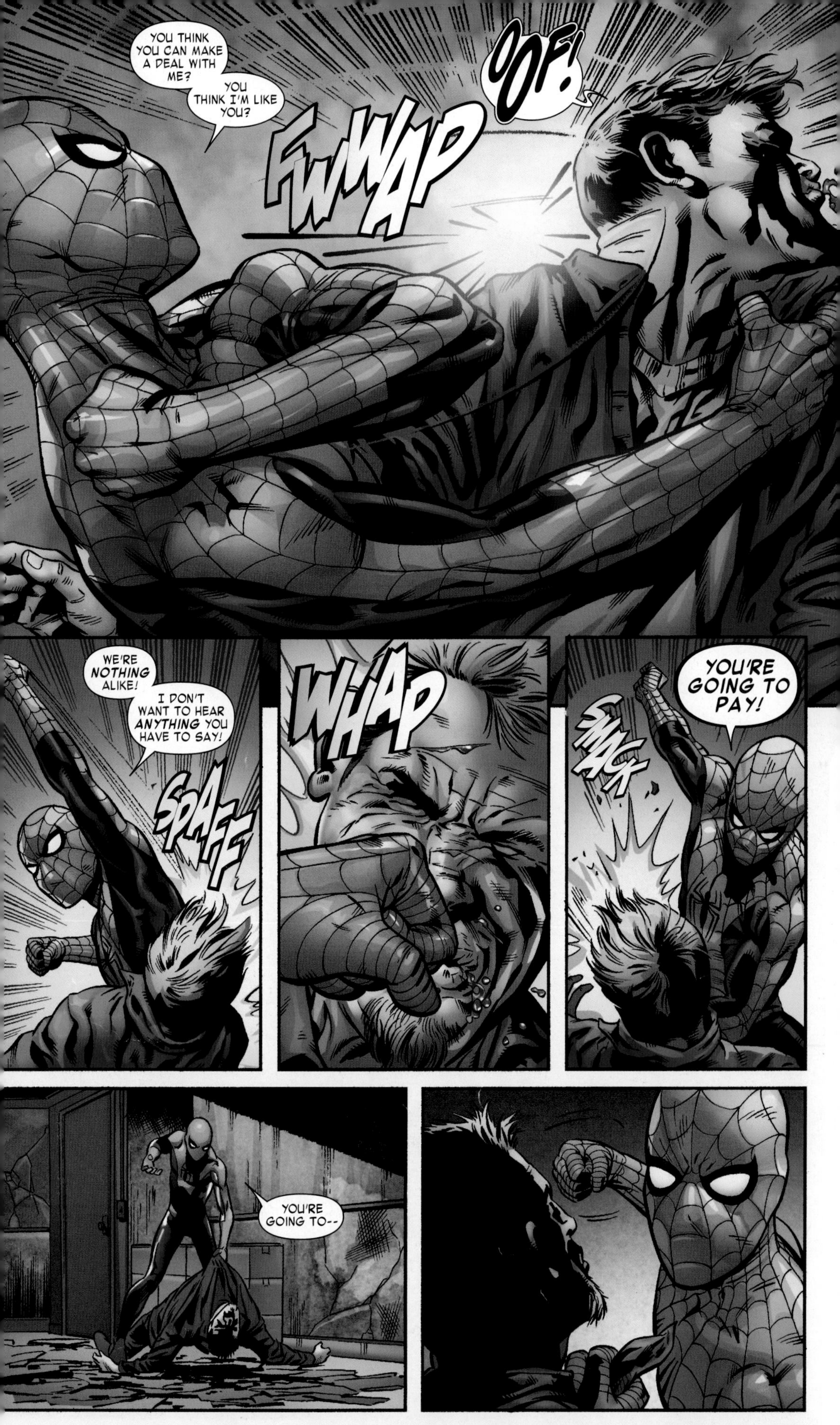
YOU THINK YOU CAN MAKE A DEAL WITH ME?
YOU THINK I'M LIKE YOU?
FWWAP
OOF!
WE'RE NOTHING ALIKE!
I DON'T WANT TO HEAR ANYTHING YOU HAVE TO SAY!
SPAFF
WHAP
YOU'RE GOING TO PAY!
SMACK
YOU'RE GOING TO--

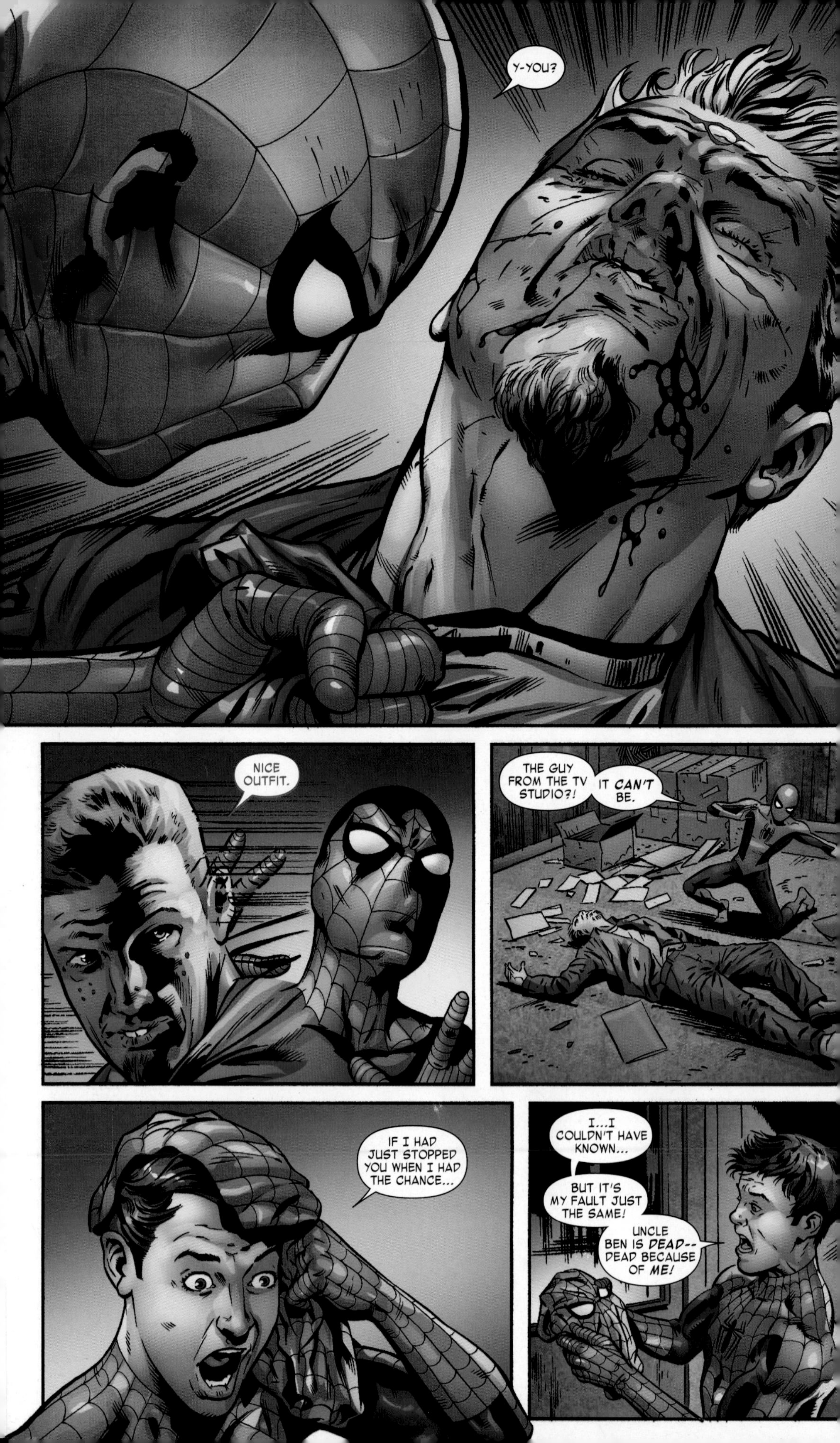
Y-YOU?
NICE OUTFIT.
THE GUY FROM THE TV STUDIO?!
IT *CAN'T* BE.
IF I HAD JUST STOPPED YOU WHEN I HAD THE CHANCE...
I...I COULDN'T HAVE KNOWN...
BUT IT'S MY FAULT JUST THE SAME!
UNCLE BEN IS *DEAD*-- DEAD BECAUSE OF *ME!*

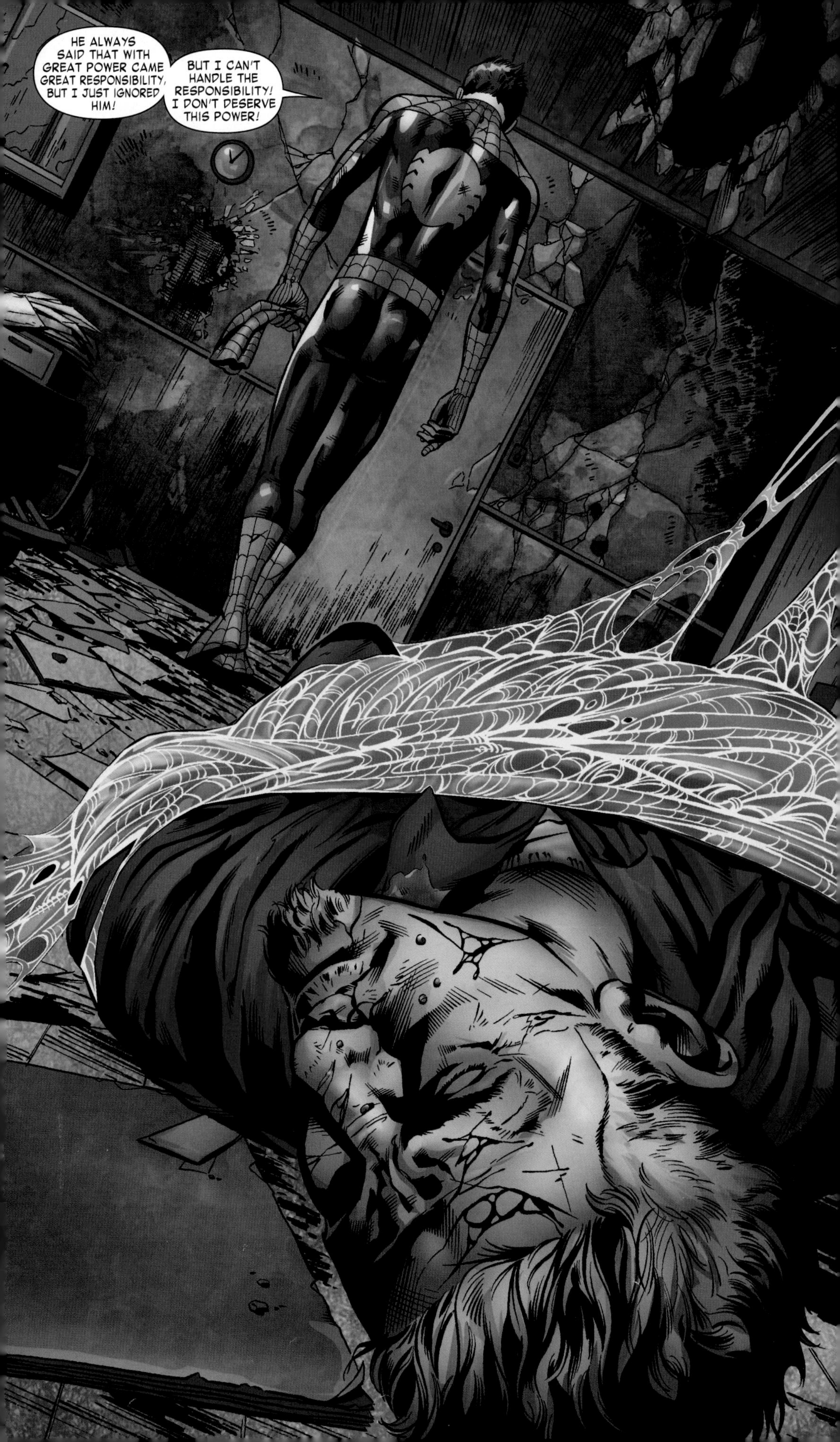
HE ALWAYS SAID THAT WITH GREAT POWER CAME GREAT RESPONSIBILITY, BUT I JUST IGNORED HIM!
BUT I CAN'T HANDLE THE RESPONSIBILITY! I DON'T DESERVE THIS POWER!

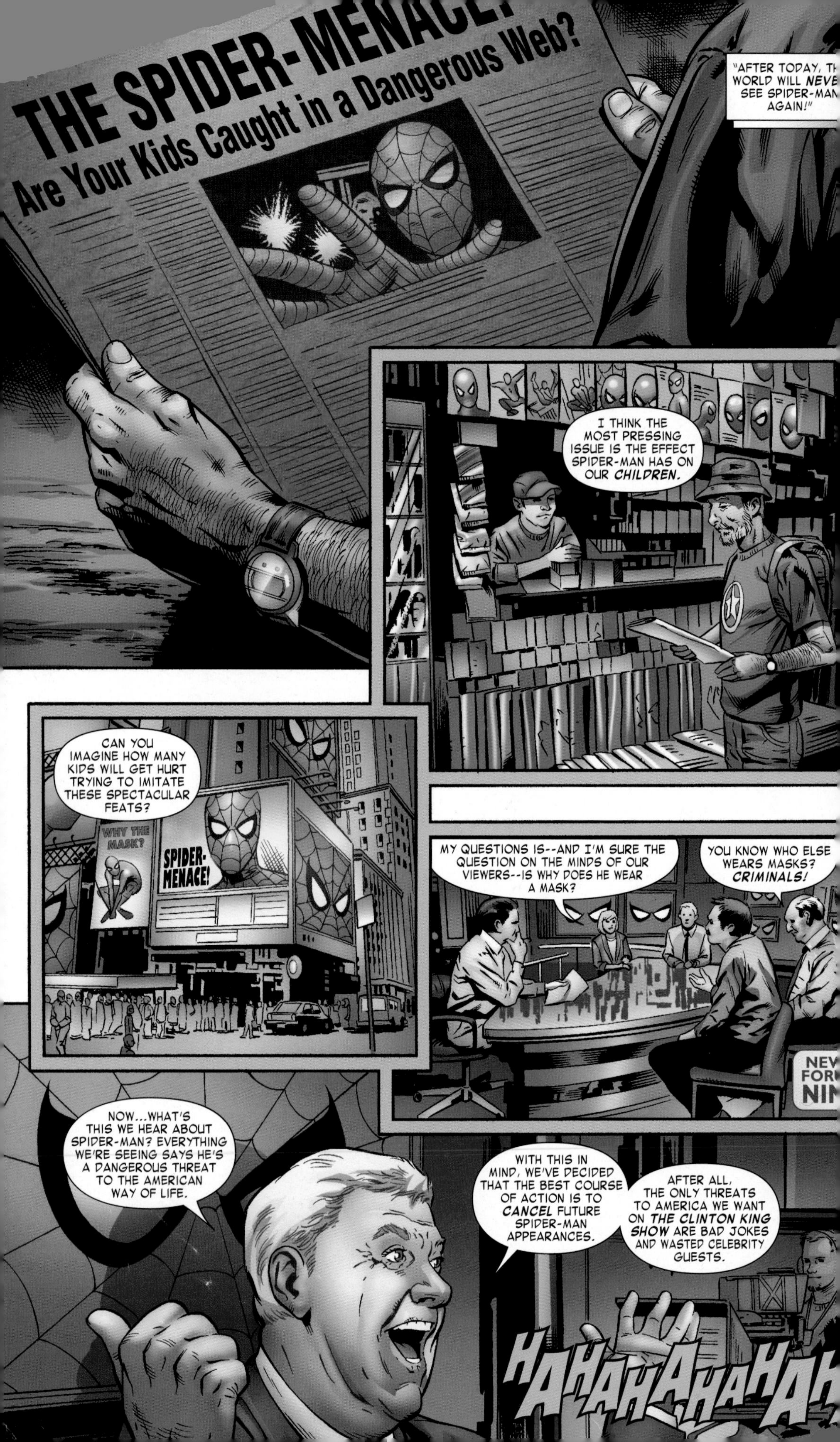
THE SPIDER-MENACE!
Are Your Kids Caught in a Dangerous Web?
"AFTER TODAY, TH WORLD WILL NEVE SEE SPIDER-MAN AGAIN!"
I THINK THE MOST PRESSING ISSUE IS THE EFFECT SPIDER-MAN HAS ON OUR CHILDREN.
CAN YOU IMAGINE HOW MANY KIDS WILL GET HURT TRYING TO IMITATE THESE SPECTACULAR FEATS?
WHY THE MASK?
SPIDER-MENACE!
MY QUESTIONS IS--AND I'M SURE THE QUESTION ON THE MINDS OF OUR VIEWERS--IS WHY DOES HE WEAR A MASK?
YOU KNOW WHO ELSE WEARS MASKS? CRIMINALS!
NOW...WHAT'S THIS WE HEAR ABOUT SPIDER-MAN? EVERYTHING WE'RE SEEING SAYS HE'S A DANGEROUS THREAT TO THE AMERICAN WAY OF LIFE.
WITH THIS IN MIND, WE'VE DECIDED THAT THE BEST COURSE OF ACTION IS TO CANCEL FUTURE SPIDER-MAN APPEARANCES.
AFTER ALL, THE ONLY THREATS TO AMERICA WE WANT ON THE CLINTON KING SHOW ARE BAD JOKES AND WASTED CELEBRITY GUESTS.
HAHAHAHAHAHAH

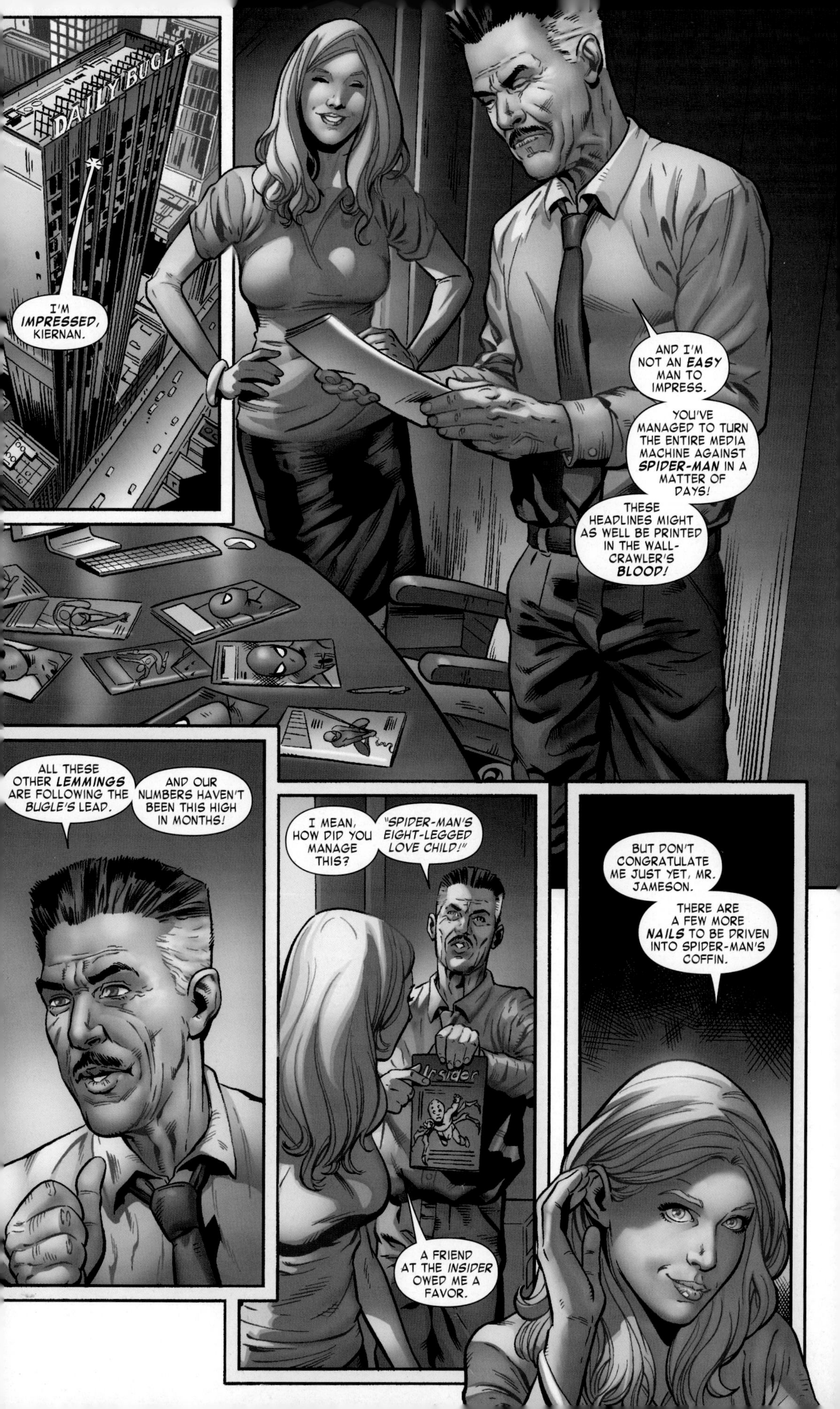
DAILY BUGLE
I'M *IMPRESSED,* KIERNAN.
AND I'M NOT AN *EASY* MAN TO IMPRESS.
YOU'VE MANAGED TO TURN THE ENTIRE MEDIA MACHINE AGAINST *SPIDER-MAN* IN A MATTER OF DAYS!
THESE HEADLINES MIGHT AS WELL BE PRINTED IN THE WALL-CRAWLER'S *BLOOD!*
ALL THESE OTHER *LEMMINGS* ARE FOLLOWING THE *BUGLE'S* LEAD.
AND OUR NUMBERS HAVEN'T BEEN THIS HIGH IN MONTHS!
I MEAN, HOW DID YOU MANAGE THIS?
"SPIDER-MAN'S EIGHT-LEGGED LOVE CHILD!"
Insider
A FRIEND AT THE *INSIDER* OWED ME A FAVOR.
BUT DON'T CONGRATULATE ME JUST YET, MR. JAMESON.
THERE ARE A FEW MORE *NAILS* TO BE DRIVEN INTO SPIDER-MAN'S COFFIN.

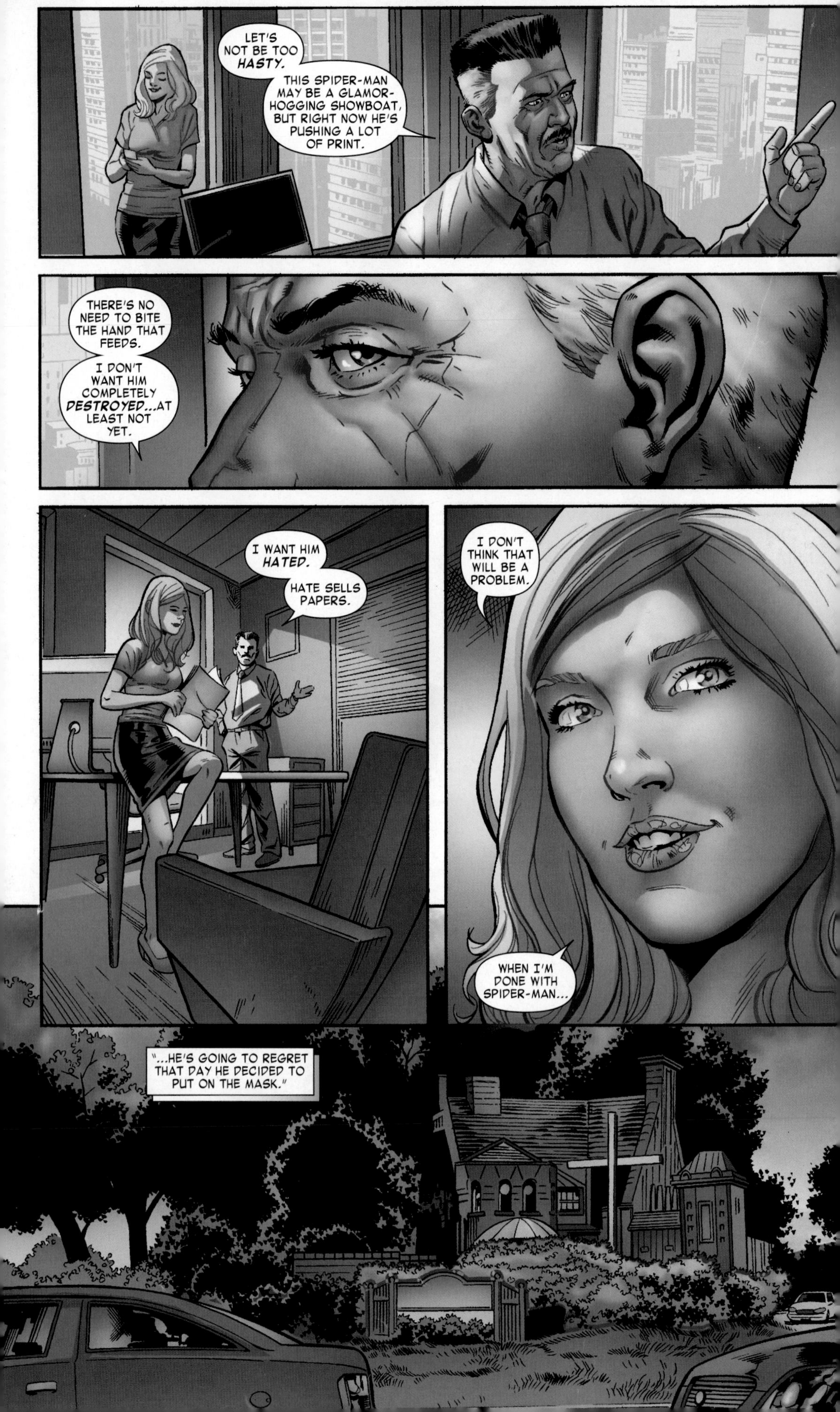
LET'S NOT BE TOO HASTY.
THIS SPIDER-MAN MAY BE A GLAMOR-HOGGING SHOWBOAT, BUT RIGHT NOW HE'S PUSHING A LOT OF PRINT.
THERE'S NO NEED TO BITE THE HAND THAT FEEDS.
I DON'T WANT HIM COMPLETELY DESTROYED...AT LEAST NOT YET.
I WANT HIM HATED.
HATE SELLS PAPERS.
I DON'T THINK THAT WILL BE A PROBLEM.
WHEN I'M DONE WITH SPIDER-MAN...
"...HE'S GOING TO REGRET THAT DAY HE DECIDED TO PUT ON THE MASK."

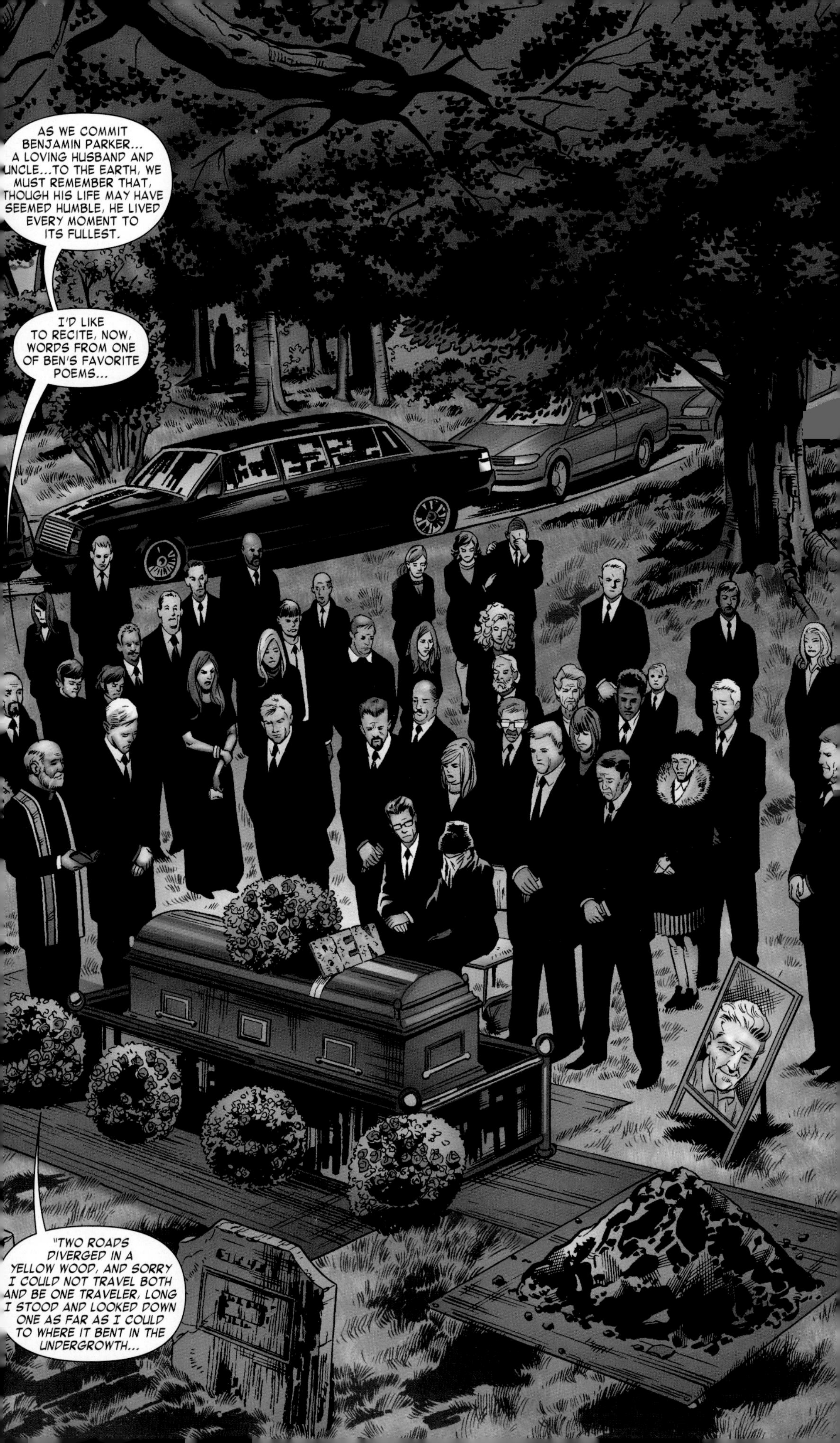
AS WE COMMIT BENJAMIN PARKER... A LOVING HUSBAND AND UNCLE...TO THE EARTH, WE MUST REMEMBER THAT, THOUGH HIS LIFE MAY HAVE SEEMED HUMBLE, HE LIVED EVERY MOMENT TO ITS FULLEST.
I'D LIKE TO RECITE, NOW, WORDS FROM ONE OF BEN'S FAVORITE POEMS...
BEN
"TWO ROADS DIVERGED IN A YELLOW WOOD, AND SORRY I COULD NOT TRAVEL BOTH AND BE ONE TRAVELER, LONG I STOOD AND LOOKED DOWN ONE AS FAR AS I COULD TO WHERE IT BENT IN THE UNDERGROWTH...

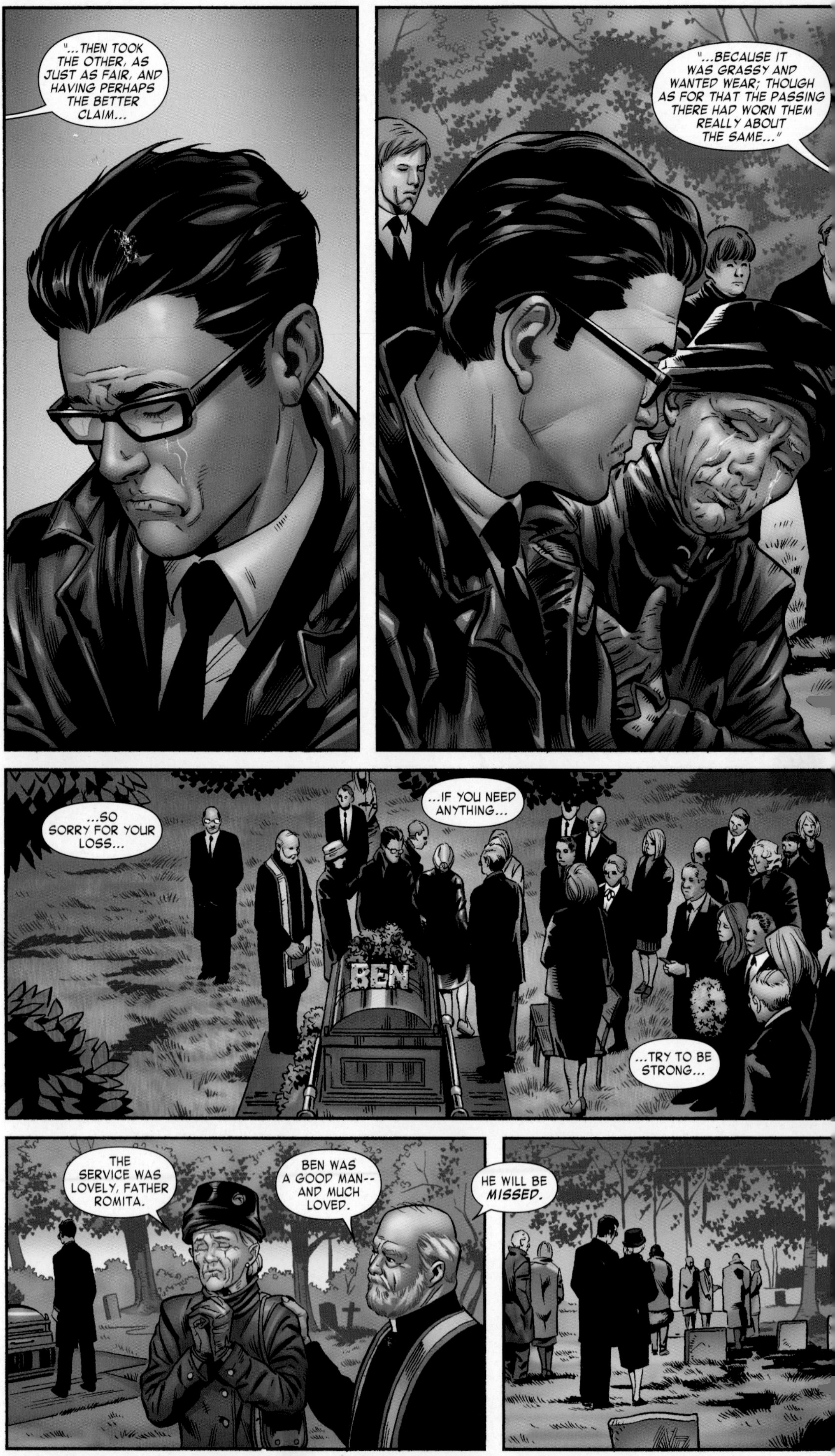
"...THEN TOOK THE OTHER, AS JUST AS FAIR, AND HAVING PERHAPS THE BETTER CLAIM...
"...BECAUSE IT WAS GRASSY AND WANTED WEAR; THOUGH AS FOR THAT THE PASSING THERE HAD WORN THEM REALLY ABOUT THE SAME..."
...SO SORRY FOR YOUR LOSS...
...IF YOU NEED ANYTHING...
BEN
...TRY TO BE STRONG...
THE SERVICE WAS LOVELY, FATHER ROMITA.
BEN WAS A GOOD MAN-- AND MUCH LOVED.
HE WILL BE *MISSED*.

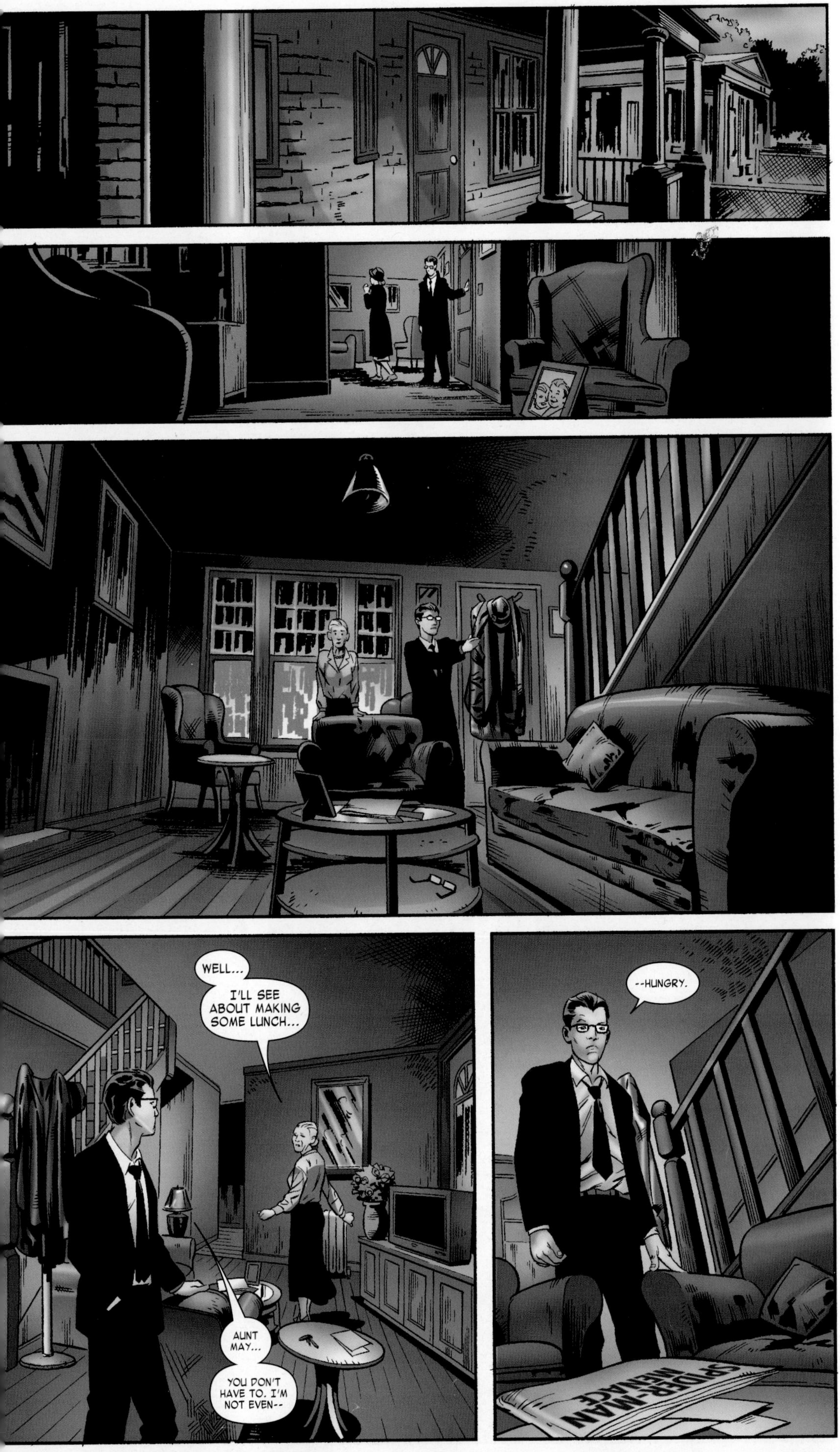

WELL...
I'LL SEE ABOUT MAKING SOME LUNCH...
AUNT MAY...
YOU DON'T HAVE TO. I'M NOT EVEN--
--HUNGRY.
SPIDER-MAN MENACE

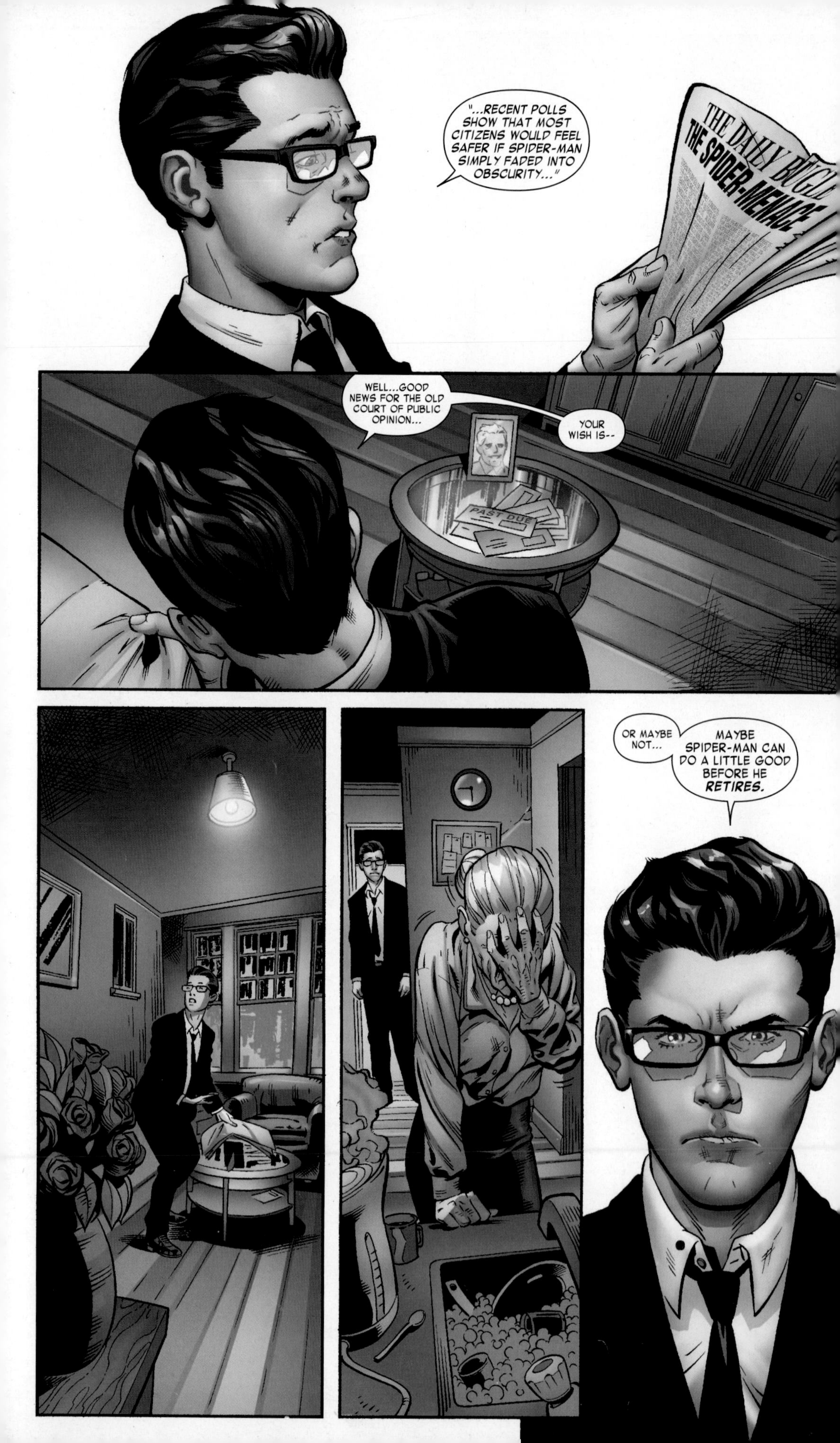
"...RECENT POLLS SHOW THAT MOST CITIZENS WOULD FEEL SAFER IF SPIDER-MAN SIMPLY FADED INTO OBSCURITY..."
THE DAILY BUGLE
THE SPIDER-MENACE
WELL...GOOD NEWS FOR THE OLD COURT OF PUBLIC OPINION...
YOUR WISH IS--
PAST DUE
OR MAYBE NOT...
MAYBE SPIDER-MAN CAN DO A LITTLE GOOD BEFORE HE RETIRES.

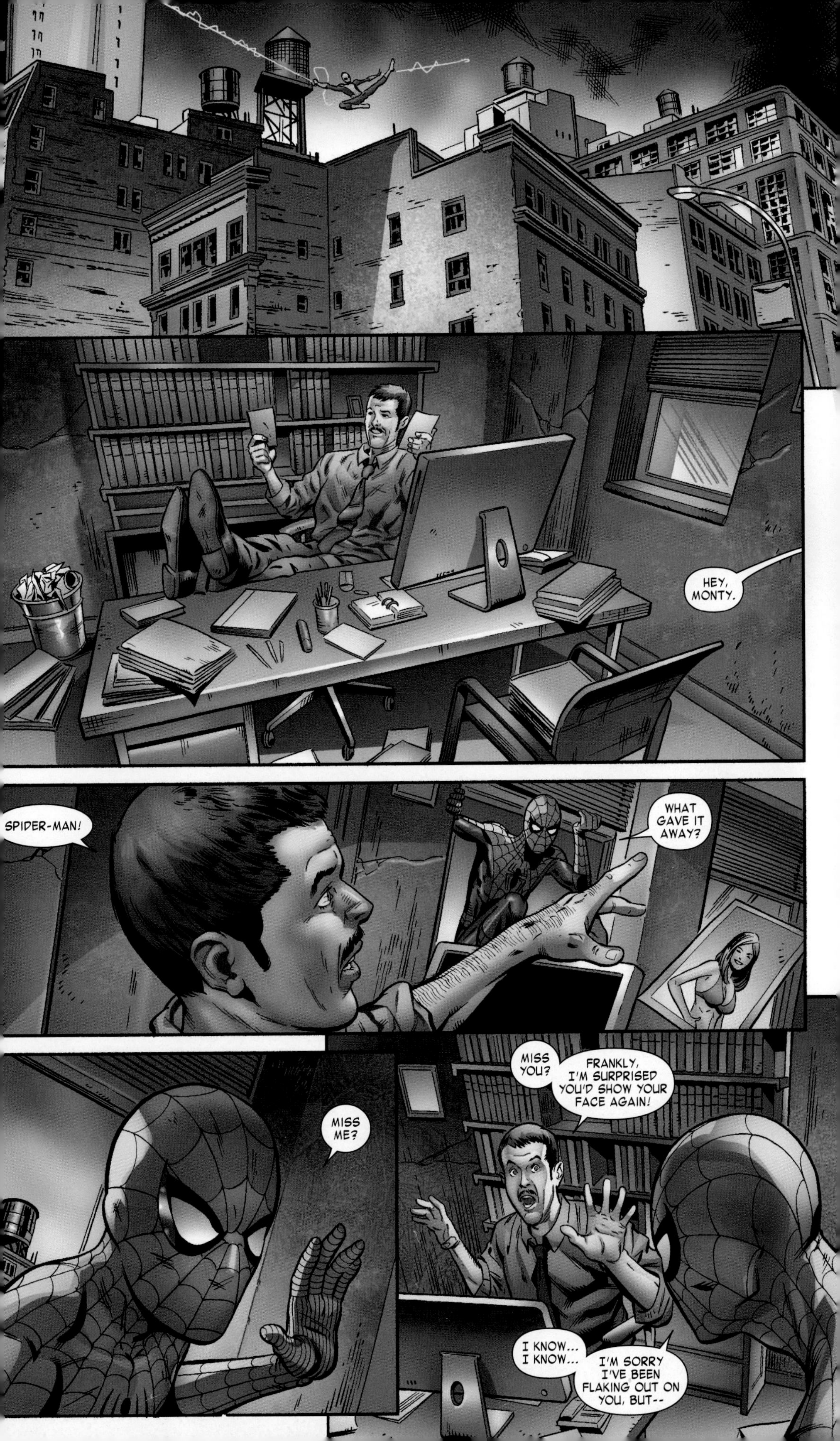
HEY, MONTY.
SPIDER-MAN!
WHAT GAVE IT AWAY?
MISS ME?
MISS YOU?
FRANKLY, I'M SURPRISED YOU'D SHOW YOUR FACE AGAIN!
I KNOW... I KNOW...
I'M SORRY I'VE BEEN FLAKING OUT ON YOU, BUT--

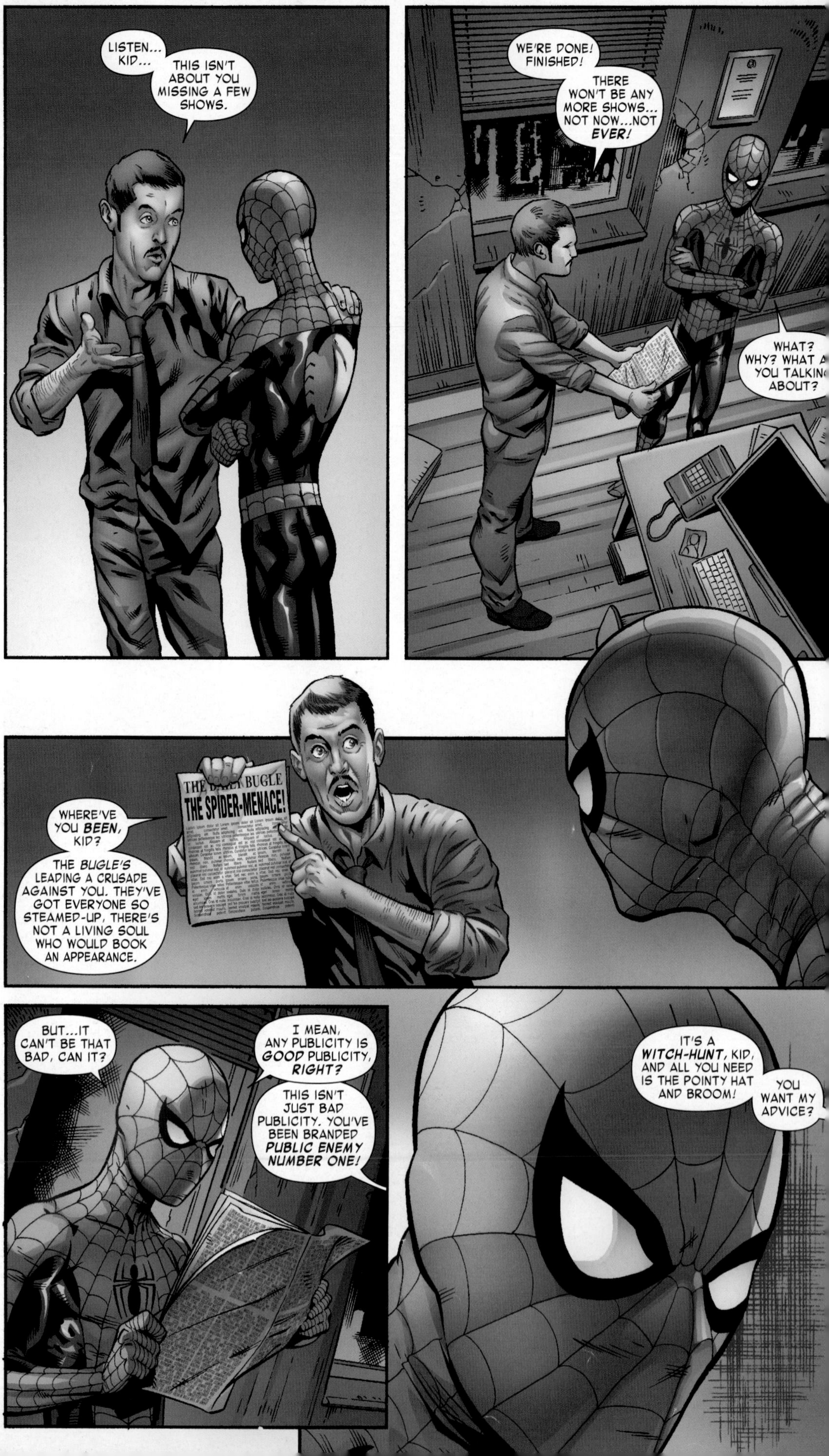
LISTEN... KID...
THIS ISN'T ABOUT YOU MISSING A FEW SHOWS.
WE'RE DONE! FINISHED!
THERE WON'T BE ANY MORE SHOWS... NOT NOW...NOT EVER!
WHAT? WHY? WHAT A YOU TALKIN ABOUT?
THE SPIDER-MENACE!
WHERE'VE YOU BEEN, KID?
THE BUGLE'S LEADING A CRUSADE AGAINST YOU. THEY'VE GOT EVERYONE SO STEAMED-UP, THERE'S NOT A LIVING SOUL WHO WOULD BOOK AN APPEARANCE.
BUT...IT CAN'T BE THAT BAD, CAN IT?
I MEAN, ANY PUBLICITY IS GOOD PUBLICITY, RIGHT?
THIS ISN'T JUST BAD PUBLICITY. YOU'VE BEEN BRANDED PUBLIC ENEMY NUMBER ONE!
IT'S A WITCH-HUNT, KID, AND ALL YOU NEED IS THE POINTY HAT AND BROOM!
YOU WANT MY ADVICE?

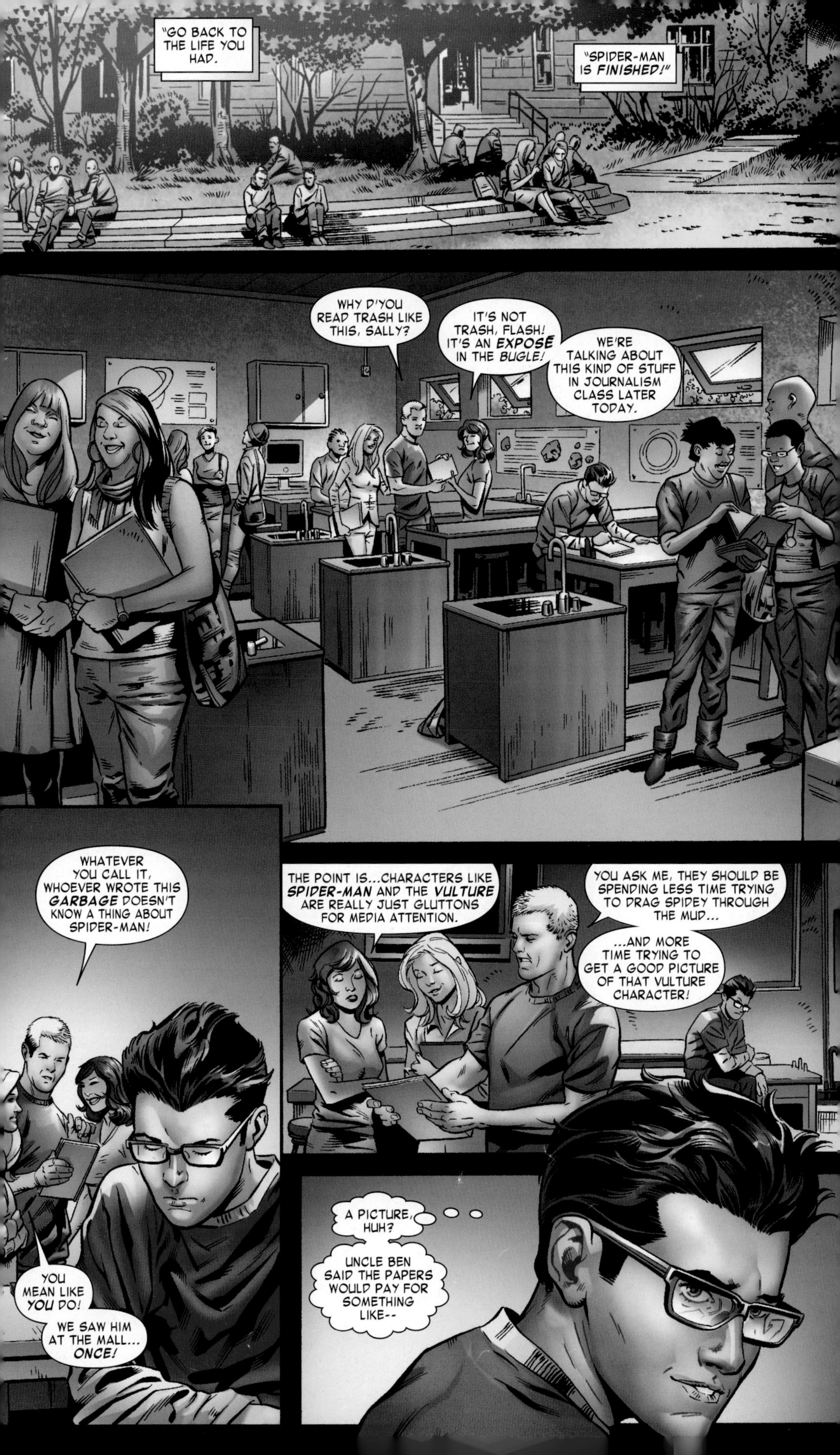
"GO BACK TO THE LIFE YOU HAD.
"SPIDER-MAN IS FINISHED!"
WHY D'YOU READ TRASH LIKE THIS, SALLY?
IT'S NOT TRASH, FLASH! IT'S AN EXPOSÉ IN THE BUGLE!
WE'RE TALKING ABOUT THIS KIND OF STUFF IN JOURNALISM CLASS LATER TODAY.
WHATEVER YOU CALL IT, WHOEVER WROTE THIS GARBAGE DOESN'T KNOW A THING ABOUT SPIDER-MAN!
YOU MEAN LIKE YOU DO!
WE SAW HIM AT THE MALL... ONCE!
THE POINT IS...CHARACTERS LIKE SPIDER-MAN AND THE VULTURE ARE REALLY JUST GLUTTONS FOR MEDIA ATTENTION.
YOU ASK ME, THEY SHOULD BE SPENDING LESS TIME TRYING TO DRAG SPIDEY THROUGH THE MUD...
...AND MORE TIME TRYING TO GET A GOOD PICTURE OF THAT VULTURE CHARACTER!
A PICTURE, HUH?
UNCLE BEN SAID THE PAPERS WOULD PAY FOR SOMETHING LIKE--

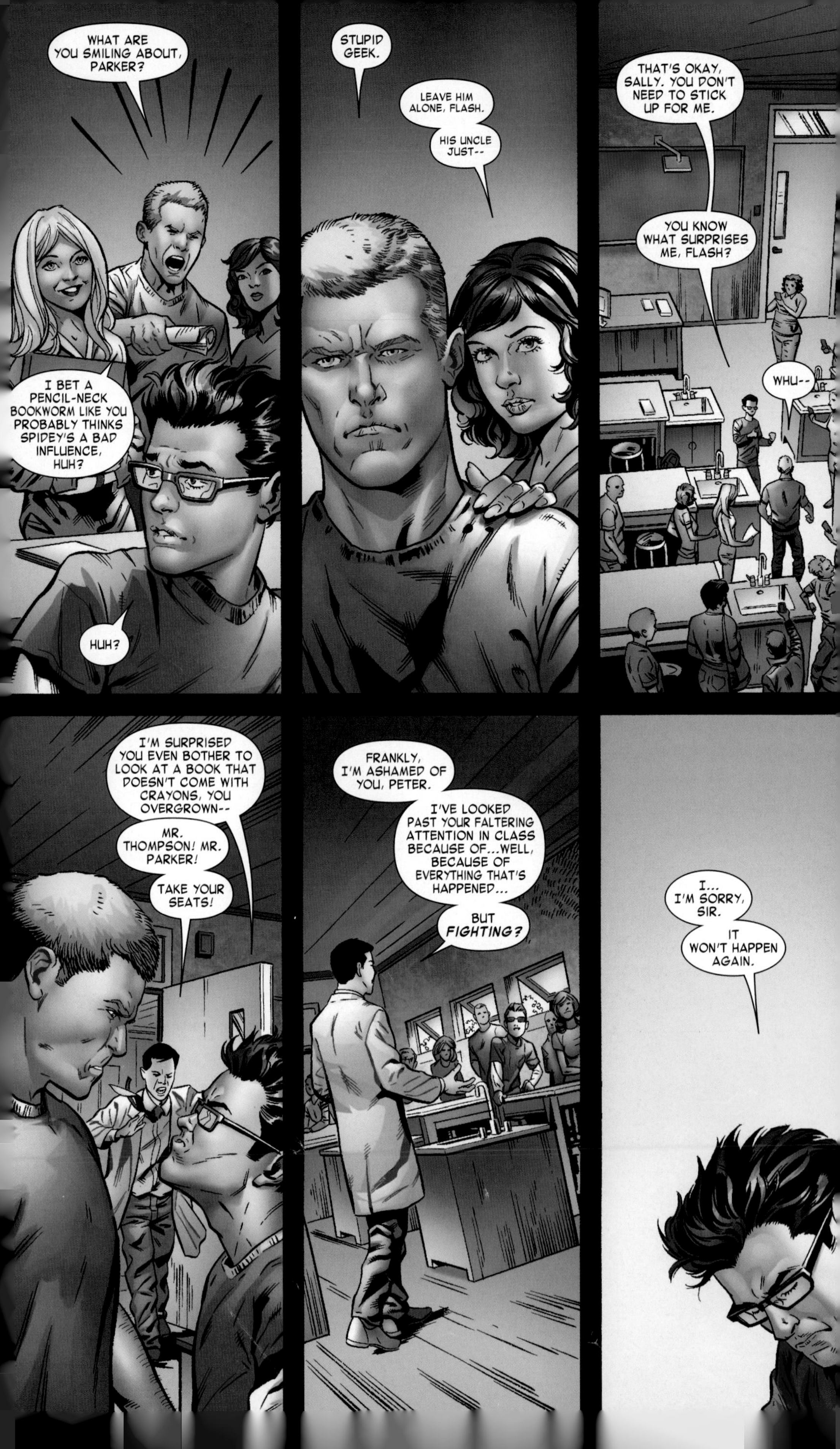
WHAT ARE YOU SMILING ABOUT, PARKER?
I BET A PENCIL-NECK BOOKWORM LIKE YOU PROBABLY THINKS SPIDEY'S A BAD INFLUENCE, HUH?
HUH?
STUPID GEEK.
LEAVE HIM ALONE, FLASH.
HIS UNCLE JUST--
THAT'S OKAY, SALLY. YOU DON'T NEED TO STICK UP FOR ME.
YOU KNOW WHAT SURPRISES ME, FLASH?
WHU--
I'M SURPRISED YOU EVEN BOTHER TO LOOK AT A BOOK THAT DOESN'T COME WITH CRAYONS, YOU OVERGROWN--
MR. THOMPSON! MR. PARKER!
TAKE YOUR SEATS!
FRANKLY, I'M ASHAMED OF YOU, PETER.
I'VE LOOKED PAST YOUR FALTERING ATTENTION IN CLASS BECAUSE OF...WELL, BECAUSE OF EVERYTHING THAT'S HAPPENED...
BUT FIGHTING?
I... I'M SORRY, SIR.
IT WON'T HAPPEN AGAIN.

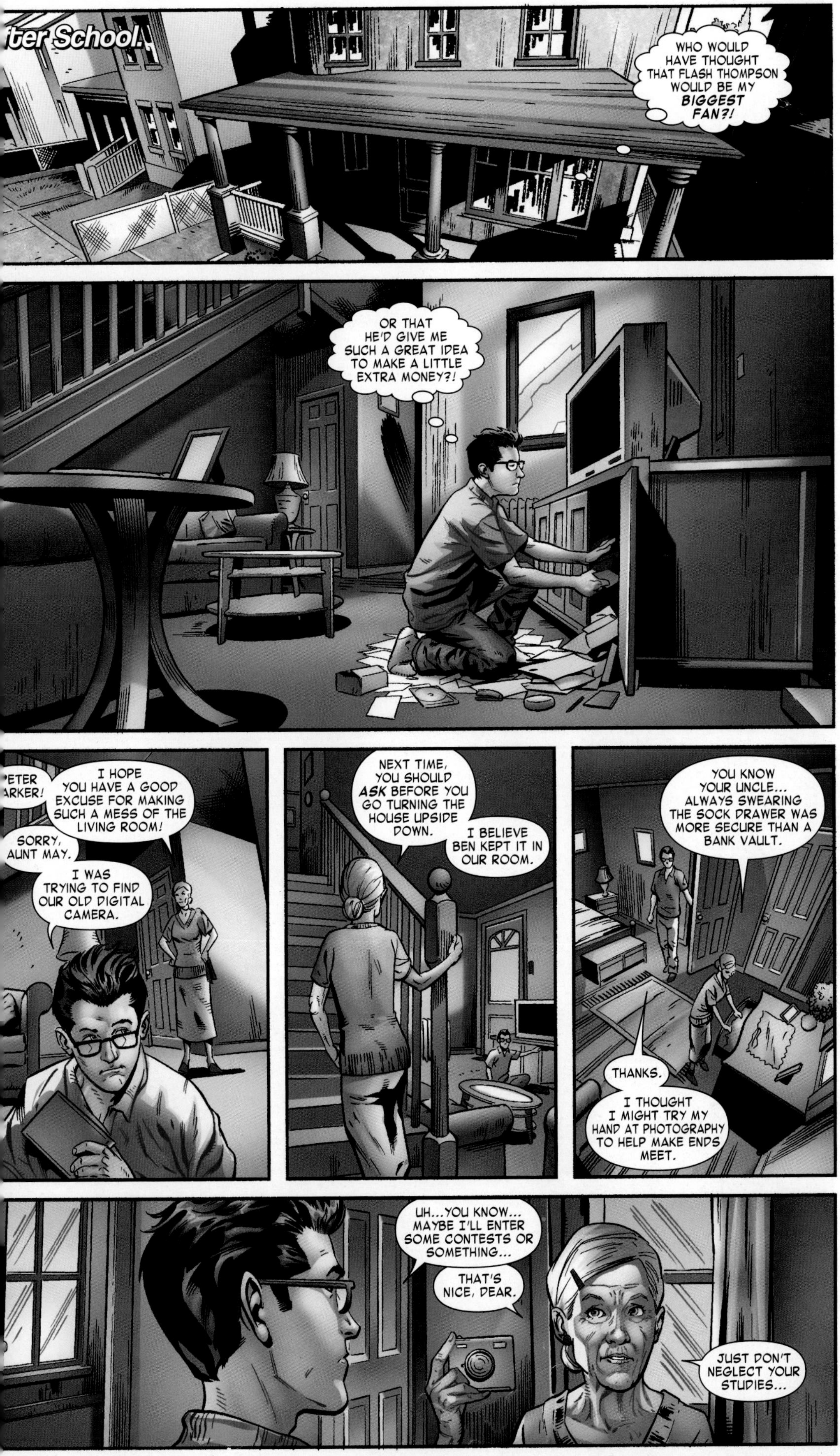
ter School.
WHO WOULD HAVE THOUGHT THAT FLASH THOMPSON WOULD BE MY BIGGEST FAN?!
OR THAT HE'D GIVE ME SUCH A GREAT IDEA TO MAKE A LITTLE EXTRA MONEY?!
ETER ARKER!
I HOPE YOU HAVE A GOOD EXCUSE FOR MAKING SUCH A MESS OF THE LIVING ROOM!
SORRY, AUNT MAY.
I WAS TRYING TO FIND OUR OLD DIGITAL CAMERA.
NEXT TIME, YOU SHOULD ASK BEFORE YOU GO TURNING THE HOUSE UPSIDE DOWN.
I BELIEVE BEN KEPT IT IN OUR ROOM.
YOU KNOW YOUR UNCLE... ALWAYS SWEARING THE SOCK DRAWER WAS MORE SECURE THAN A BANK VAULT.
THANKS.
I THOUGHT I MIGHT TRY MY HAND AT PHOTOGRAPHY TO HELP MAKE ENDS MEET.
UH...YOU KNOW... MAYBE I'LL ENTER SOME CONTESTS OR SOMETHING...
THAT'S NICE, DEAR.
JUST DON'T NEGLECT YOUR STUDIES...

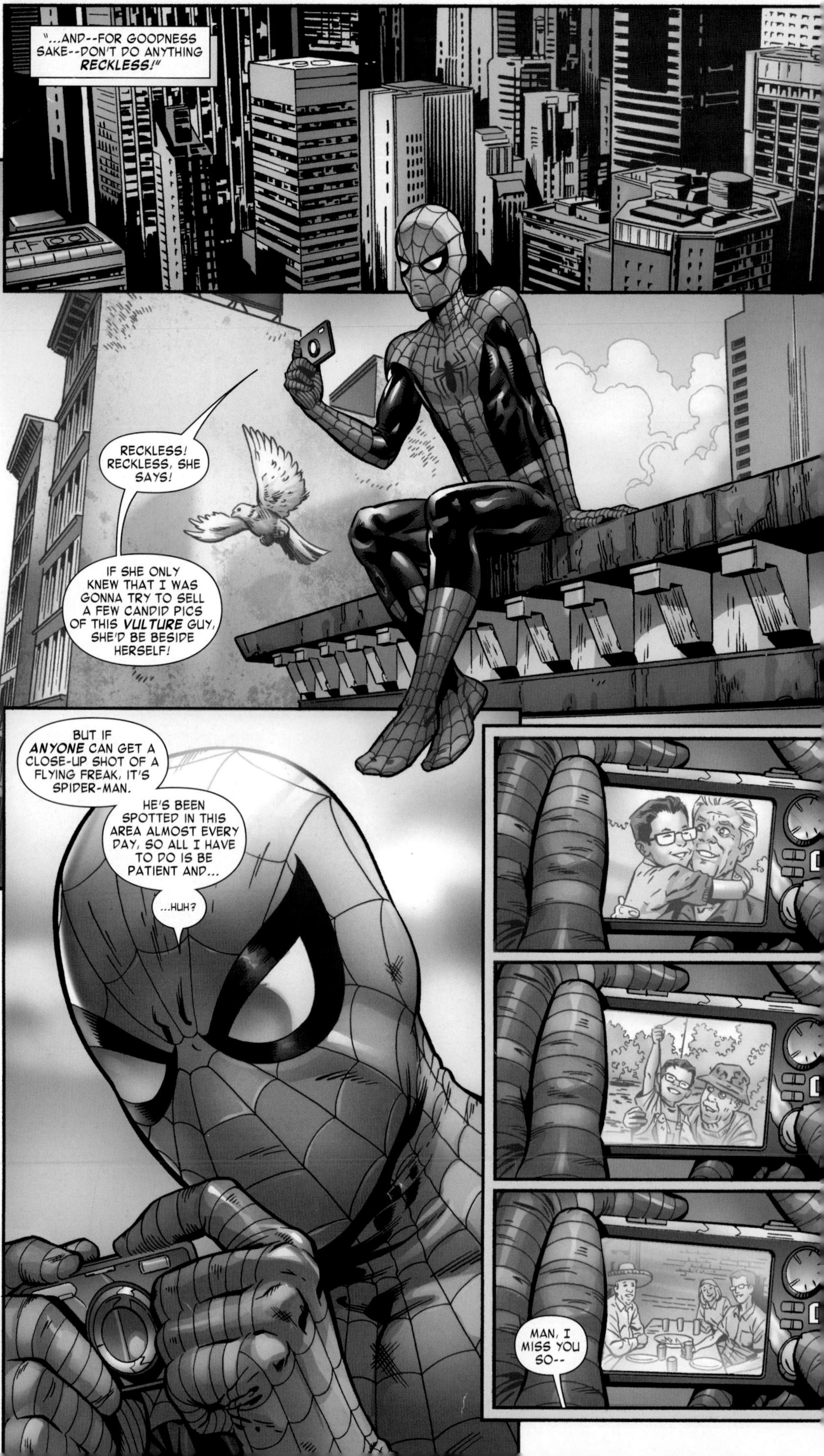
"...AND--FOR GOODNESS SAKE--DON'T DO ANYTHING RECKLESS!"
RECKLESS! RECKLESS, SHE SAYS!
IF SHE ONLY KNEW THAT I WAS GONNA TRY TO SELL A FEW CANDID PICS OF THIS VULTURE GUY, SHE'D BE BESIDE HERSELF!
BUT IF ANYONE CAN GET A CLOSE-UP SHOT OF A FLYING FREAK, IT'S SPIDER-MAN.
HE'S BEEN SPOTTED IN THIS AREA ALMOST EVERY DAY, SO ALL I HAVE TO DO IS BE PATIENT AND...
...HUH?
MAN, I MISS YOU SO--

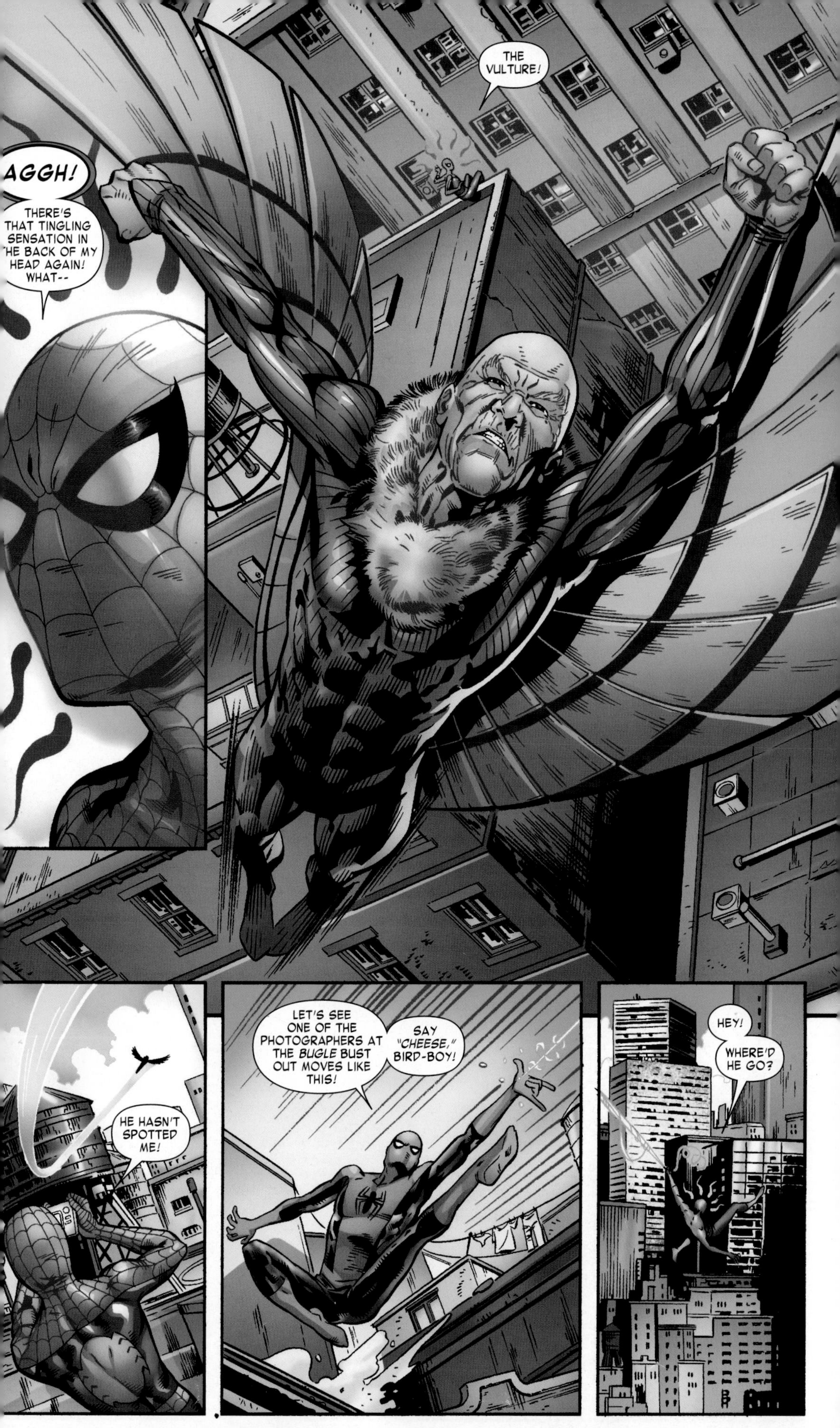
AGGH!
THERE'S THAT TINGLING SENSATION IN THE BACK OF MY HEAD AGAIN! WHAT--
THE VULTURE!
HE HASN'T SPOTTED ME!
LET'S SEE ONE OF THE PHOTOGRAPHERS AT THE *BUGLE* BUST OUT MOVES LIKE THIS!
SAY *"CHEESE,"* BIRD-BOY!
HEY!
WHERE'D HE GO?

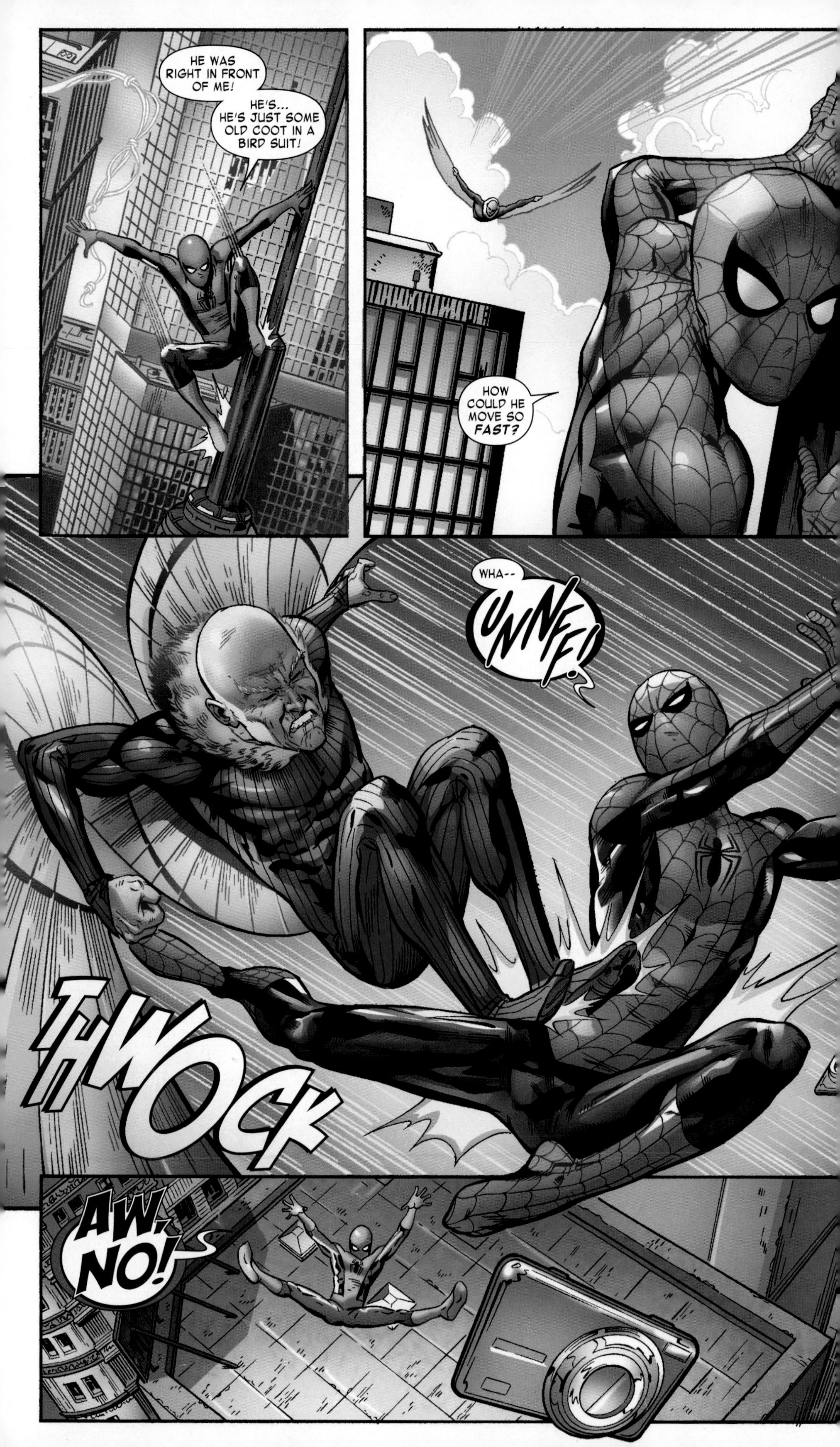

HE WAS RIGHT IN FRONT OF ME!
HE'S... HE'S JUST SOME OLD COOT IN A BIRD SUIT!
HOW COULD HE MOVE SO FAST?
WHA--
UNNFF!
THWOCK
AW, NO!

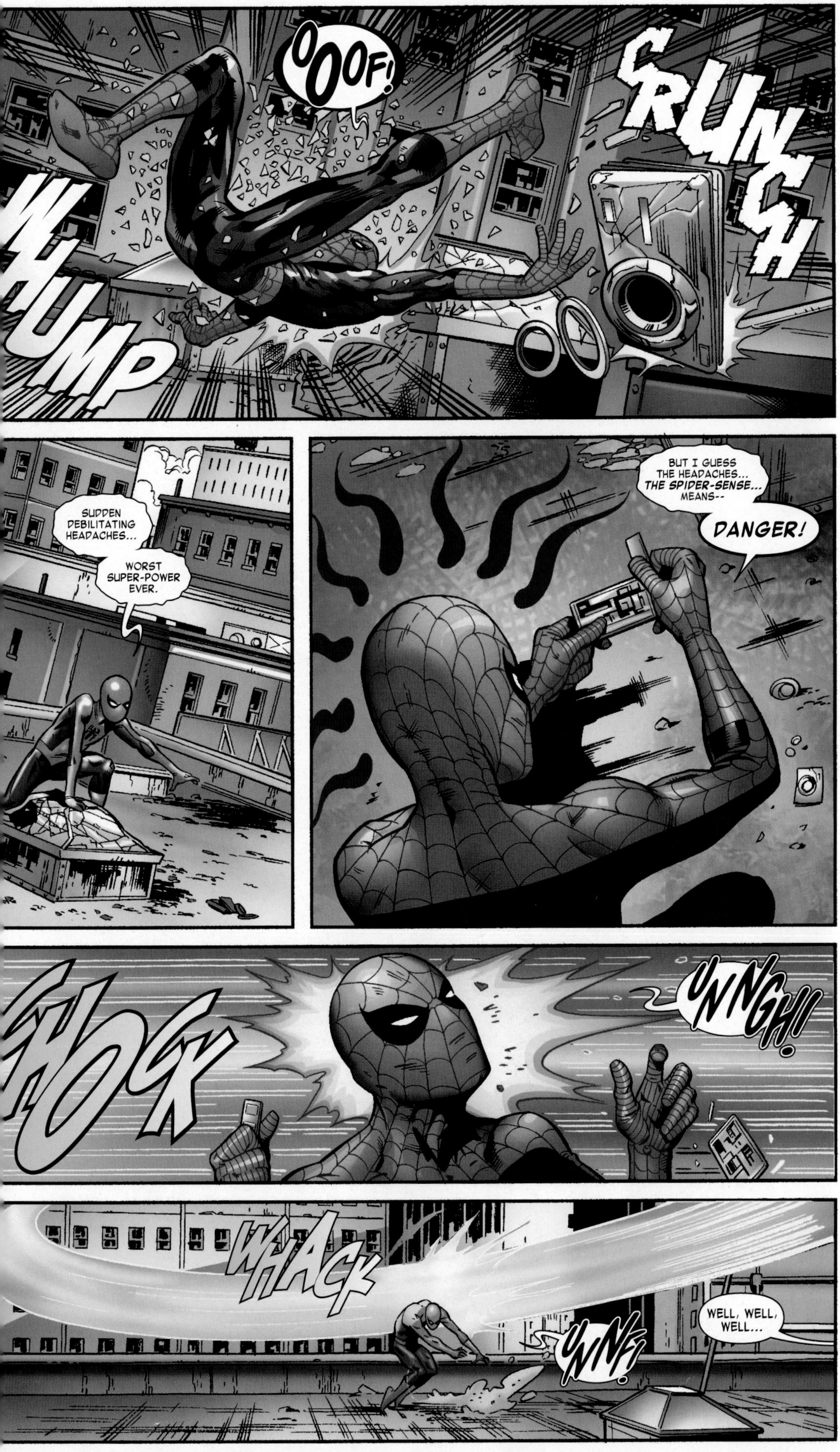
OOOF!
CRUNCH
WHUMP
SUDDEN DEBILITATING HEADACHES...
WORST SUPER-POWER EVER.
BUT I GUESS THE HEADACHES... THE SPIDER-SENSE... MEANS--
DANGER!
CHOCK
UNNGH!
WHACK
UNNF!
WELL, WELL, WELL...

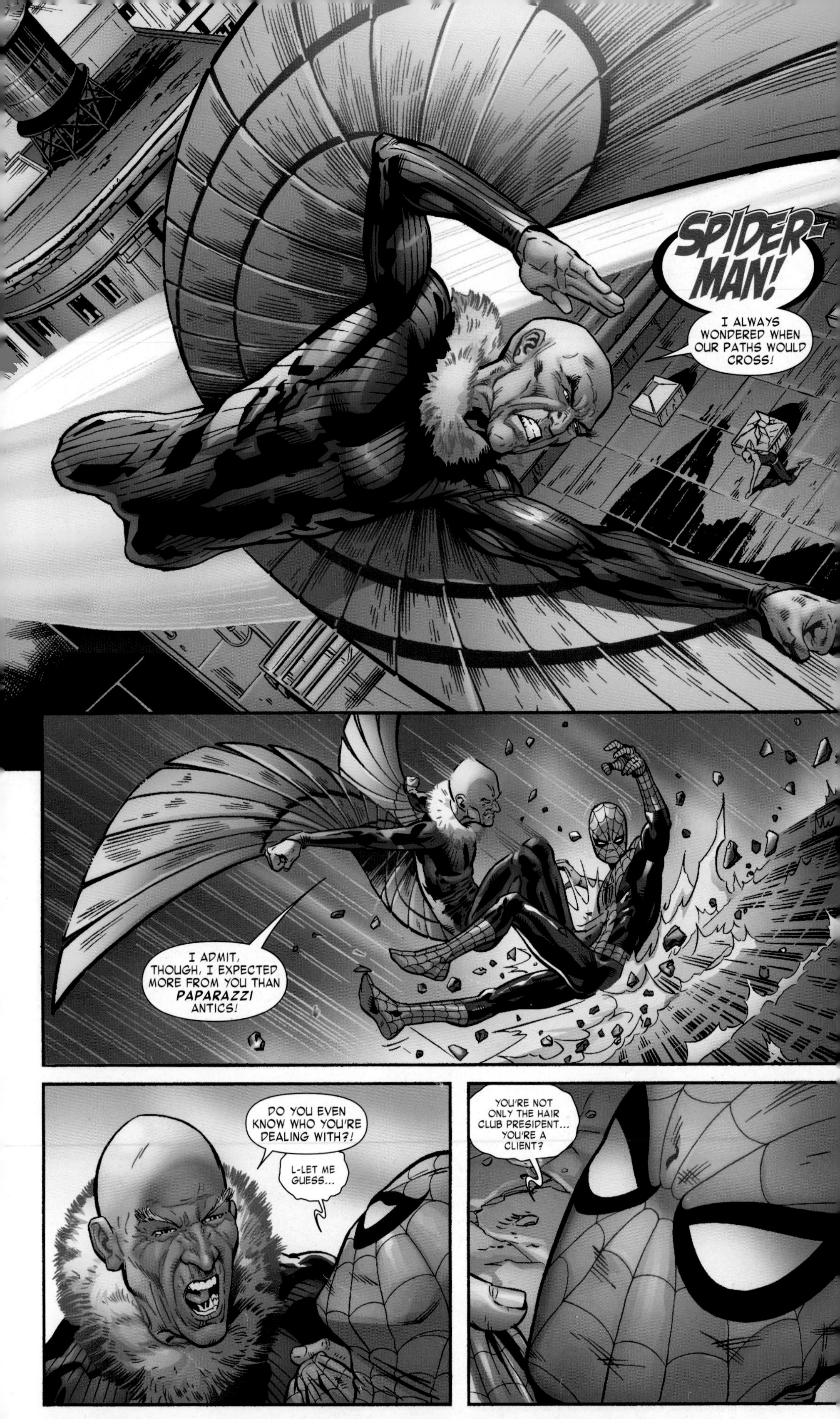
SPIDER-MAN!
I ALWAYS WONDERED WHEN OUR PATHS WOULD CROSS!
I ADMIT, THOUGH, I EXPECTED MORE FROM YOU THAN *PAPARAZZI* ANTICS!
DO YOU EVEN KNOW WHO YOU'RE DEALING WITH?!
L-LET ME GUESS...
YOU'RE NOT ONLY THE HAIR CLUB PRESIDENT... YOU'RE A CLIENT?

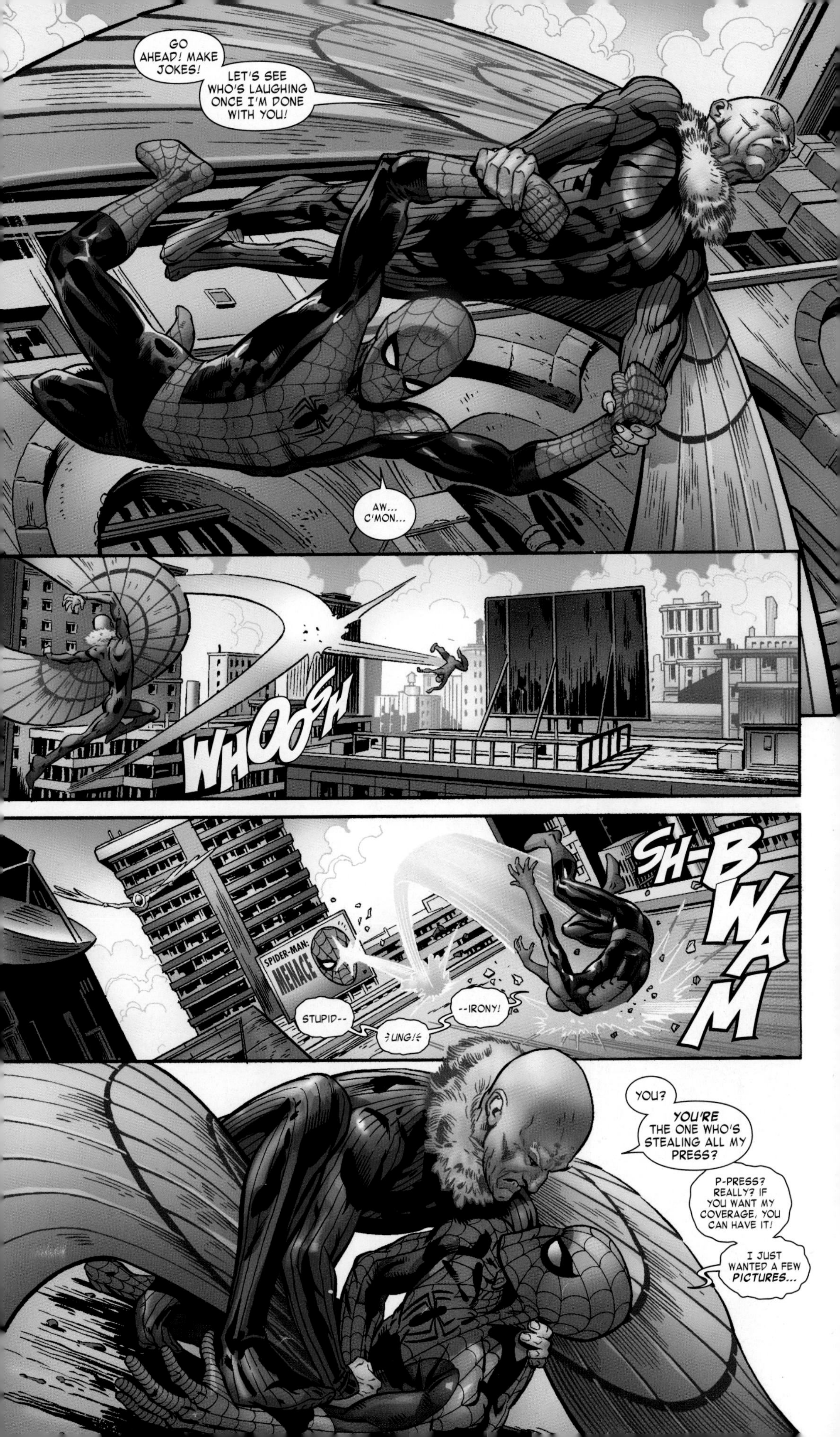
GO AHEAD! MAKE JOKES!
LET'S SEE WHO'S LAUGHING ONCE I'M DONE WITH YOU!
AW... C'MON...
WHOOSH
SH-BWAM
SPIDER-MAN: MENACE
STUPID--
UNG!
--IRONY!
YOU?
YOU'RE THE ONE WHO'S STEALING ALL MY PRESS?
P-PRESS? REALLY? IF YOU WANT MY COVERAGE, YOU CAN HAVE IT!
I JUST WANTED A FEW PICTURES...

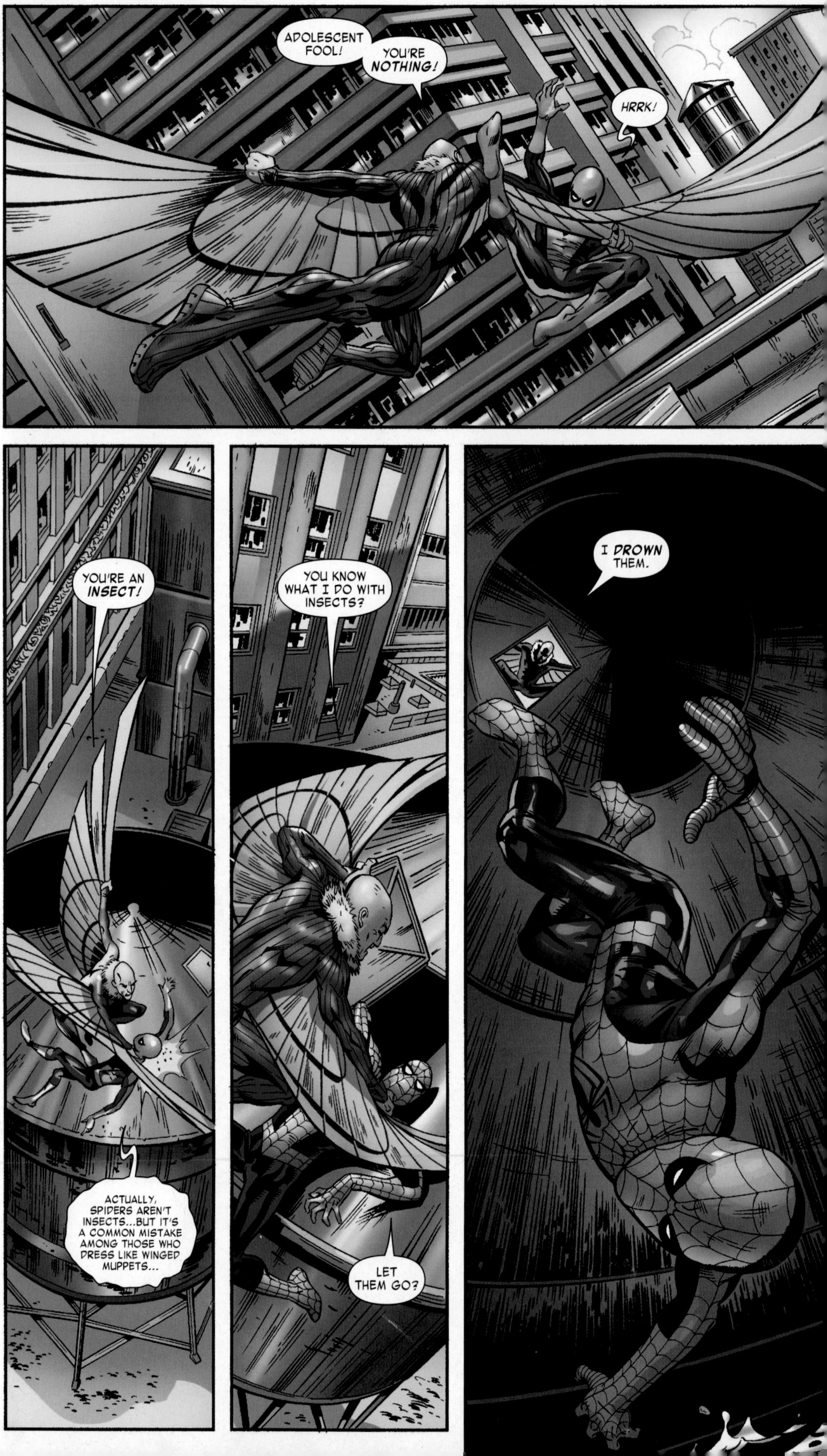
ADOLESCENT FOOL!
YOU'RE NOTHING!
HRRK!
YOU'RE AN INSECT!
ACTUALLY, SPIDERS AREN'T INSECTS...BUT IT'S A COMMON MISTAKE AMONG THOSE WHO DRESS LIKE WINGED MUPPETS...
YOU KNOW WHAT I DO WITH INSECTS?
LET THEM GO?
I DROWN THEM.

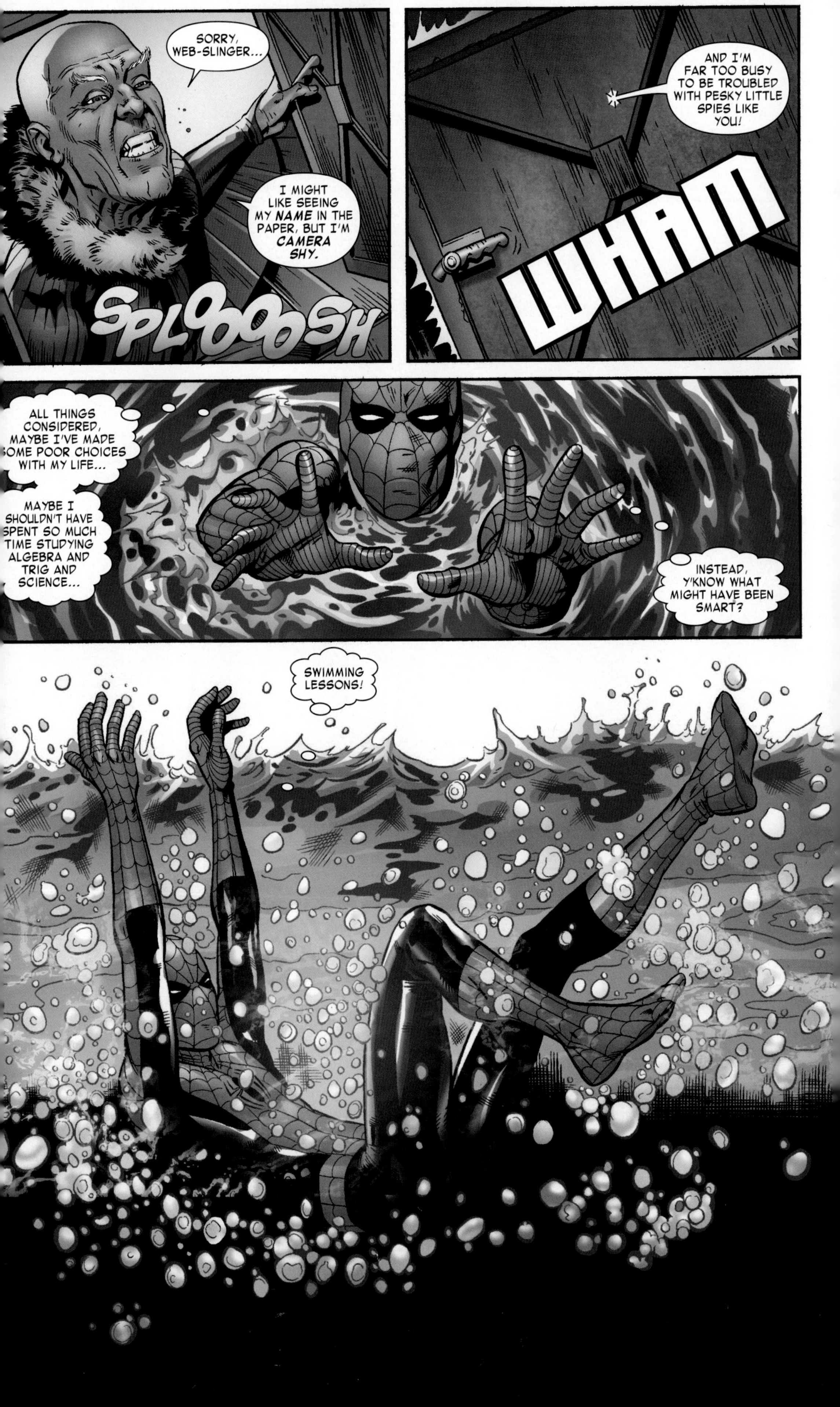
SORRY, WEB-SLINGER...
I MIGHT LIKE SEEING MY NAME IN THE PAPER, BUT I'M CAMERA SHY.
SPLOOOOSH
AND I'M FAR TOO BUSY TO BE TROUBLED WITH PESKY LITTLE SPIES LIKE YOU!
WHAM
ALL THINGS CONSIDERED, MAYBE I'VE MADE SOME POOR CHOICES WITH MY LIFE...
MAYBE I SHOULDN'T HAVE SPENT SO MUCH TIME STUDYING ALGEBRA AND TRIG AND SCIENCE...
INSTEAD, Y'KNOW WHAT MIGHT HAVE BEEN SMART?
SWIMMING LESSONS!

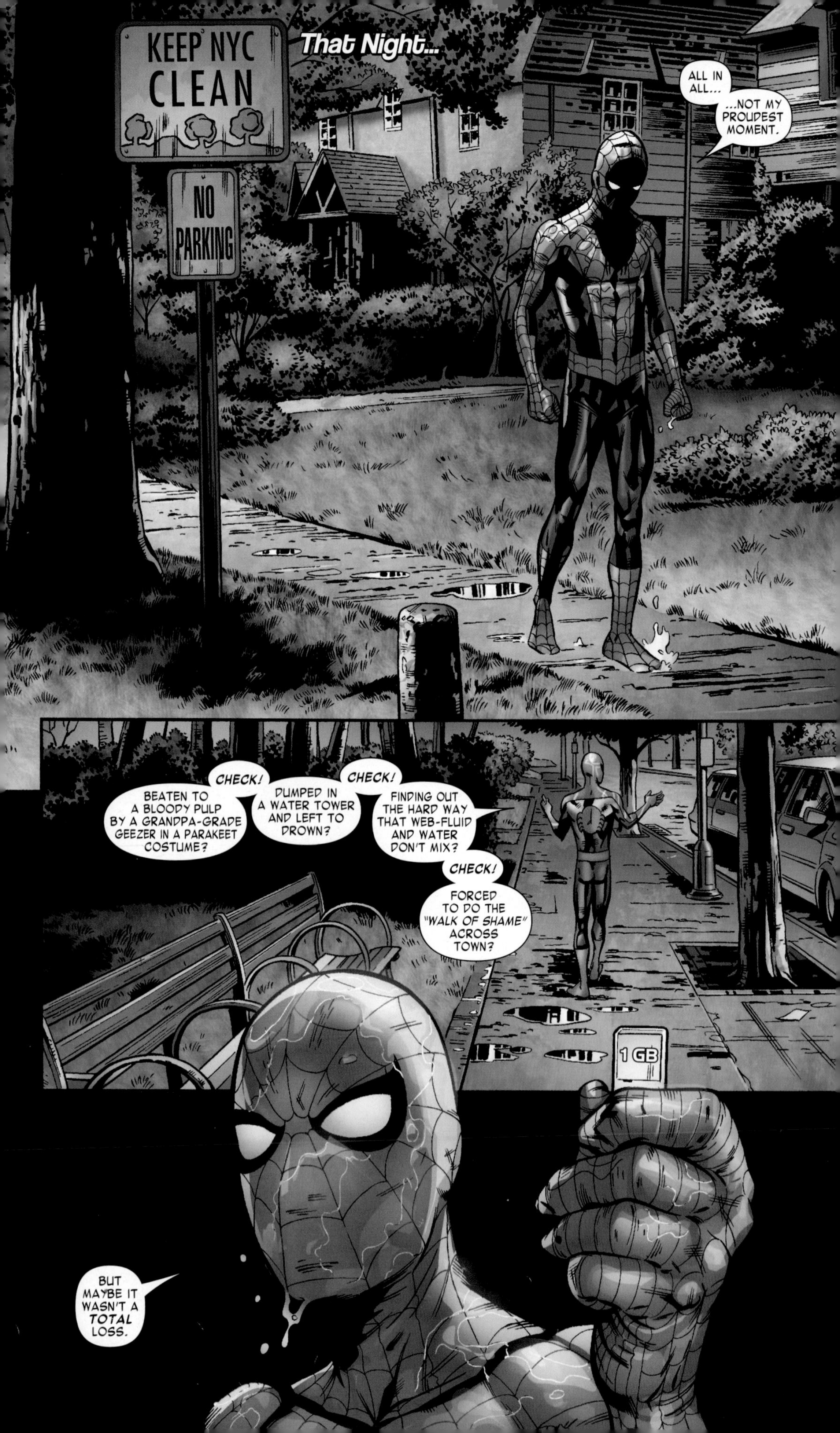
KEEP NYC CLEAN
NO PARKING
That Night...
ALL IN ALL...
...NOT MY PROUDEST MOMENT.
BEATEN TO A BLOODY PULP BY A GRANDPA-GRADE GEEZER IN A PARAKEET COSTUME?
CHECK!
DUMPED IN A WATER TOWER AND LEFT TO DROWN?
CHECK!
FINDING OUT THE HARD WAY THAT WEB-FLUID AND WATER DON'T MIX?
CHECK!
FORCED TO DO THE "WALK OF SHAME" ACROSS TOWN?
1 GB
BUT MAYBE IT WASN'T A *TOTAL* LOSS.

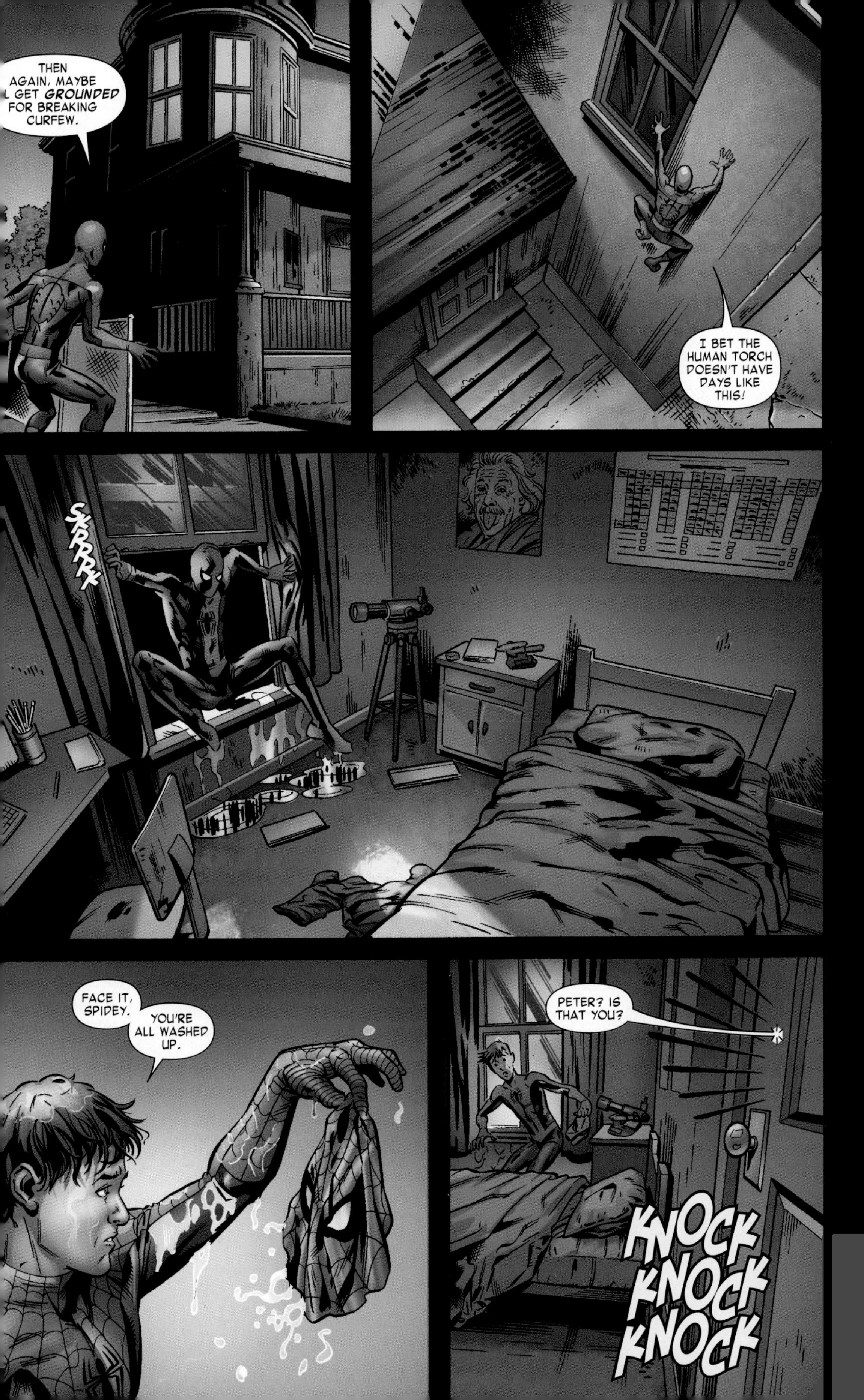
THEN AGAIN, MAYBE I'LL GET GROUNDED FOR BREAKING CURFEW.
I BET THE HUMAN TORCH DOESN'T HAVE DAYS LIKE THIS!
SKRRRK
FACE IT, SPIDEY.
YOU'RE ALL WASHED UP.
PETER? IS THAT YOU?
KNOCK KNOCK KNOCK

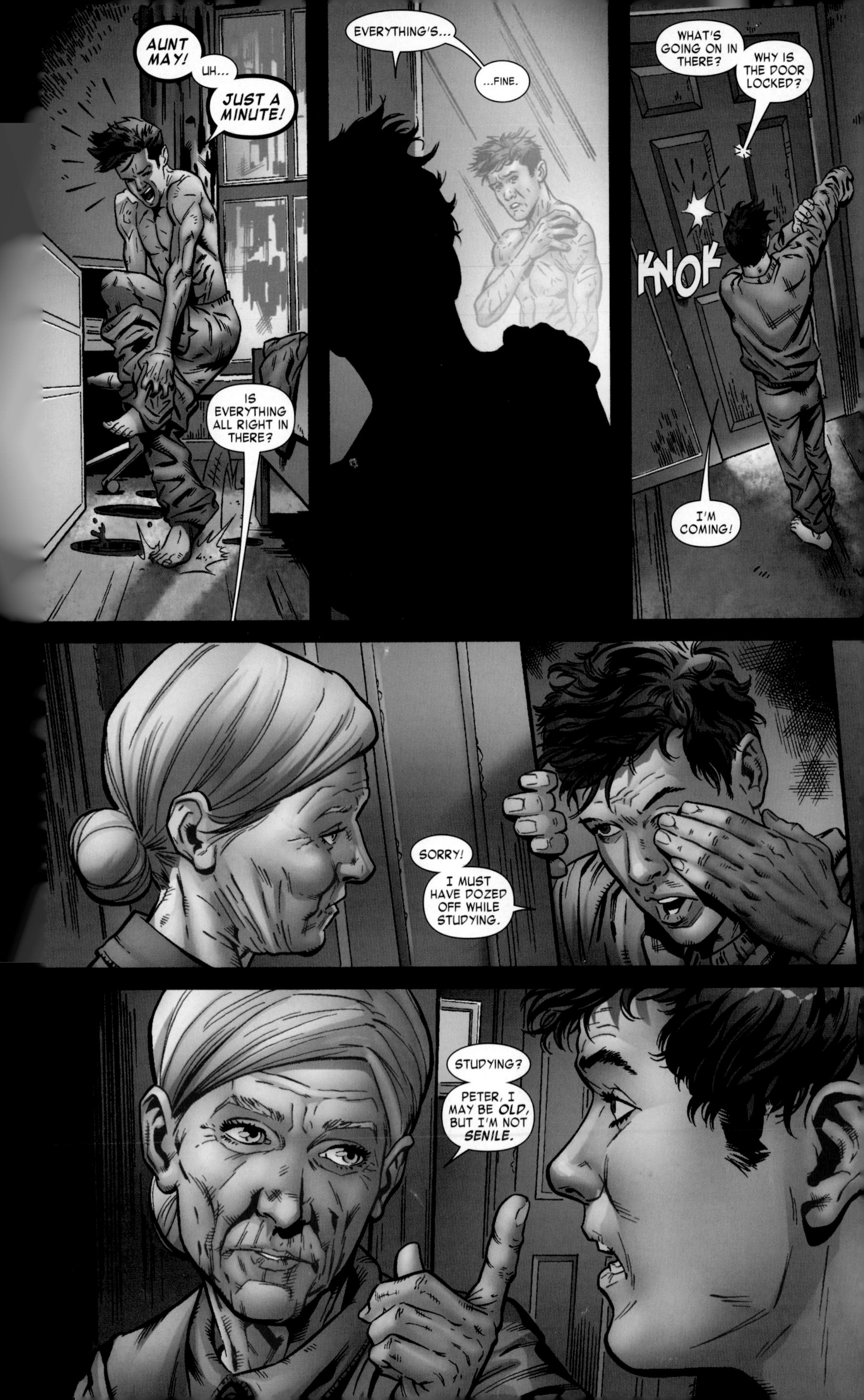
AUNT MAY!
UH...
JUST A MINUTE!
IS EVERYTHING ALL RIGHT IN THERE?
EVERYTHING'S...
...FINE.
WHAT'S GOING ON IN THERE?
WHY IS THE DOOR LOCKED?
KNOK
I'M COMING!
SORRY!
I MUST HAVE DOZED OFF WHILE STUDYING.
STUDYING?
PETER, I MAY BE OLD, BUT I'M NOT SENILE.

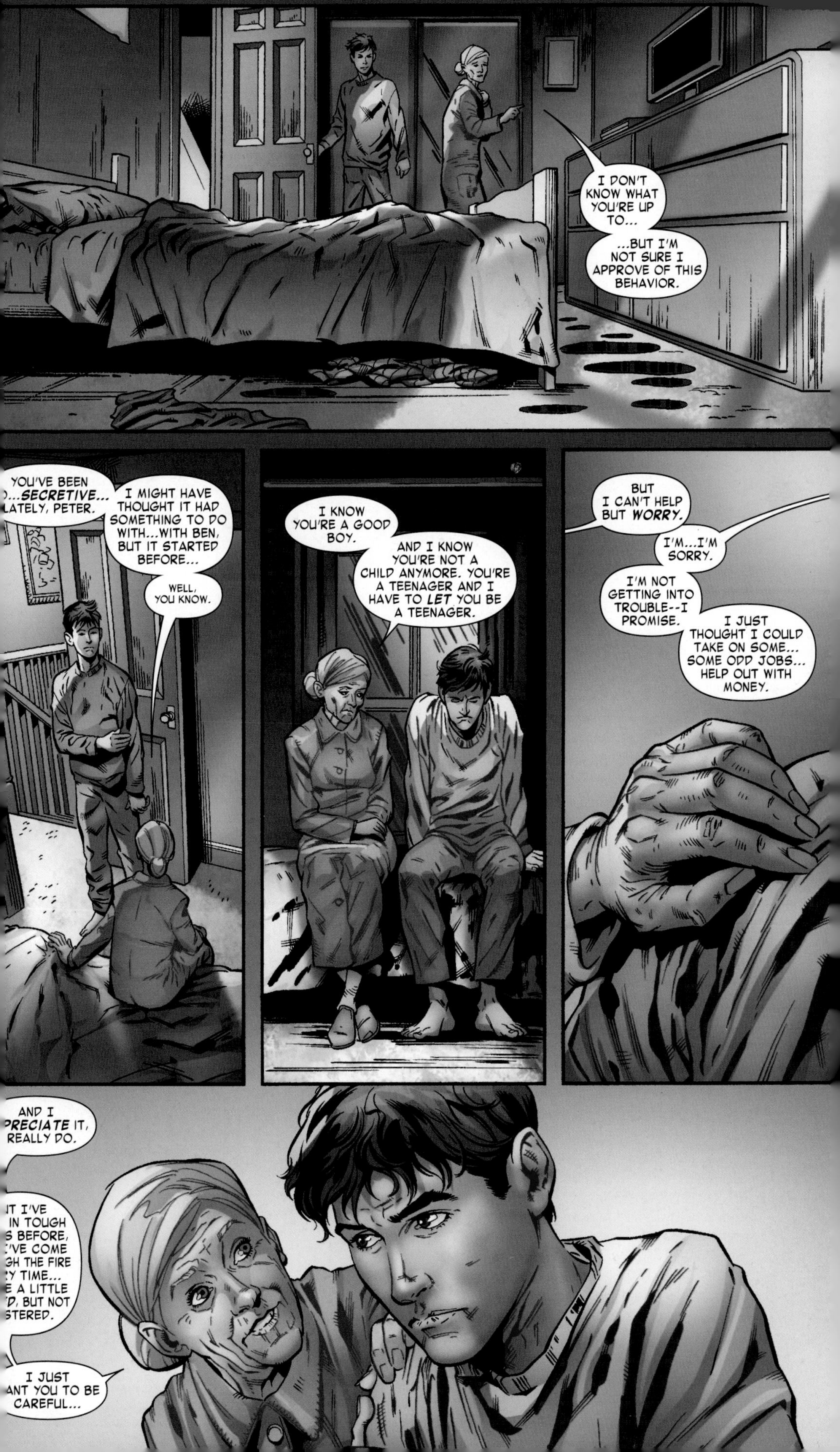

I DON'T KNOW WHAT YOU'RE UP TO...
...BUT I'M NOT SURE I APPROVE OF THIS BEHAVIOR.
YOU'VE BEEN ...SECRETIVE... LATELY, PETER.
I MIGHT HAVE THOUGHT IT HAD SOMETHING TO DO WITH...WITH BEN, BUT IT STARTED BEFORE...
WELL, YOU KNOW.
I KNOW YOU'RE A GOOD BOY.
AND I KNOW YOU'RE NOT A CHILD ANYMORE. YOU'RE A TEENAGER AND I HAVE TO LET YOU BE A TEENAGER.
BUT I CAN'T HELP BUT WORRY.
I'M...I'M SORRY.
I'M NOT GETTING INTO TROUBLE--I PROMISE.
I JUST THOUGHT I COULD TAKE ON SOME... SOME ODD JOBS... HELP OUT WITH MONEY.
AND I PRECIATE IT, REALLY DO.
IN TOUGH BEFORE, I'VE COME THE FIRE TIME... A LITTLE BUT NOT STERED.
I JUST ANT YOU TO BE CAREFUL...

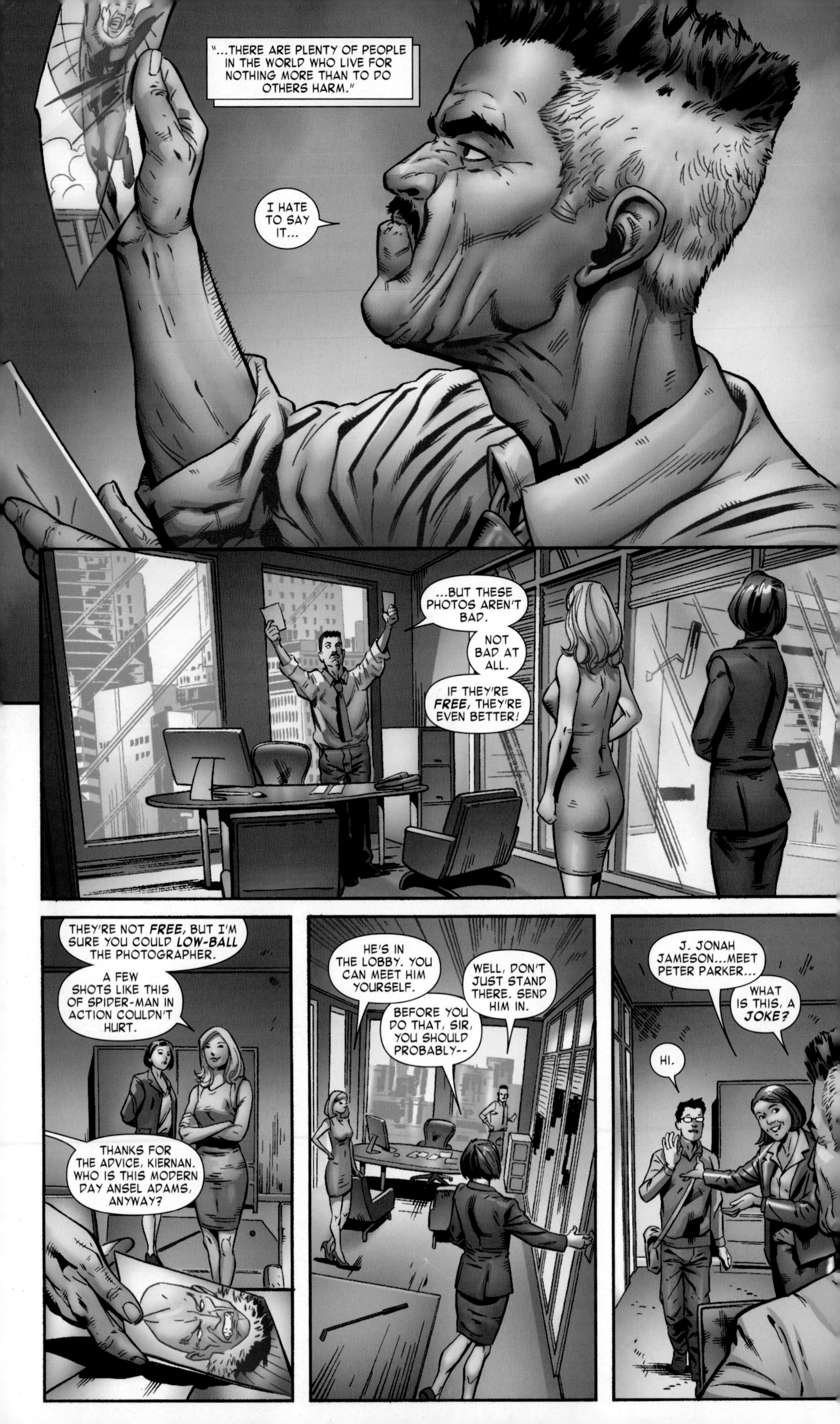
"...THERE ARE PLENTY OF PEOPLE IN THE WORLD WHO LIVE FOR NOTHING MORE THAN TO DO OTHERS HARM."
I HATE TO SAY IT...
...BUT THESE PHOTOS AREN'T BAD.
NOT BAD AT ALL.
IF THEY'RE FREE, THEY'RE EVEN BETTER!
THEY'RE NOT FREE, BUT I'M SURE YOU COULD LOW-BALL THE PHOTOGRAPHER.
A FEW SHOTS LIKE THIS OF SPIDER-MAN IN ACTION COULDN'T HURT.
THANKS FOR THE ADVICE, KIERNAN. WHO IS THIS MODERN DAY ANSEL ADAMS, ANYWAY?
HE'S IN THE LOBBY. YOU CAN MEET HIM YOURSELF.
WELL, DON'T JUST STAND THERE. SEND HIM IN.
BEFORE YOU DO THAT, SIR, YOU SHOULD PROBABLY--
J. JONAH JAMESON...MEET PETER PARKER...
WHAT IS THIS, A JOKE?
HI.

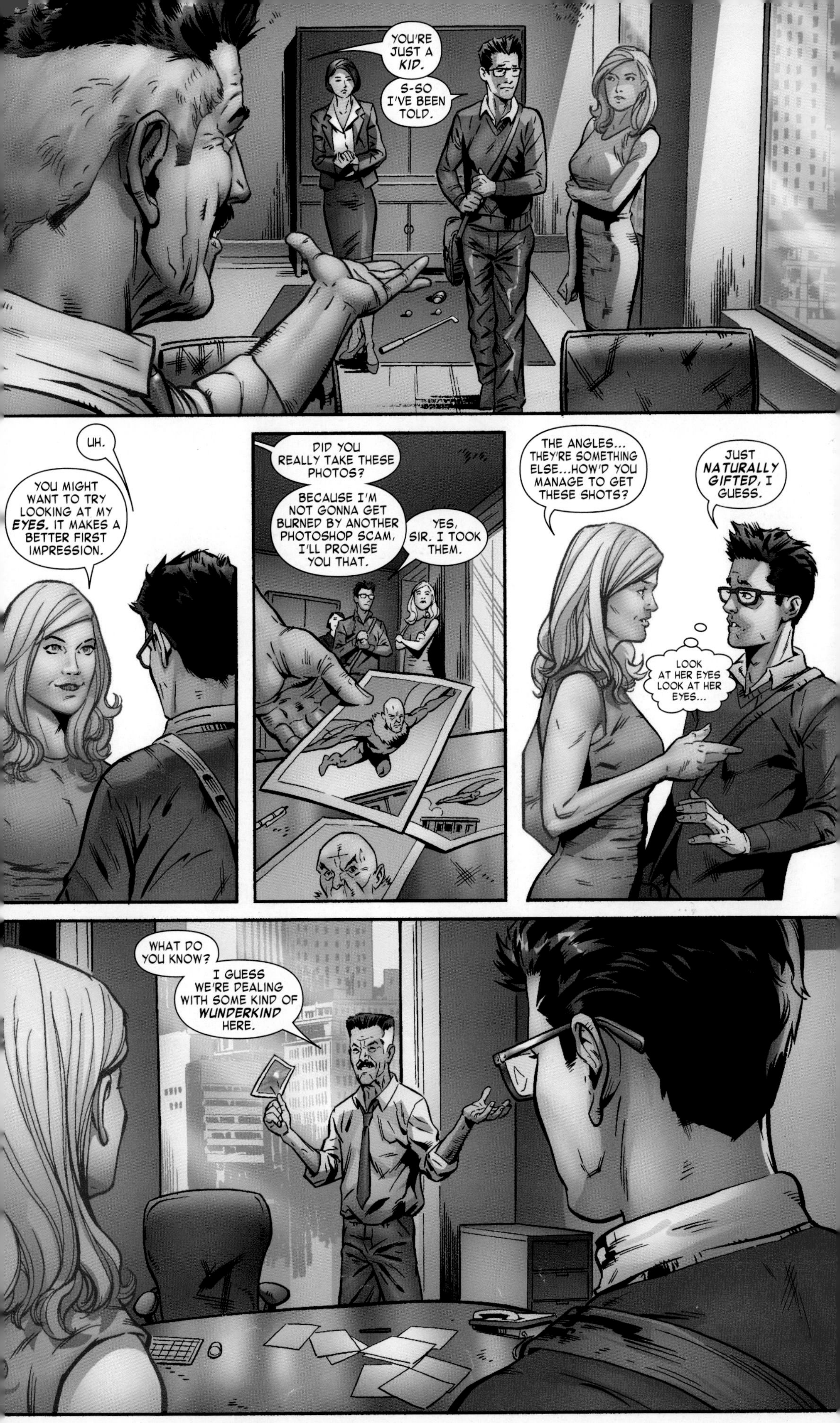
YOU'RE JUST A KID.
S-SO I'VE BEEN TOLD.
UH.
YOU MIGHT WANT TO TRY LOOKING AT MY EYES. IT MAKES A BETTER FIRST IMPRESSION.
DID YOU REALLY TAKE THESE PHOTOS?
BECAUSE I'M NOT GONNA GET BURNED BY ANOTHER PHOTOSHOP SCAM, I'LL PROMISE YOU THAT.
YES, SIR. I TOOK THEM.
THE ANGLES... THEY'RE SOMETHING ELSE...HOW'D YOU MANAGE TO GET THESE SHOTS?
JUST NATURALLY GIFTED, I GUESS.
LOOK AT HER EYES LOOK AT HER EYES...
WHAT DO YOU KNOW?
I GUESS WE'RE DEALING WITH SOME KIND OF WUNDERKIND HERE.

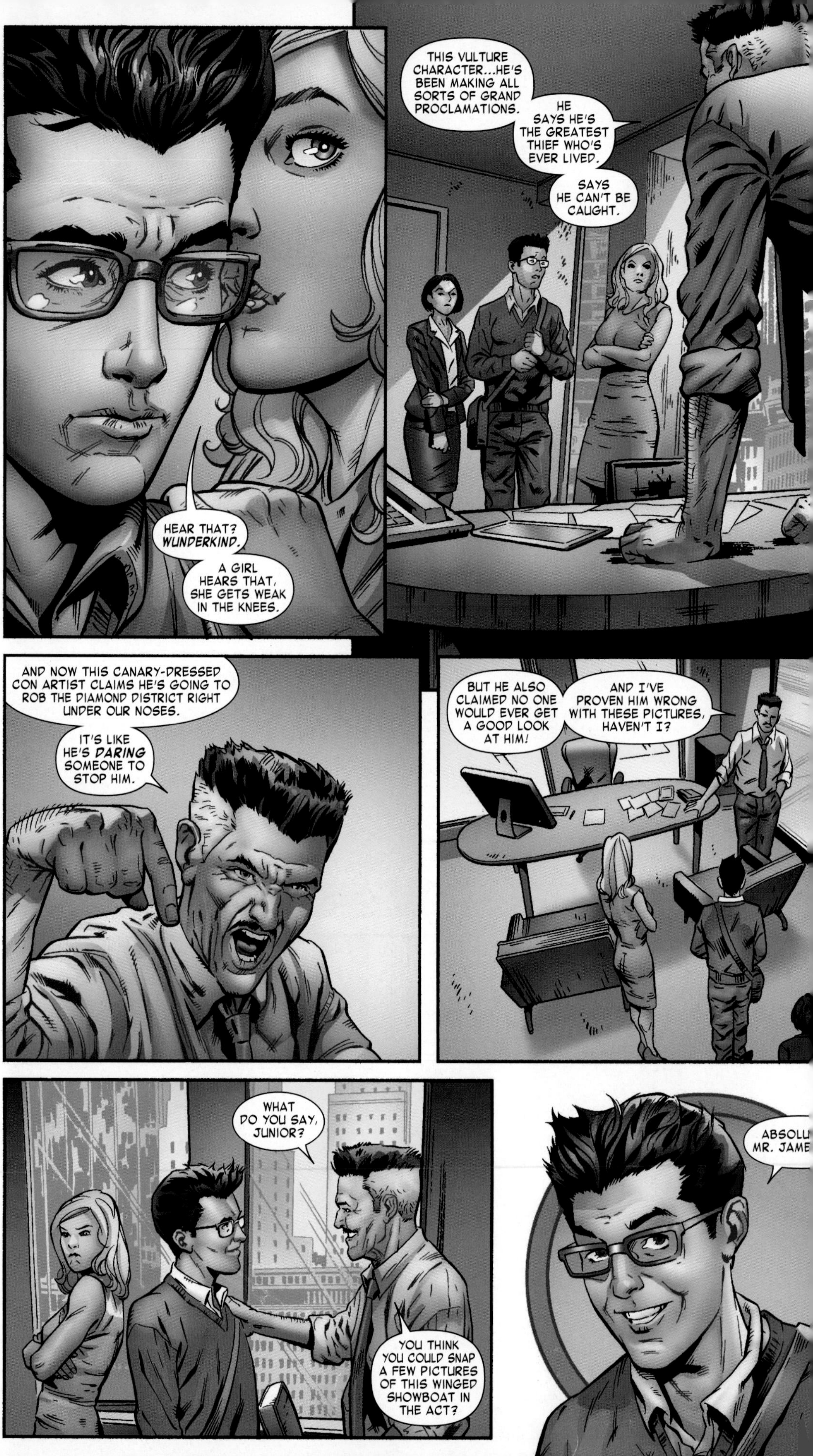
THIS VULTURE CHARACTER...HE'S BEEN MAKING ALL SORTS OF GRAND PROCLAMATIONS.
HE SAYS HE'S THE GREATEST THIEF WHO'S EVER LIVED.
SAYS HE CAN'T BE CAUGHT.
HEAR THAT? *WUNDERKIND.*
A GIRL HEARS THAT, SHE GETS WEAK IN THE KNEES.
AND NOW THIS CANARY-DRESSED CON ARTIST CLAIMS HE'S GOING TO ROB THE DIAMOND DISTRICT RIGHT UNDER OUR NOSES.
IT'S LIKE HE'S *DARING* SOMEONE TO STOP HIM.
BUT HE ALSO CLAIMED NO ONE WOULD EVER GET A GOOD LOOK AT HIM!
AND I'VE PROVEN HIM WRONG WITH THESE PICTURES, HAVEN'T I?
WHAT DO YOU SAY, JUNIOR?
YOU THINK YOU COULD SNAP A FEW PICTURES OF THIS WINGED SHOWBOAT IN THE ACT?
ABSOLU
MR. JAME

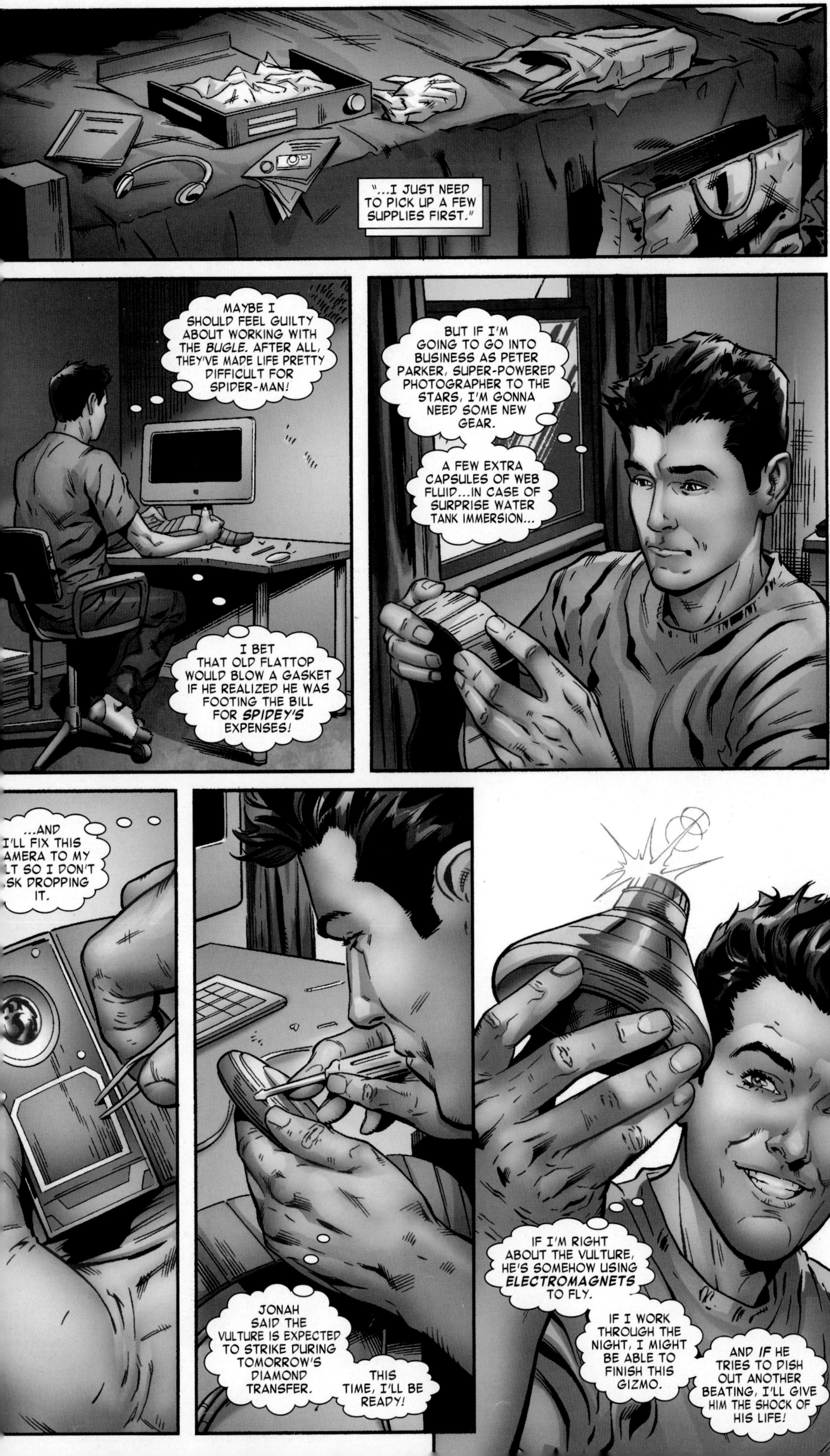
"...I JUST NEED TO PICK UP A FEW SUPPLIES FIRST."
MAYBE I SHOULD FEEL GUILTY ABOUT WORKING WITH THE BUGLE. AFTER ALL, THEY'VE MADE LIFE PRETTY DIFFICULT FOR SPIDER-MAN!
I BET THAT OLD FLATTOP WOULD BLOW A GASKET IF HE REALIZED HE WAS FOOTING THE BILL FOR SPIDEY'S EXPENSES!
BUT IF I'M GOING TO GO INTO BUSINESS AS PETER PARKER, SUPER-POWERED PHOTOGRAPHER TO THE STARS, I'M GONNA NEED SOME NEW GEAR.
A FEW EXTRA CAPSULES OF WEB FLUID...IN CASE OF SURPRISE WATER TANK IMMERSION...
...AND I'LL FIX THIS AMERA TO MY LT SO I DON'T SK DROPPING IT.
JONAH SAID THE VULTURE IS EXPECTED TO STRIKE DURING TOMORROW'S DIAMOND TRANSFER.
THIS TIME, I'LL BE READY!
IF I'M RIGHT ABOUT THE VULTURE, HE'S SOMEHOW USING ELECTROMAGNETS TO FLY.
IF I WORK THROUGH THE NIGHT, I MIGHT BE ABLE TO FINISH THIS GIZMO.
AND IF HE TRIES TO DISH OUT ANOTHER BEATING, I'LL GIVE HIM THE SHOCK OF HIS LIFE!

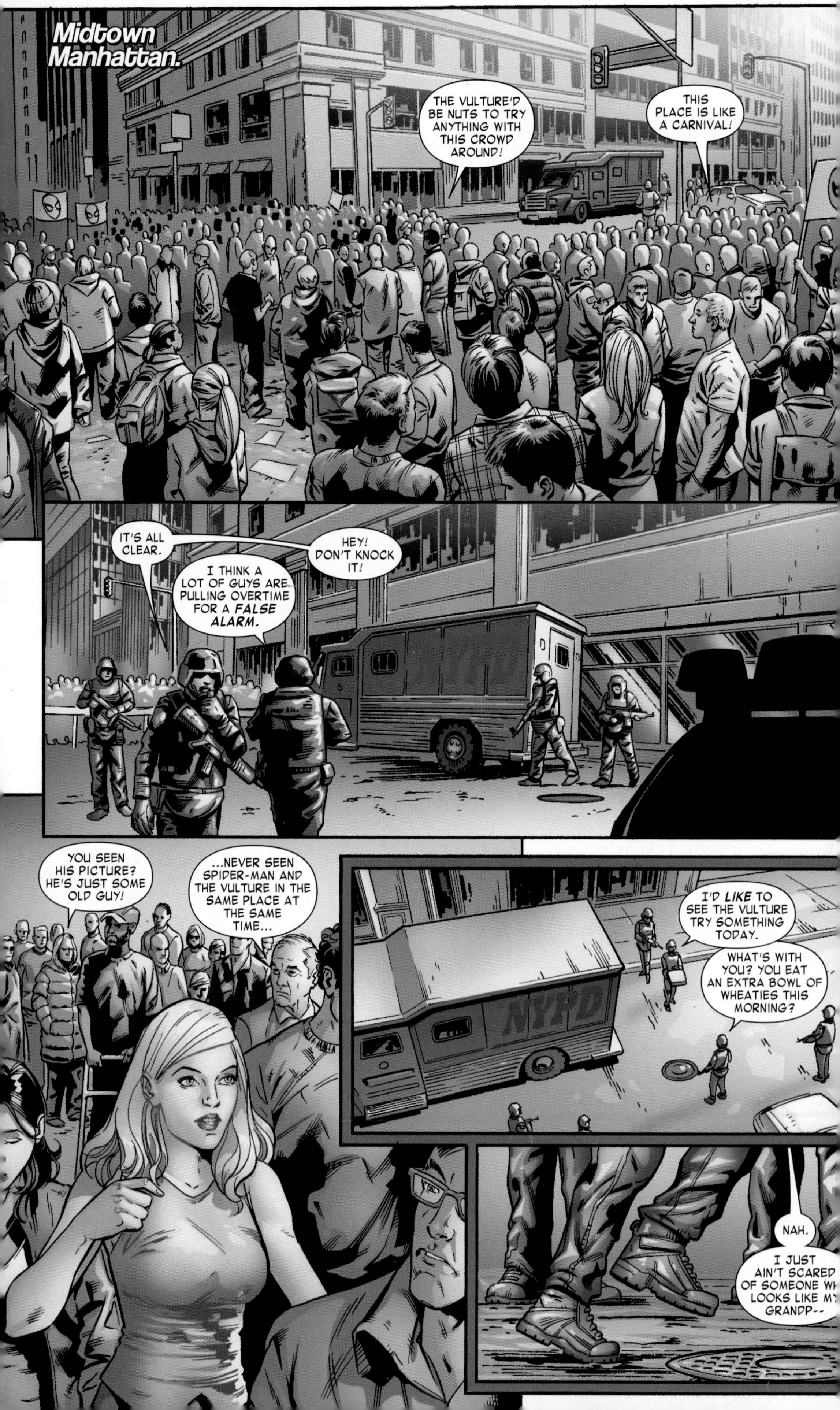

Midtown Manhattan.
THE VULTURE'D BE NUTS TO TRY ANYTHING WITH THIS CROWD AROUND!
THIS PLACE IS LIKE A CARNIVAL!
IT'S ALL CLEAR.
I THINK A LOT OF GUYS ARE PULLING OVERTIME FOR A *FALSE ALARM.*
HEY! DON'T KNOCK IT!
YOU SEEN HIS PICTURE? HE'S JUST SOME OLD GUY!
...NEVER SEEN SPIDER-MAN AND THE VULTURE IN THE SAME PLACE AT THE SAME TIME...
I'D *LIKE* TO SEE THE VULTURE TRY SOMETHING TODAY.
WHAT'S WITH YOU? YOU EAT AN EXTRA BOWL OF WHEATIES THIS MORNING?
NAH.
I JUST AIN'T SCARED OF SOMEONE WH LOOKS LIKE MY GRANDP--

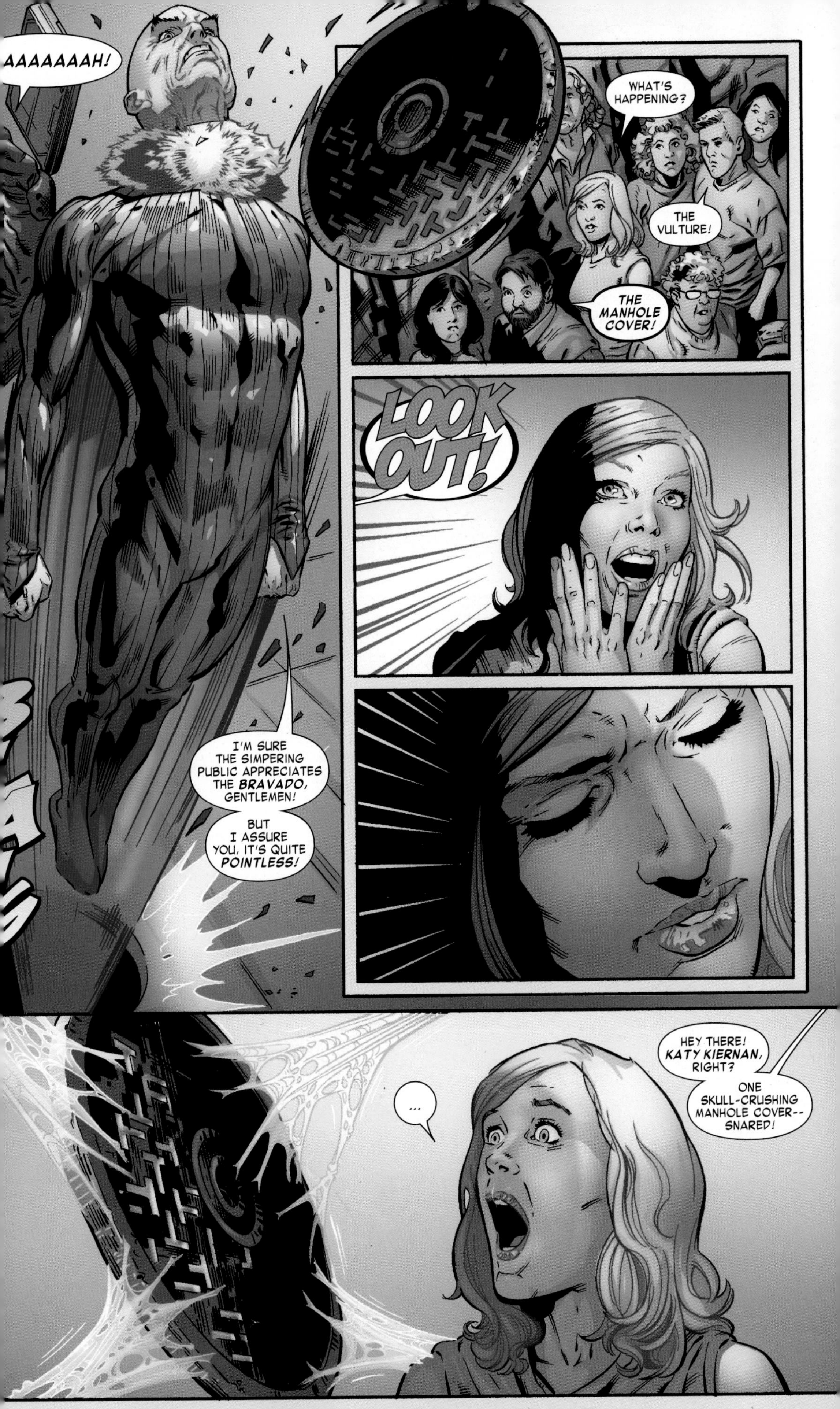
AAAAAAAH!
WHAT'S HAPPENING?
THE VULTURE!
THE MANHOLE COVER!
LOOK OUT!
I'M SURE THE SIMPERING PUBLIC APPRECIATES THE BRAVADO, GENTLEMEN!
BUT I ASSURE YOU, IT'S QUITE POINTLESS!
HEY THERE! KATY KIERNAN, RIGHT?
ONE SKULL-CRUSHING MANHOLE COVER-- SNARED!
...

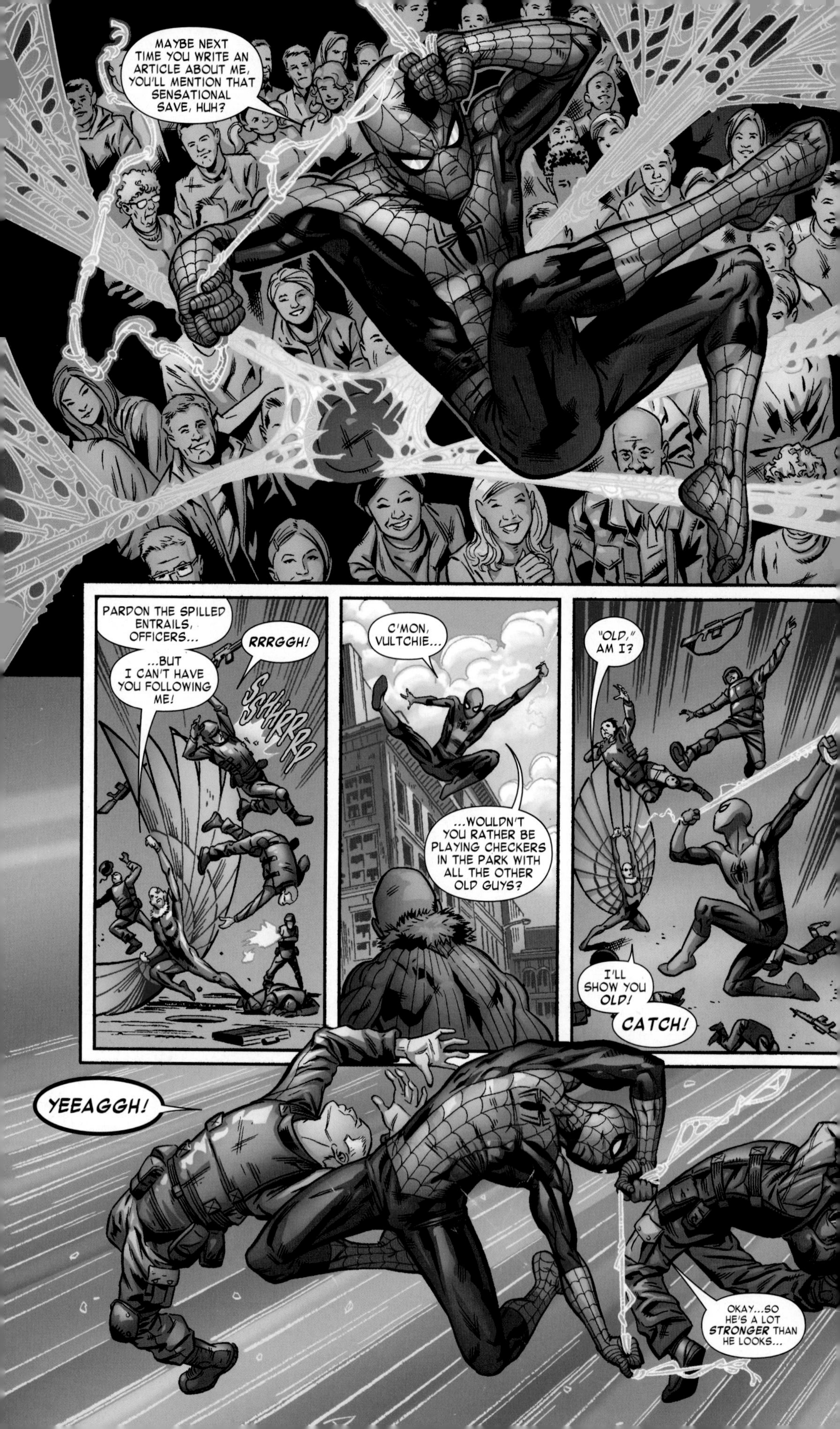
MAYBE NEXT TIME YOU WRITE AN ARTICLE ABOUT ME, YOU'LL MENTION THAT SENSATIONAL SAVE, HUH?
PARDON THE SPILLED ENTRAILS, OFFICERS...
...BUT I CAN'T HAVE YOU FOLLOWING ME!
RRRGGH!
SSHRRRP
C'MON, VULTCHIE...
...WOULDN'T YOU RATHER BE PLAYING CHECKERS IN THE PARK WITH ALL THE OTHER OLD GUYS?
"OLD," AM I?
I'LL SHOW YOU OLD!
CATCH!
YEEAGGH!
OKAY...SO HE'S A LOT STRONGER THAN HE LOOKS...

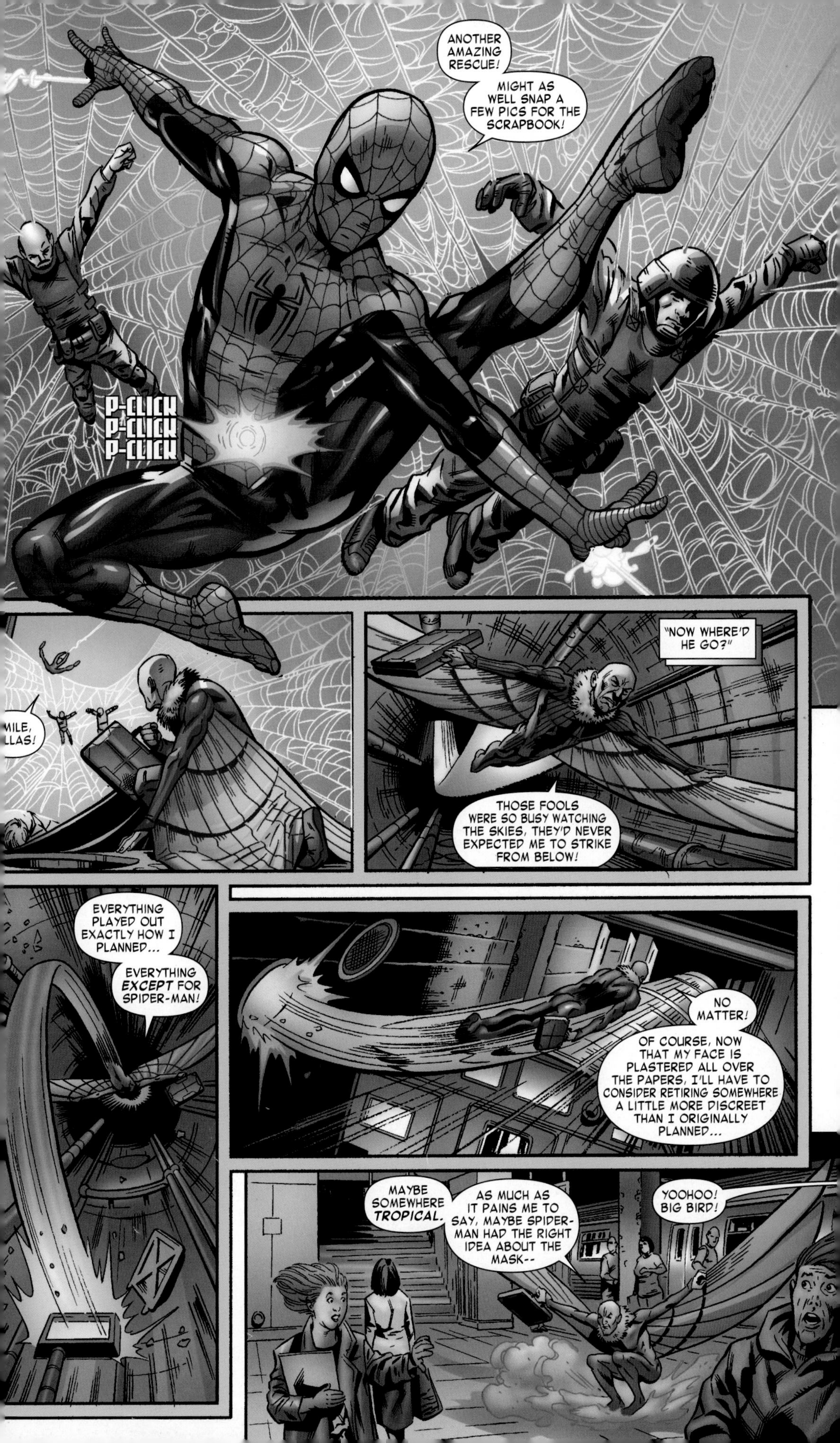

ANOTHER AMAZING RESCUE!
MIGHT AS WELL SNAP A FEW PICS FOR THE SCRAPBOOK!
P-CLICK P-CLICK P-CLICK
MILE, LLAS!
"NOW WHERE'D HE GO?"
THOSE FOOLS WERE SO BUSY WATCHING THE SKIES, THEY'D NEVER EXPECTED ME TO STRIKE FROM BELOW!
EVERYTHING PLAYED OUT EXACTLY HOW I PLANNED...
EVERYTHING *EXCEPT* FOR SPIDER-MAN!
NO MATTER!
OF COURSE, NOW THAT MY FACE IS PLASTERED ALL OVER THE PAPERS, I'LL HAVE TO CONSIDER RETIRING SOMEWHERE A LITTLE MORE DISCREET THAN I ORIGINALLY PLANNED...
MAYBE SOMEWHERE *TROPICAL*.
AS MUCH AS IT PAINS ME TO SAY, MAYBE SPIDER-MAN HAD THE RIGHT IDEA ABOUT THE MASK--
YOOHOO! BIG BIRD!

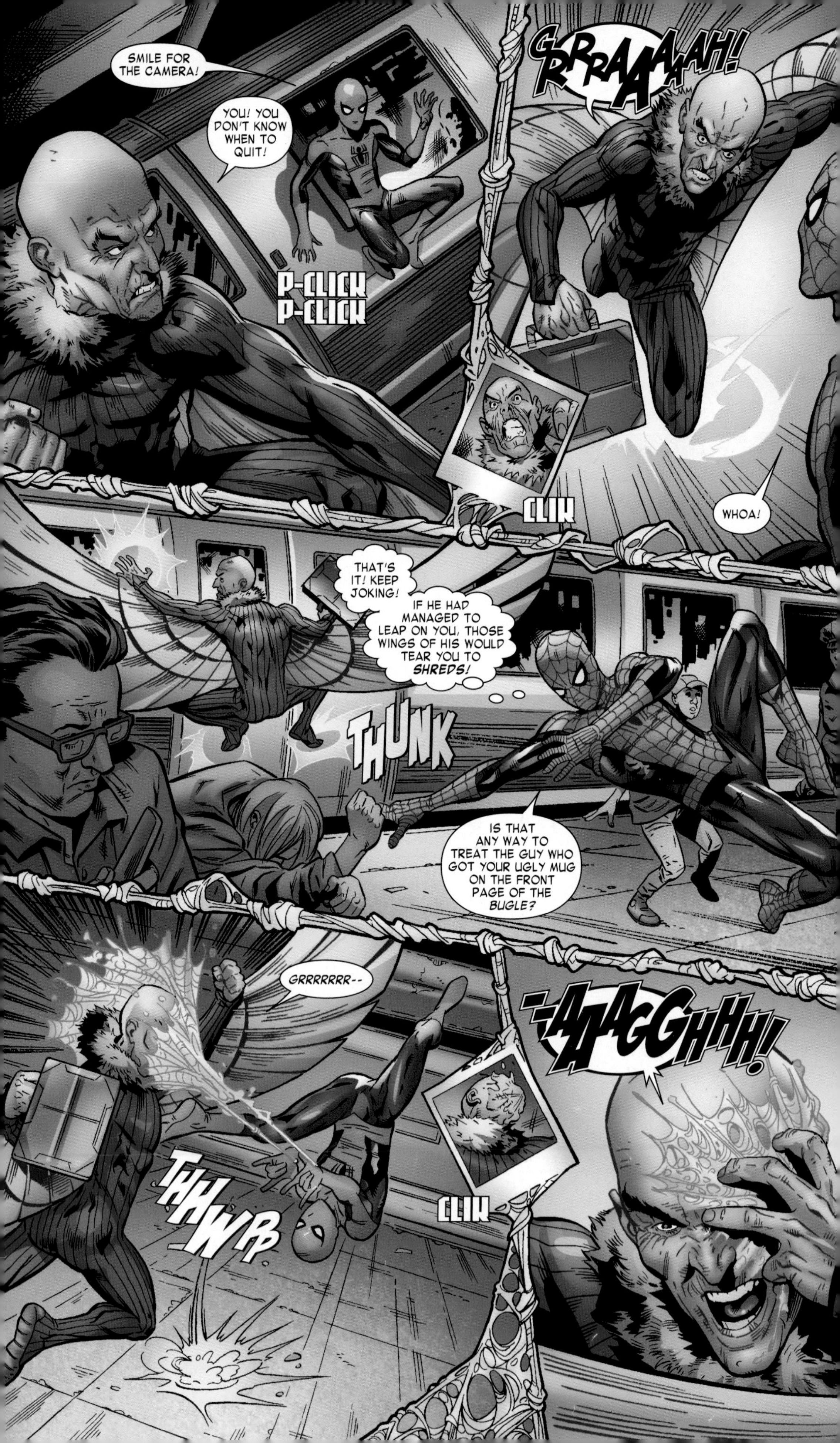

SMILE FOR THE CAMERA!
YOU! YOU DON'T KNOW WHEN TO QUIT!
P-CLICK P-CLICK
GRRRAAAAAAH!
CLIK
WHOA!
THAT'S IT! KEEP JOKING!
IF HE HAD MANAGED TO LEAP ON YOU, THOSE WINGS OF HIS WOULD TEAR YOU TO SHREDS!
THUNK
IS THAT ANY WAY TO TREAT THE GUY WHO GOT YOUR UGLY MUG ON THE FRONT PAGE OF THE BUGLE?
GRRRRRRR--
--AAAGGHHH!
THHWPP
CLIK

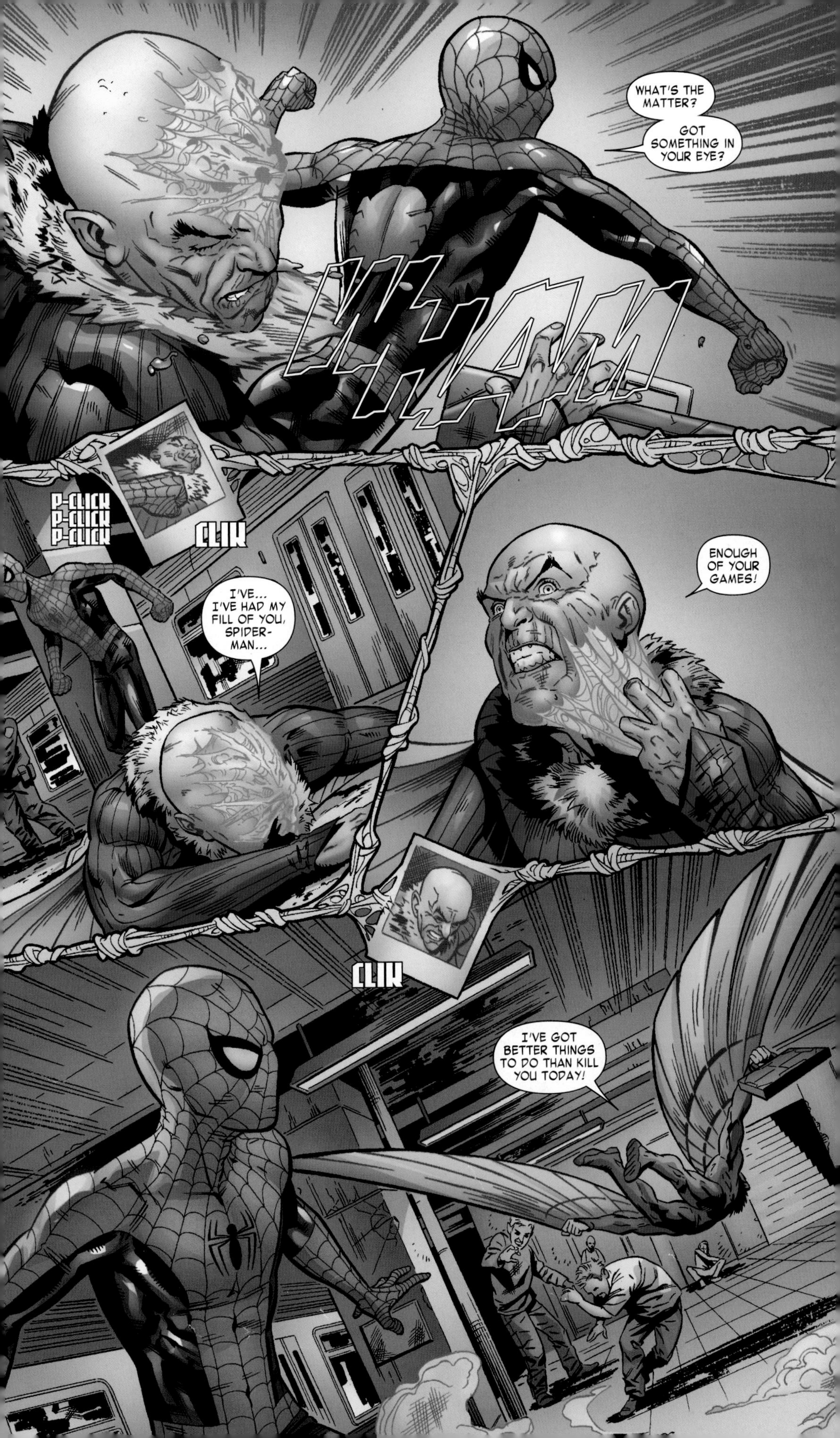
WHAT'S THE MATTER?
GOT SOMETHING IN YOUR EYE?
WHAM
P-CLICK
P-CLICK
P-CLICK
CLIK
ENOUGH OF YOUR GAMES!
I'VE... I'VE HAD MY FILL OF YOU, SPIDER-MAN...
CLIK
I'VE GOT BETTER THINGS TO DO THAN KILL YOU TODAY!

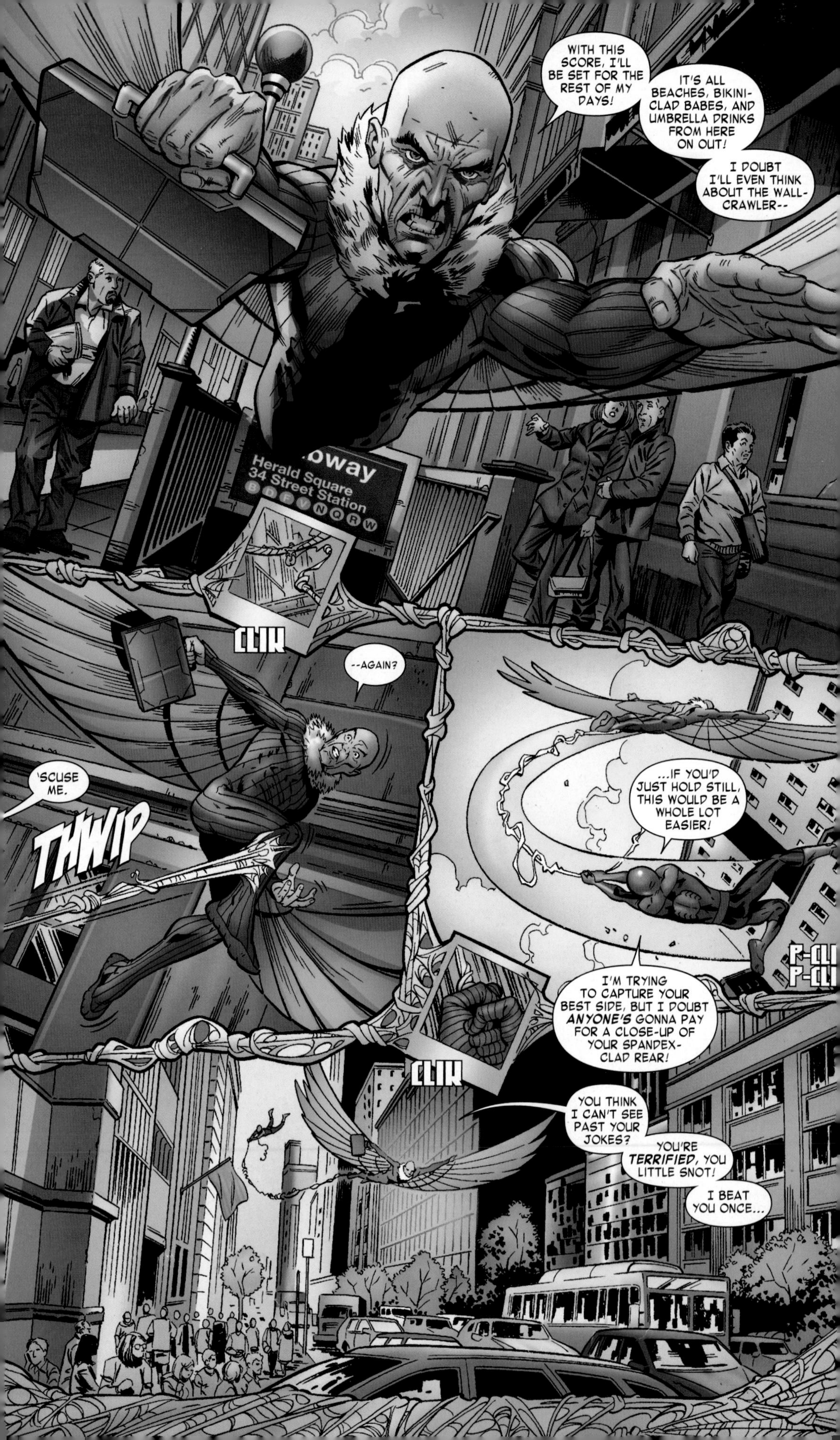
WITH THIS SCORE, I'LL BE SET FOR THE REST OF MY DAYS!
IT'S ALL BEACHES, BIKINI-CLAD BABES, AND UMBRELLA DRINKS FROM HERE ON OUT!
I DOUBT I'LL EVEN THINK ABOUT THE WALL-CRAWLER--
Herald Square
34 Street Station
CLIK
--AGAIN?
'SCUSE ME.
THWIP
...IF YOU'D JUST HOLD STILL, THIS WOULD BE A WHOLE LOT EASIER!
I'M TRYING TO CAPTURE YOUR BEST SIDE, BUT I DOUBT ANYONE'S GONNA PAY FOR A CLOSE-UP OF YOUR SPANDEX-CLAD REAR!
CLIK
YOU THINK I CAN'T SEE PAST YOUR JOKES?
YOU'RE TERRIFIED, YOU LITTLE SNOT!
I BEAT YOU ONCE...

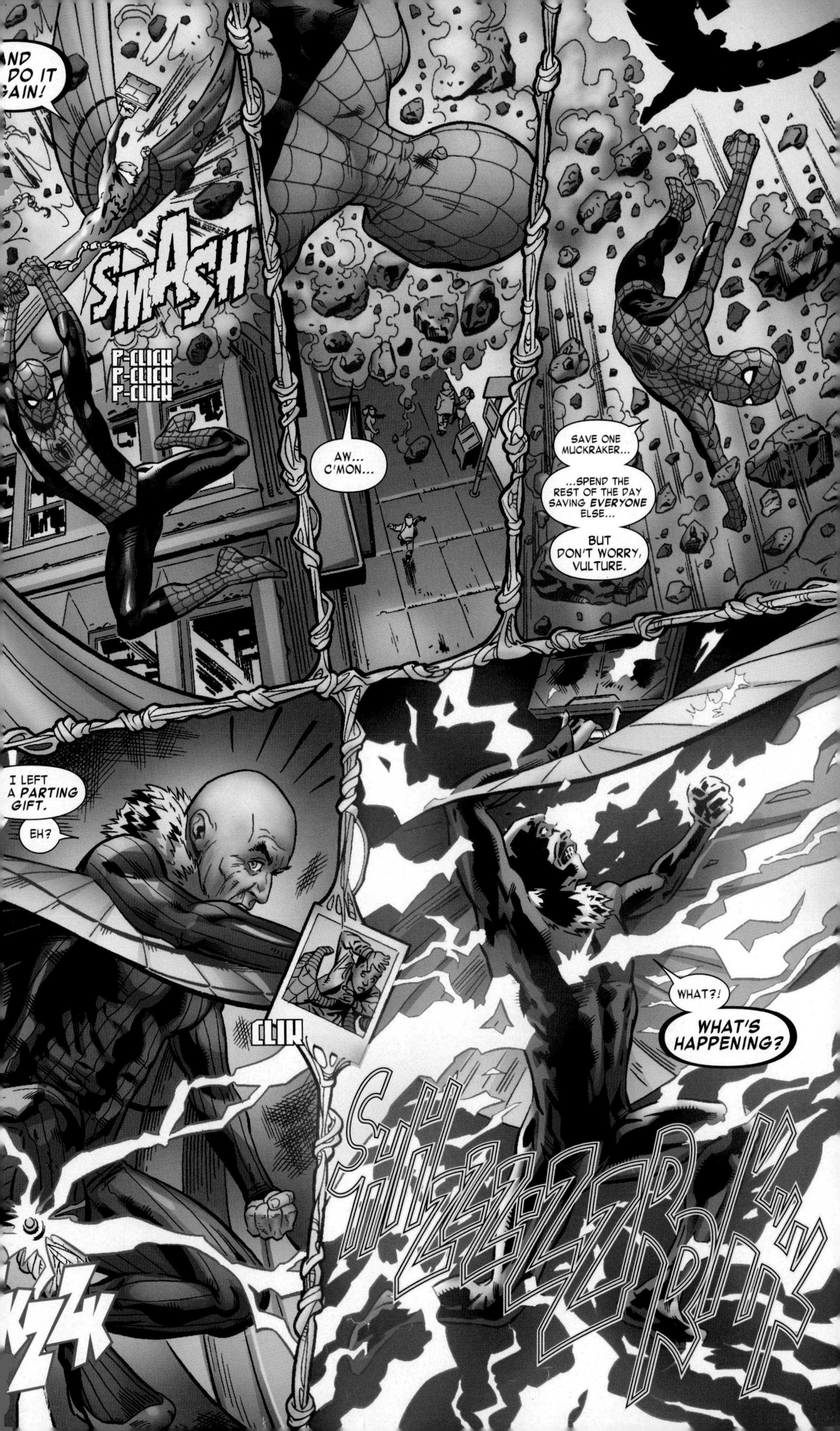
ND
DO IT
GAIN!
SMASH
P-CLICK
P-CLICK
P-CLICK
AW... C'MON...
SAVE ONE MUCKRAKER...
...SPEND THE REST OF THE DAY SAVING EVERYONE ELSE...
BUT DON'T WORRY, VULTURE.
I LEFT A PARTING GIFT.
EH?
CLIK
WHAT?!
WHAT'S HAPPENING?

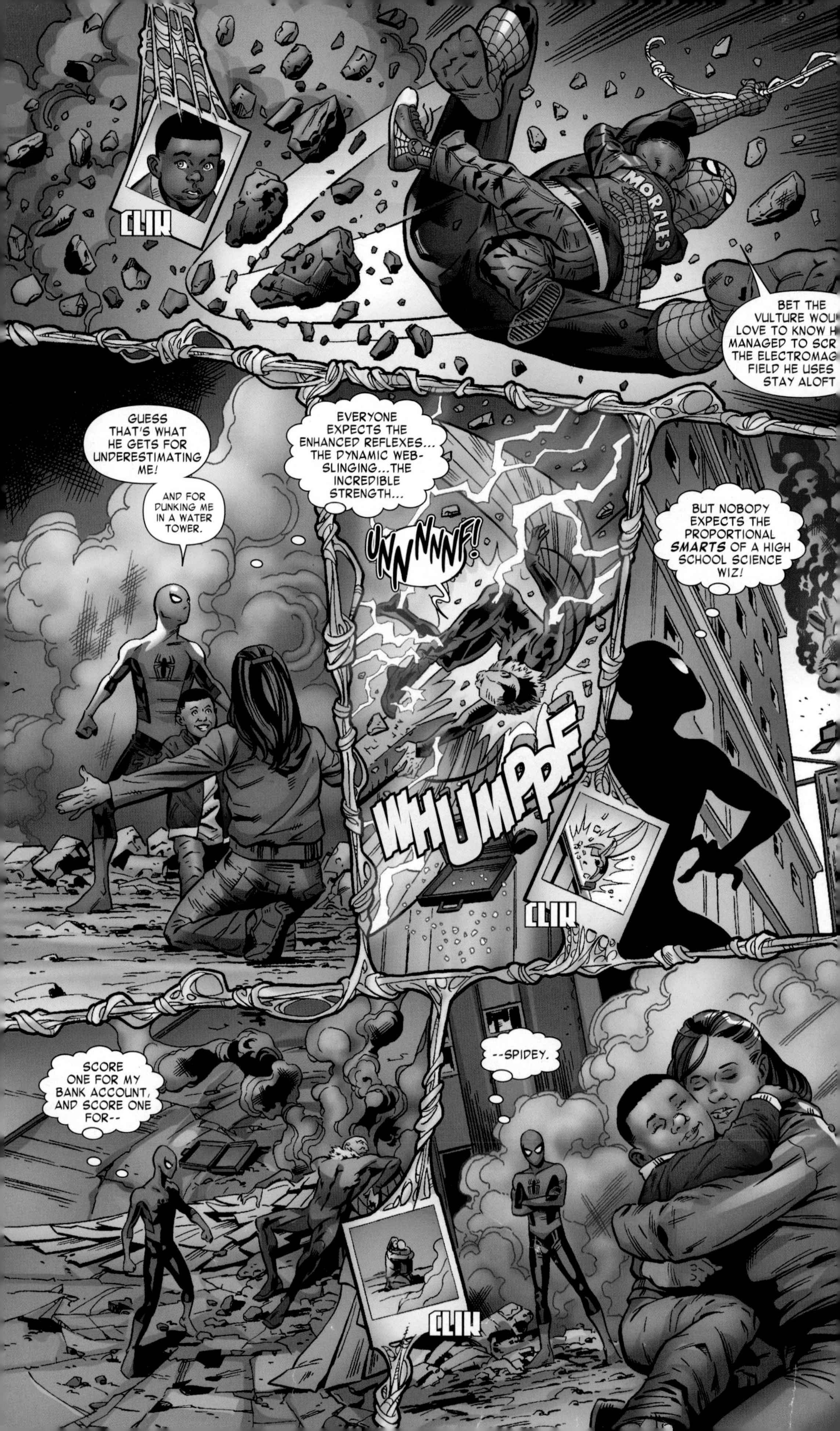
CLIK
MORALES
BET THE VULTURE WOU LOVE TO KNOW H MANAGED TO SCR THE ELECTROMAG FIELD HE USES STAY ALOFT
GUESS THAT'S WHAT HE GETS FOR UNDERESTIMATING ME!
AND FOR DUNKING ME IN A WATER TOWER.
EVERYONE EXPECTS THE ENHANCED REFLEXES... THE DYNAMIC WEB-SLINGING...THE INCREDIBLE STRENGTH...
UNNNNNF!
BUT NOBODY EXPECTS THE PROPORTIONAL SMARTS OF A HIGH SCHOOL SCIENCE WIZ!
WHUMPPF
CLIK
SCORE ONE FOR MY BANK ACCOUNT, AND SCORE ONE FOR--
--SPIDEY.
CLIK

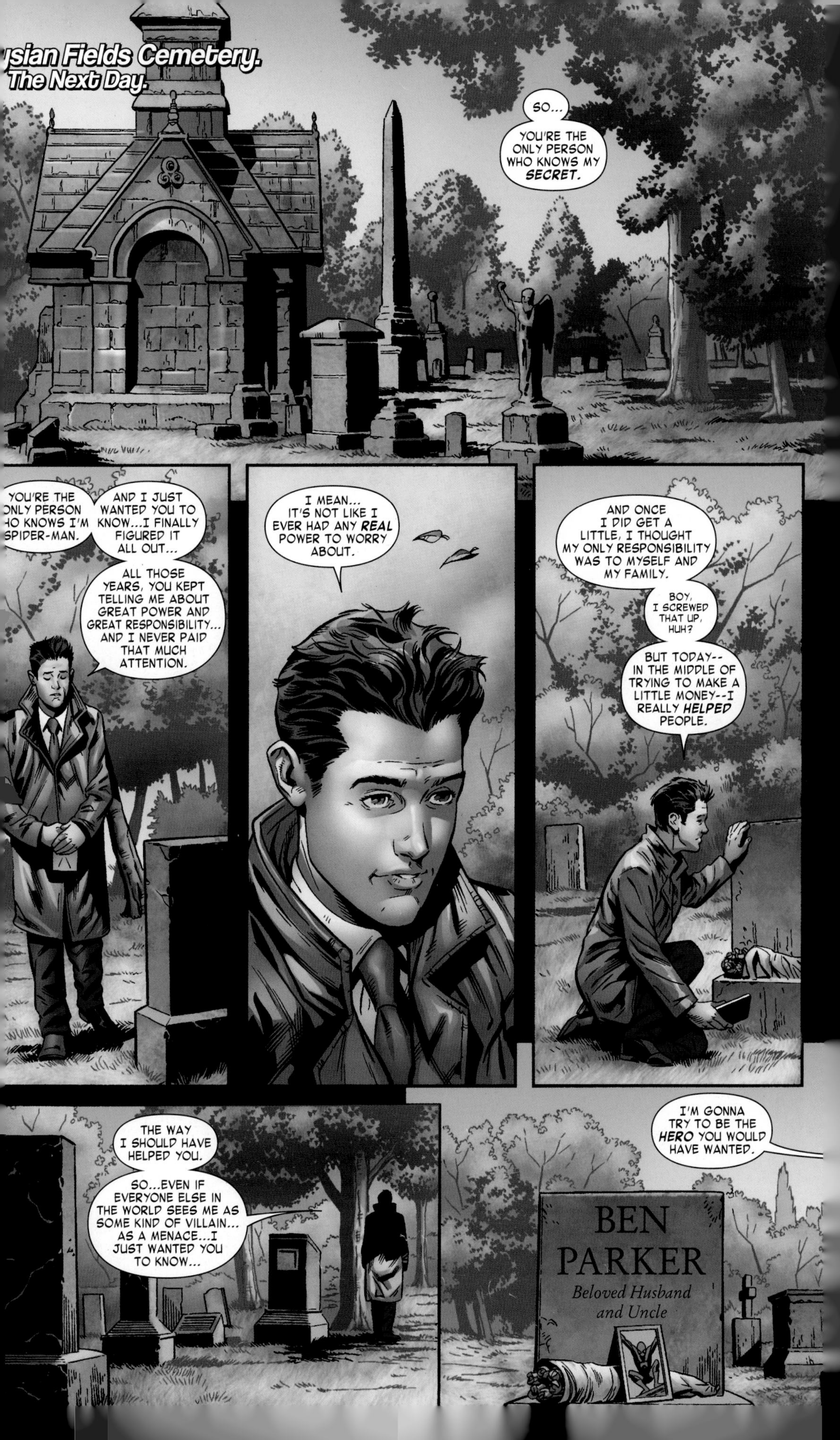

ysian Fields Cemetery. The Next Day.
SO...
YOU'RE THE ONLY PERSON WHO KNOWS MY SECRET.
YOU'RE THE ONLY PERSON HO KNOWS I'M SPIDER-MAN.
AND I JUST WANTED YOU TO KNOW...I FINALLY FIGURED IT ALL OUT...
ALL THOSE YEARS, YOU KEPT TELLING ME ABOUT GREAT POWER AND GREAT RESPONSIBILITY... AND I NEVER PAID THAT MUCH ATTENTION.
I MEAN... IT'S NOT LIKE I EVER HAD ANY REAL POWER TO WORRY ABOUT.
AND ONCE I DID GET A LITTLE, I THOUGHT MY ONLY RESPONSIBILITY WAS TO MYSELF AND MY FAMILY.
BOY, I SCREWED THAT UP, HUH?
BUT TODAY-- IN THE MIDDLE OF TRYING TO MAKE A LITTLE MONEY--I REALLY HELPED PEOPLE.
THE WAY I SHOULD HAVE HELPED YOU.
SO...EVEN IF EVERYONE ELSE IN THE WORLD SEES ME AS SOME KIND OF VILLAIN... AS A MENACE...I JUST WANTED YOU TO KNOW...
I'M GONNA TRY TO BE THE HERO YOU WOULD HAVE WANTED.
BEN PARKER
Beloved Husband and Uncle

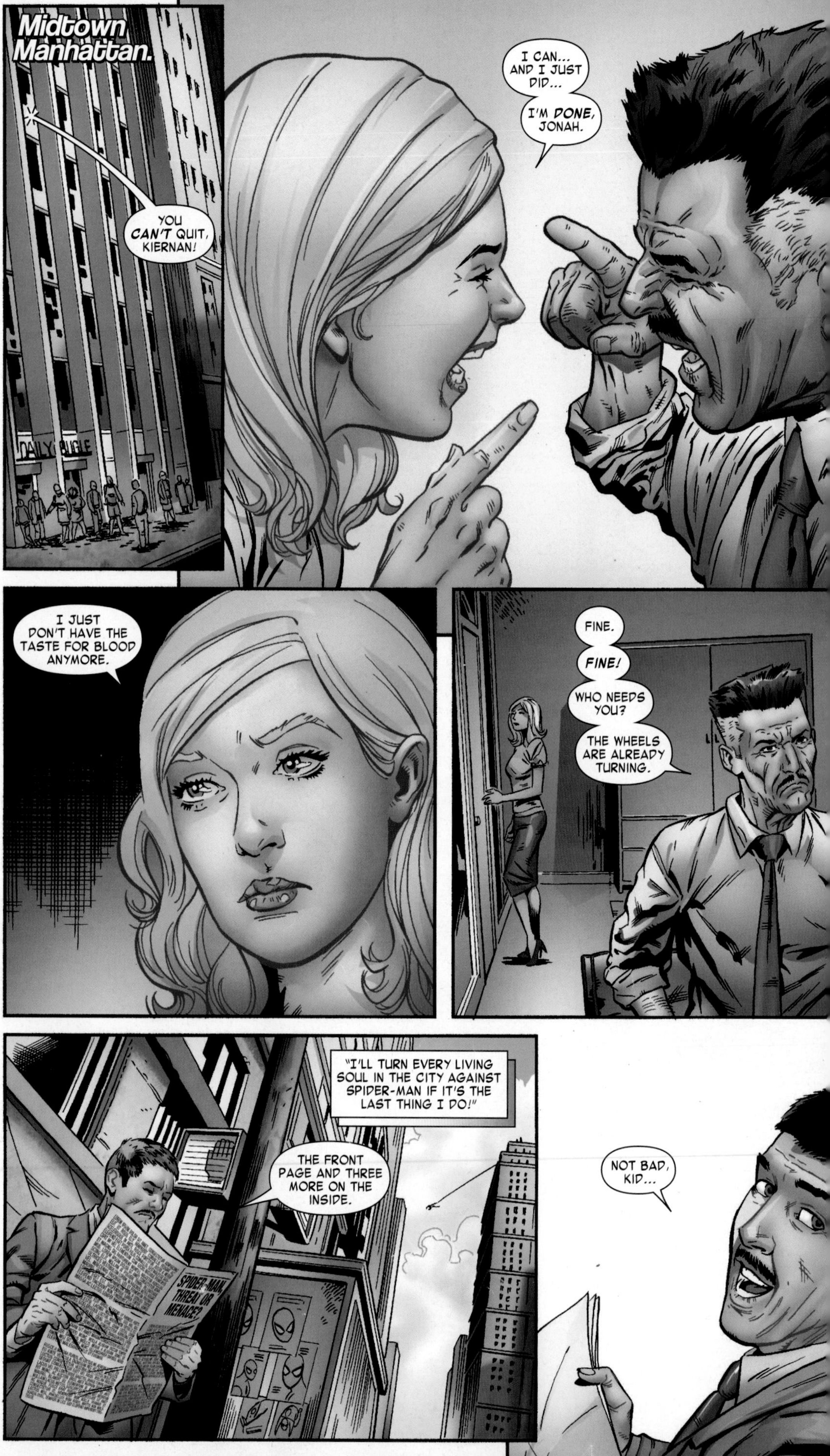
Midtown Manhattan.
DAILY BUGLE
YOU CAN'T QUIT, KIERNAN!
I CAN... AND I JUST DID...
I'M DONE, JONAH.
I JUST DON'T HAVE THE TASTE FOR BLOOD ANYMORE.
FINE.
FINE!
WHO NEEDS YOU?
THE WHEELS ARE ALREADY TURNING.
"I'LL TURN EVERY LIVING SOUL IN THE CITY AGAINST SPIDER-MAN IF IT'S THE LAST THING I DO!"
SPIDER-MAN THREAT OR MENACE?
THE FRONT PAGE AND THREE MORE ON THE INSIDE.
NOT BAD, KID...

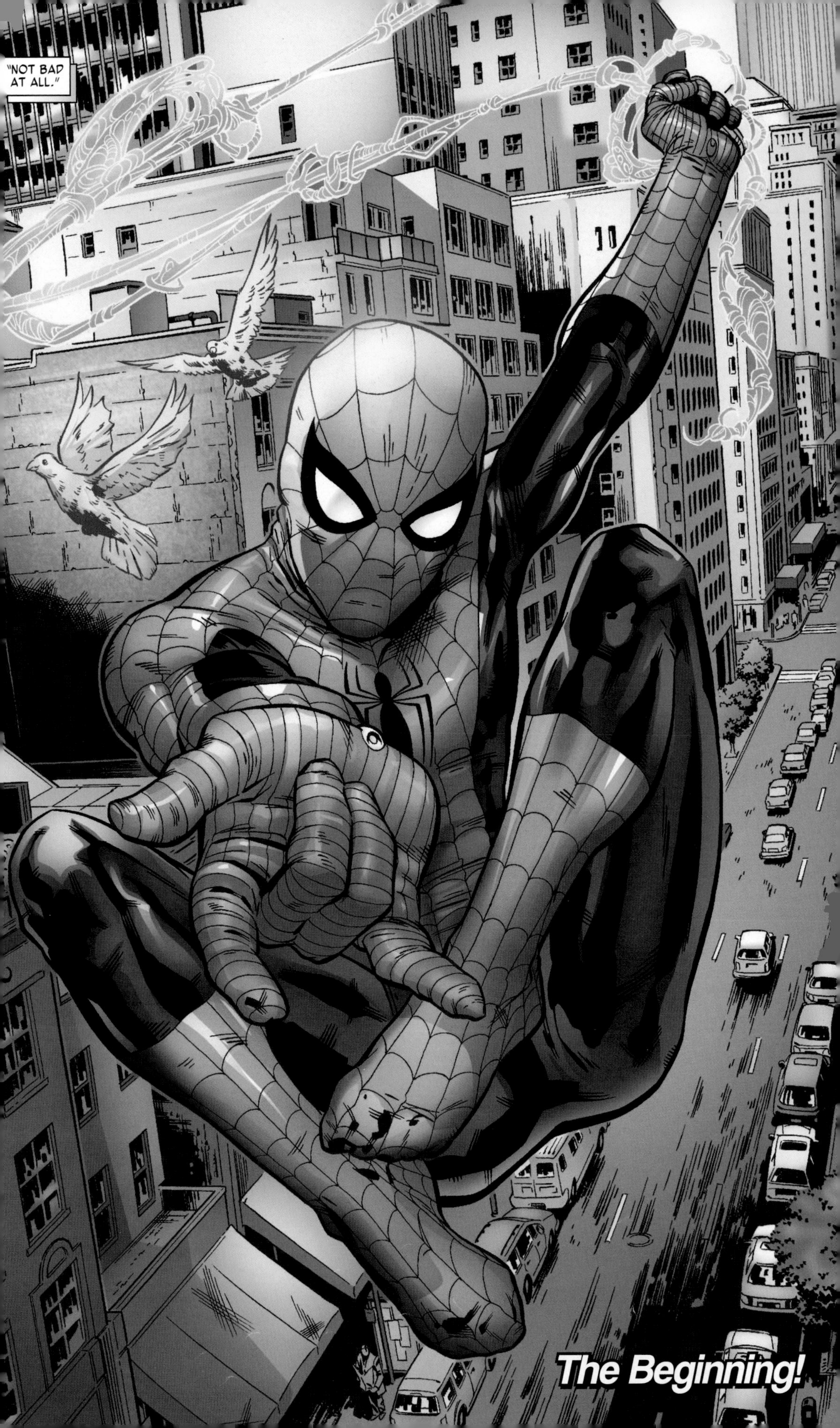
"NOT BAD AT ALL."
The Beginning!

WHERE ARE THEY NOW? *AVENGING SPIDER-MAN (2011) #1* SPIDER-MAN AND RED HULK TAKE ON A MOLOID ARMY DURING THE NEW YORK MARATHON IN THIS ACTION-PACKED EXTRAVAGANZA!

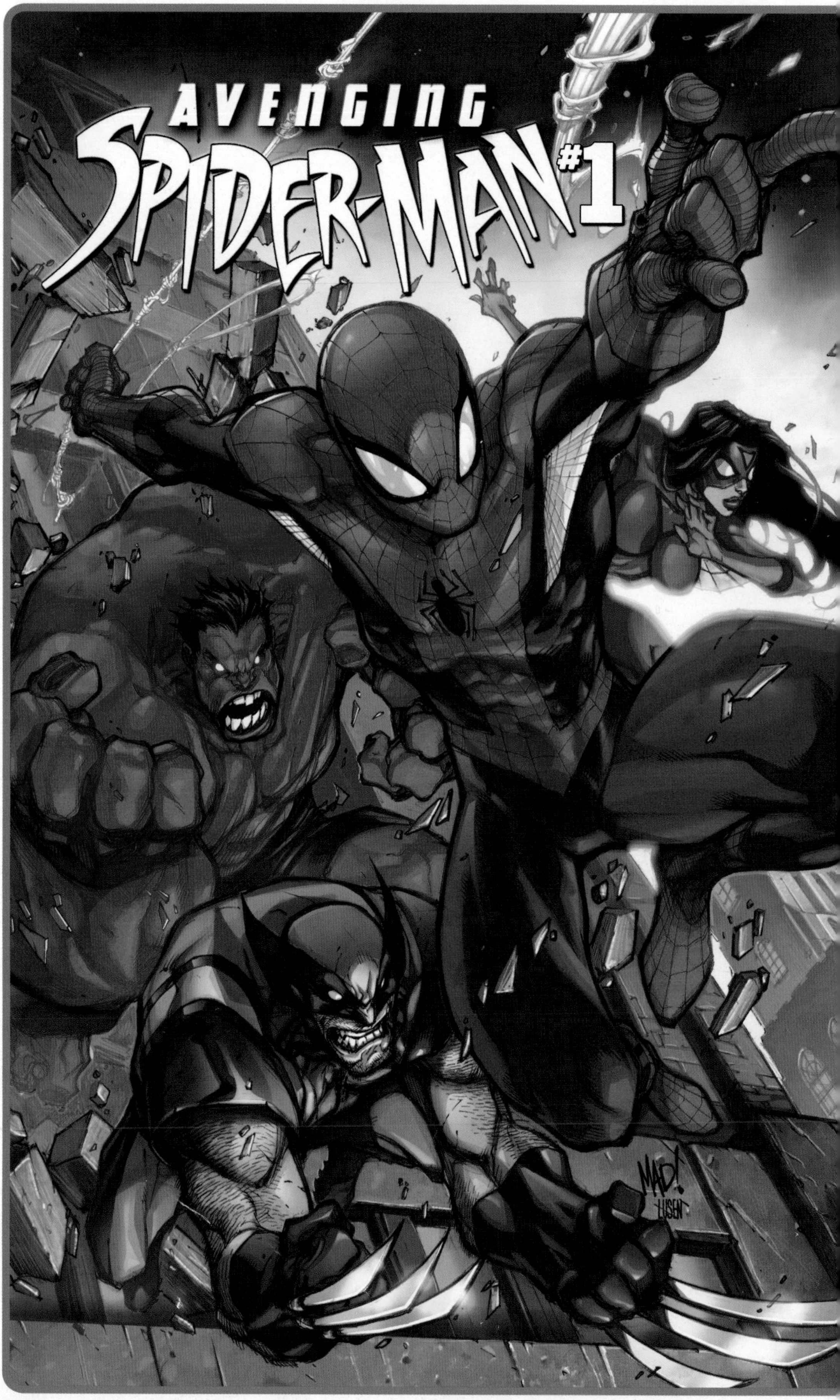
AVENGING
SPIDER-MAN #1
MAD!
LUSEN

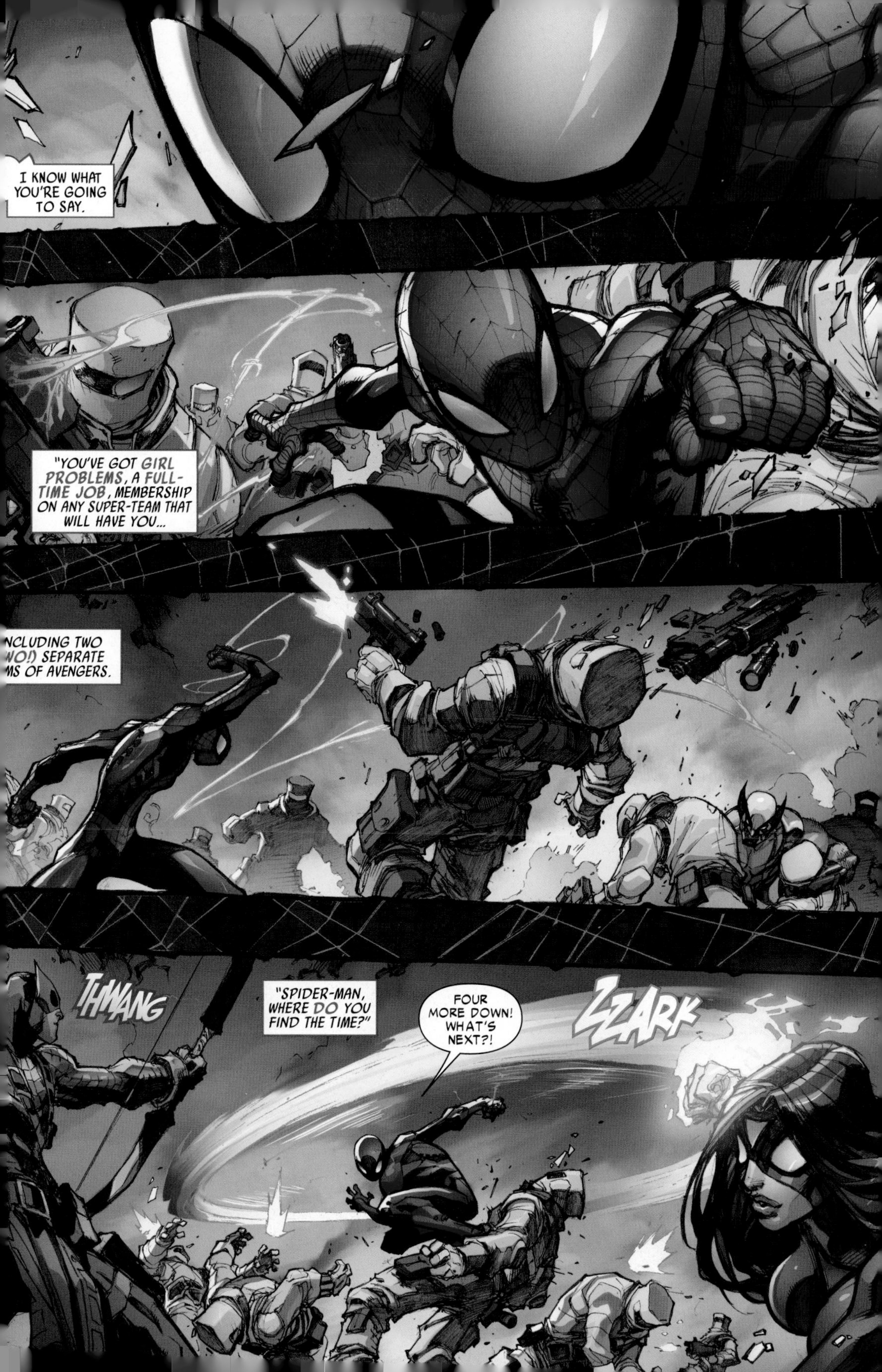

I KNOW WHAT YOU'RE GOING TO SAY.
"YOU'VE GOT GIRL PROBLEMS, A FULL-TIME JOB, MEMBERSHIP ON ANY SUPER-TEAM THAT WILL HAVE YOU...
NCLUDING TWO WO!) SEPARATE MS OF AVENGERS.
THWANG
"SPIDER-MAN, WHERE DO YOU FIND THE TIME?"
FOUR MORE DOWN! WHAT'S NEXT?!
ZZARK

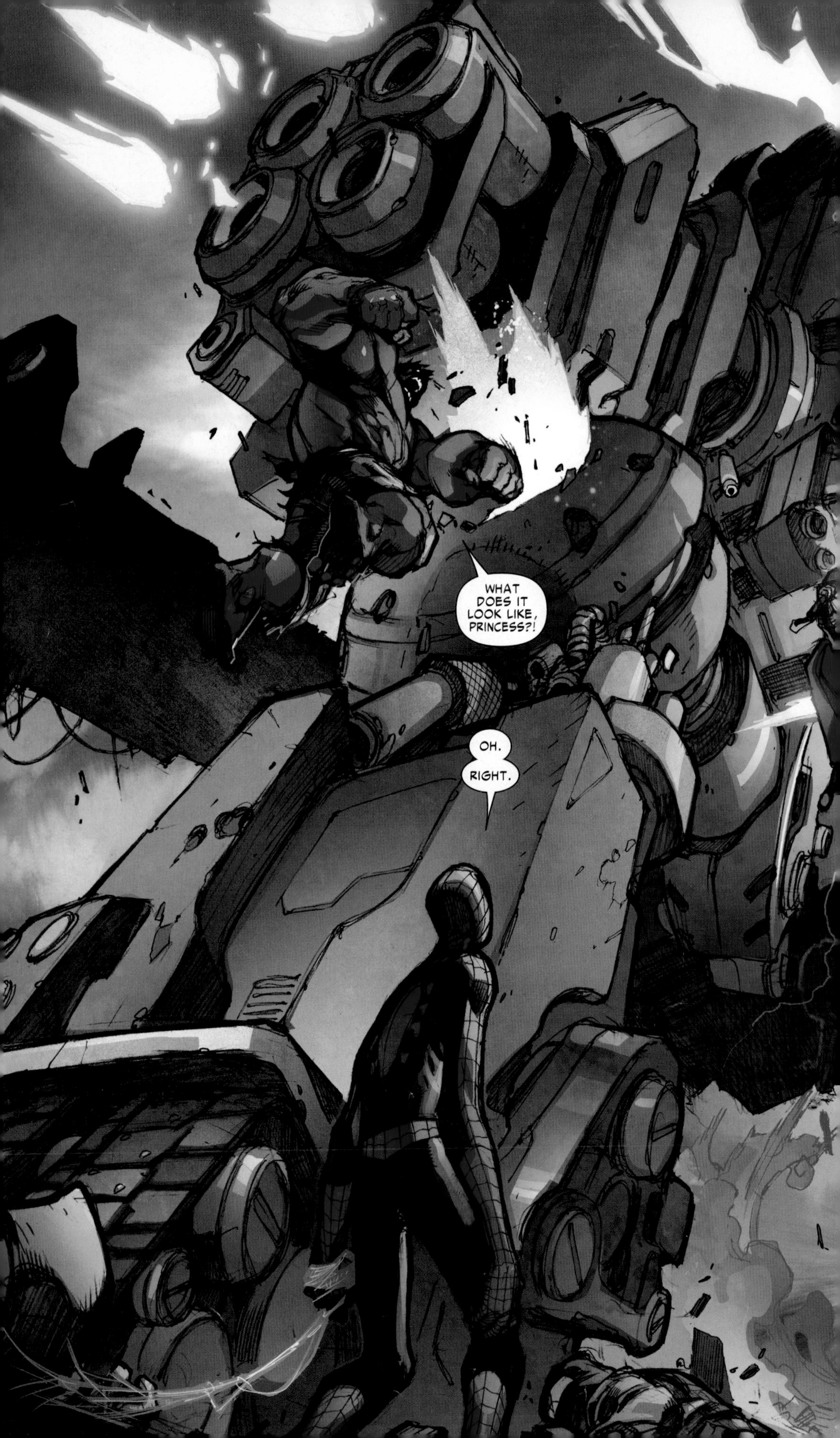
WHAT DOES IT LOOK LIKE, PRINCESS?!
OH.
RIGHT.

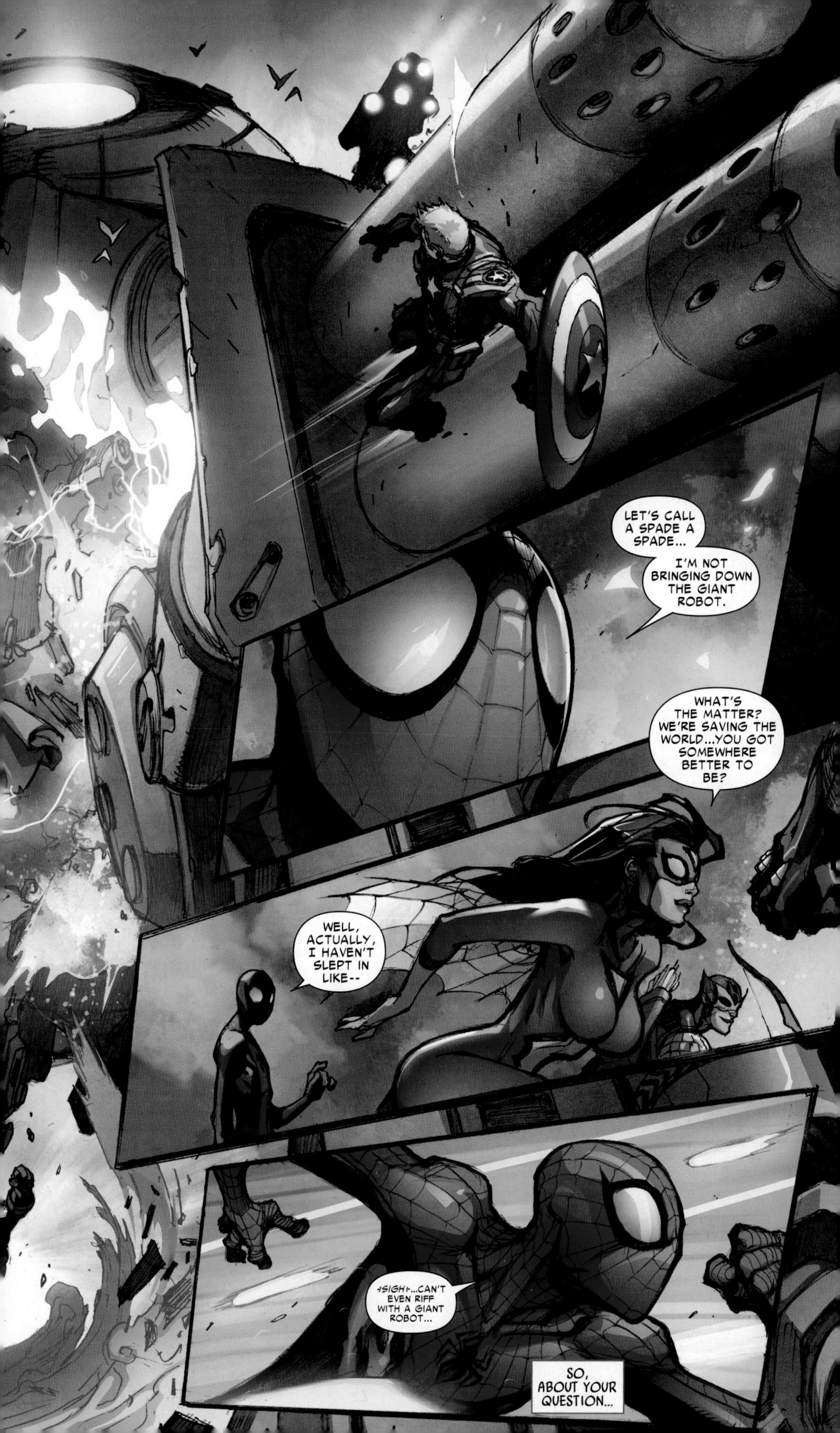
LET'S CALL A SPADE A SPADE...
I'M NOT BRINGING DOWN THE GIANT ROBOT.
WHAT'S THE MATTER? WE'RE SAVING THE WORLD...YOU GOT SOMEWHERE BETTER TO BE?
WELL, ACTUALLY, I HAVEN'T SLEPT IN LIKE--
SIGH...CAN'T EVEN RIFF WITH A GIANT ROBOT...
SO, ABOUT YOUR QUESTION...

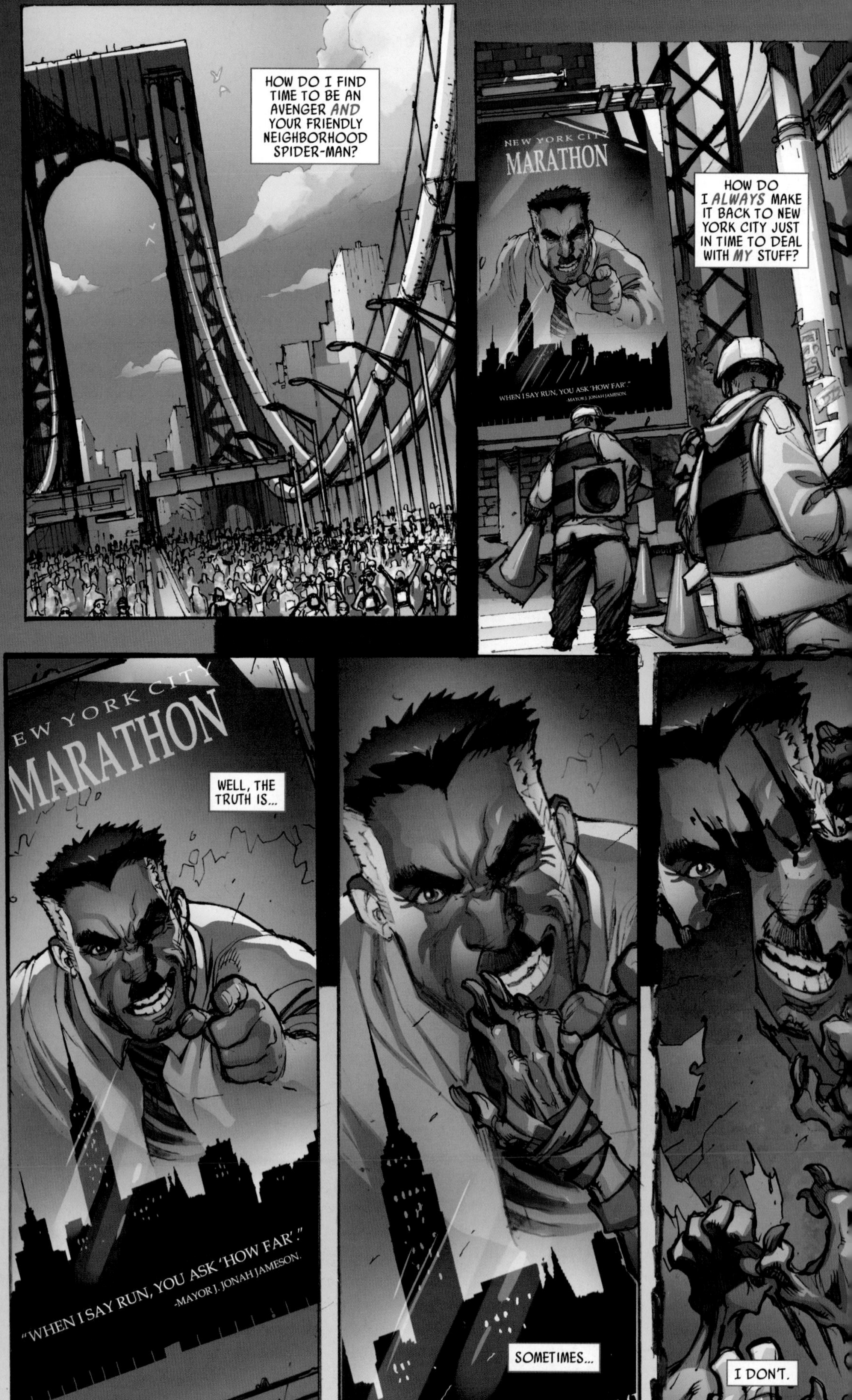
HOW DO I FIND TIME TO BE AN AVENGER AND YOUR FRIENDLY NEIGHBORHOOD SPIDER-MAN?
NEW YORK CITY MARATHON
"WHEN I SAY RUN, YOU ASK 'HOW FAR.'"
-MAYOR J. JONAH JAMESON.
HOW DO I ALWAYS MAKE IT BACK TO NEW YORK CITY JUST IN TIME TO DEAL WITH MY STUFF?
EW YORK CITY
MARATHON
WELL, THE TRUTH IS...
"WHEN I SAY RUN, YOU ASK 'HOW FAR.'"
-MAYOR J. JONAH JAMESON.
SOMETIMES...
I DON'T.

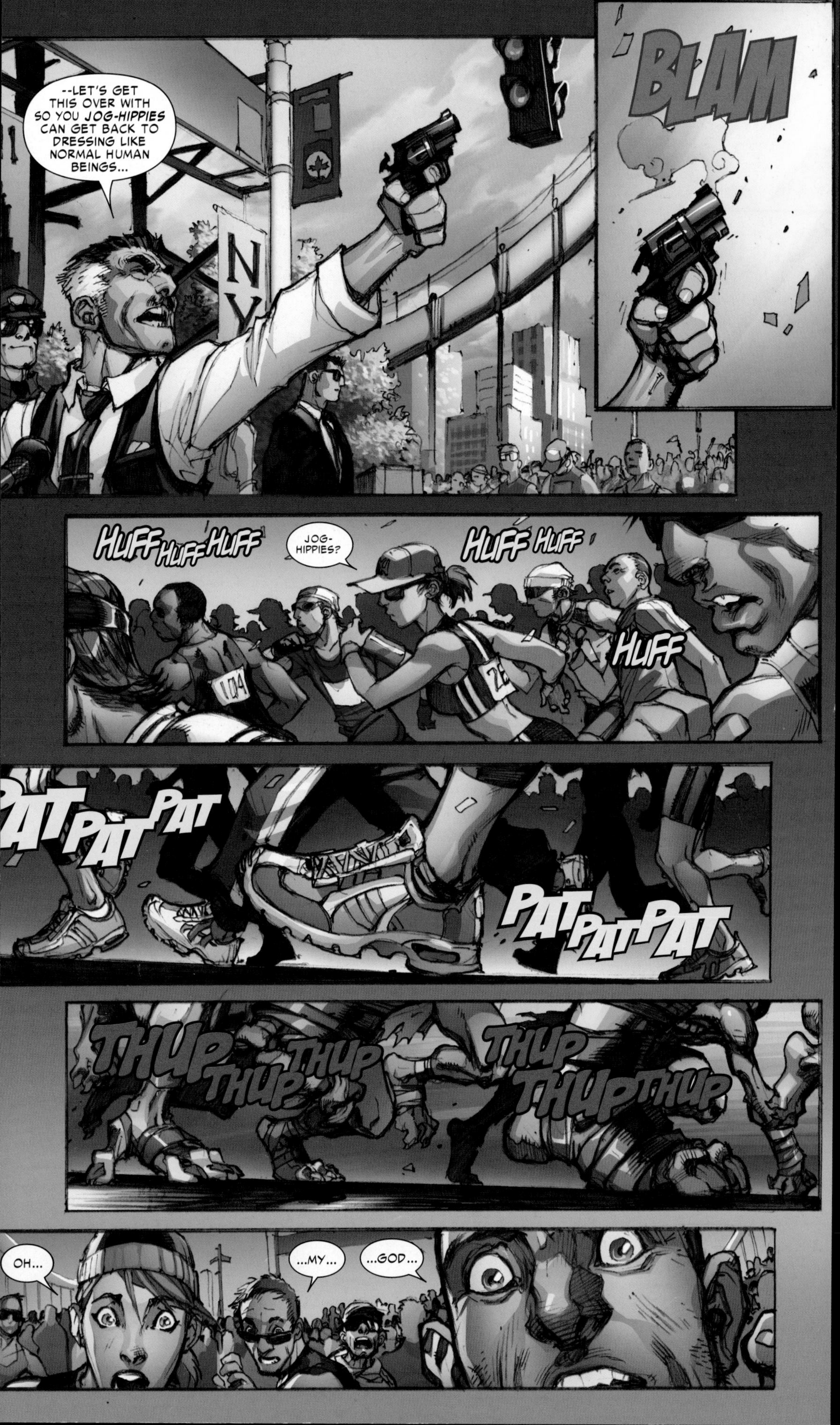
--LET'S GET THIS OVER WITH SO YOU JOG-HIPPIES CAN GET BACK TO DRESSING LIKE NORMAL HUMAN BEINGS...
BLAM
HUFF HUFF HUFF
JOG-HIPPIES?
HUFF HUFF
HUFF
PAT PAT PAT
PAT PAT PAT
THUP THUP THUP
THUP THUP THUP
OH...
...MY...
...GOD...

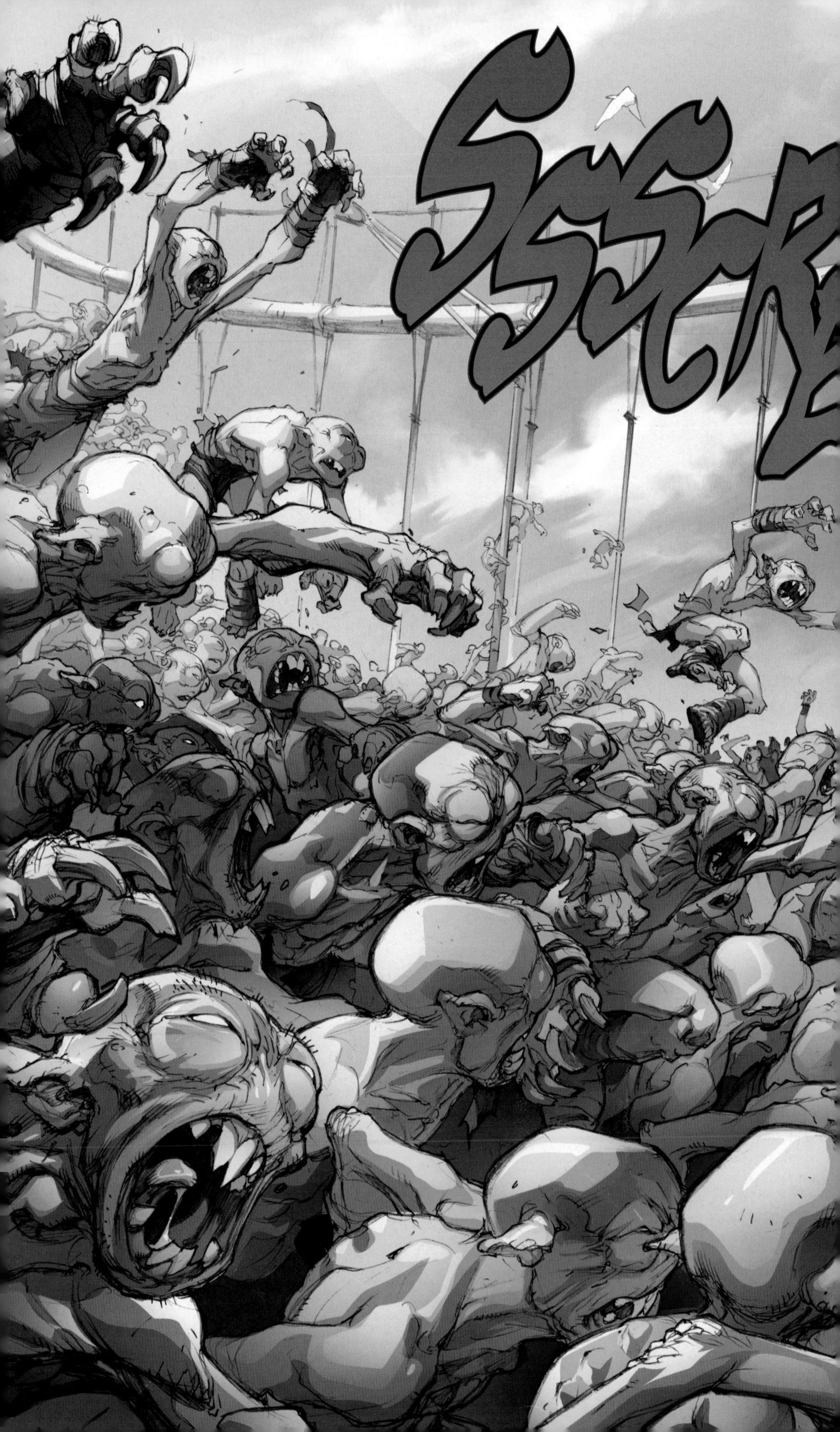
SSSCR

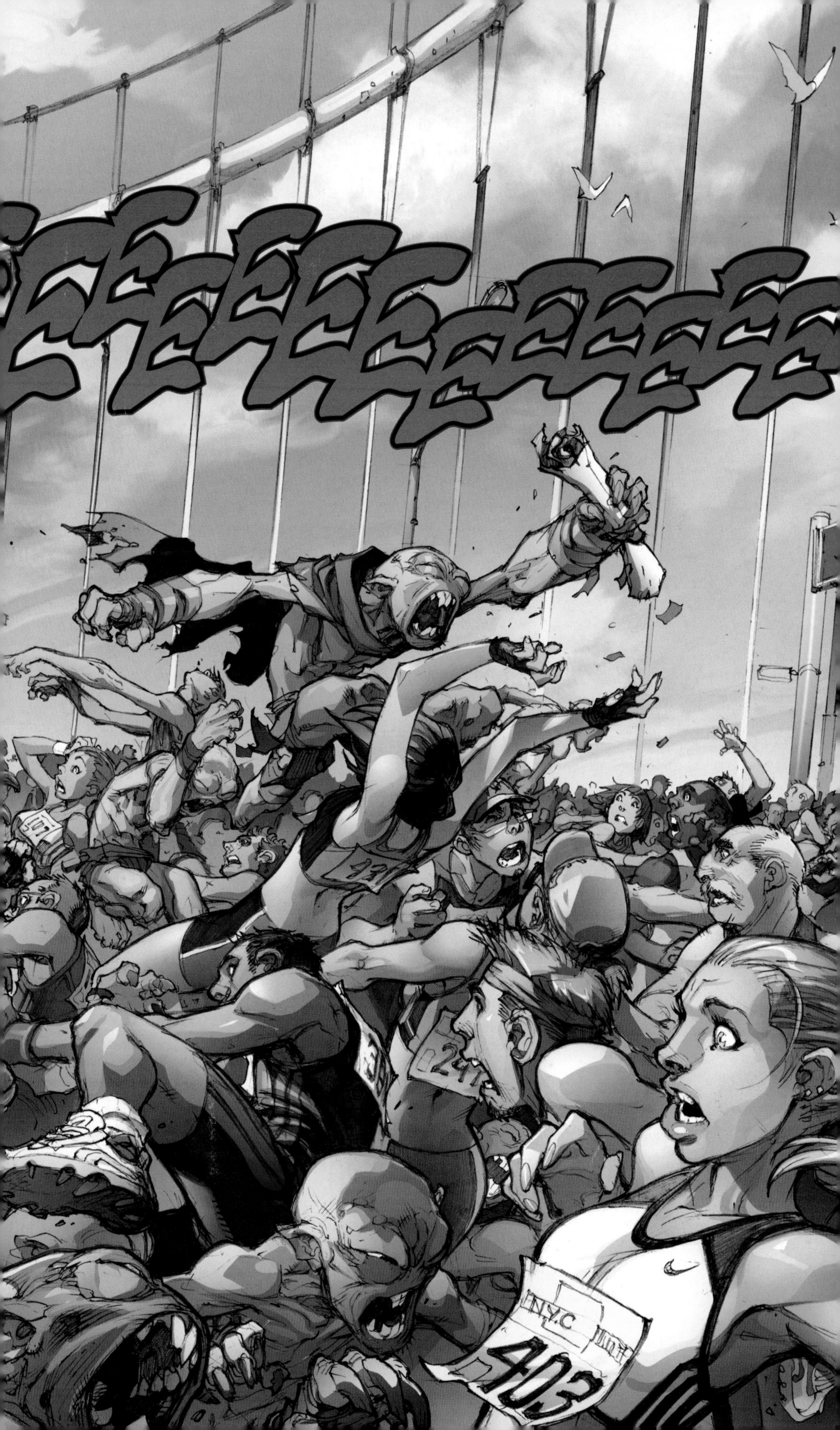
EEEEEEEEEEEE
N.Y.C
403

While attending a demonstration in radiology high school student Peter Parker was bitten a spider which had accidentally been expose to radioactive rays. Through a miracle of science, Peter soon found that he had gaine the spider's powers... and had, in effect, become a human spider! From that day on he was the...

AVENGING SPIDER-MAN

AVEN
SPIDE

WRITER: **ZEB WELLS**

COLOR ART: **FERRAN DANIEL**

PRODUCTION ASSIST: **MANNY MEDEROS**   ASSISTANT EDITOR: **ELLIE PY**

EDITOR IN CHIEF: **AXEL ALONSO**   CHIEF CREATIVE OFFICER: **JOE QUESADA**

VARIANT COVER ARTISTS: **RAMOS & DELGADO; CAMPBELL &**

BLANK VARIANT BY

eral Thaddeus "Thunderbolt" Ross was a
orated war hero who fiercely hunted the Hulk.
r several futile years of chasing the original
en Goliath, Ross sought vengeance and
le a pact for power with the evil Intelegencia.
ued with the powers of super-strength,
rgy absorption and gamma radiation…
how seeks redemption as…

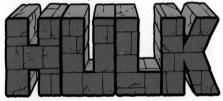

GING
R-MAN

RTIST: **JOE MADUREIRA**

LETTERER: **VC's JOE CARAMAGNA**

OR: **STEPHEN WACKER**

PUBLISHER: **DAN BUCKLEY**

EXECUTIVE EDITOR: **TOM BREVOORT**

EXECUTIVE PRODUCER: **ALAN FINE**

E QUESADA, DANNY MIKI, & RICHARD ISANOVE

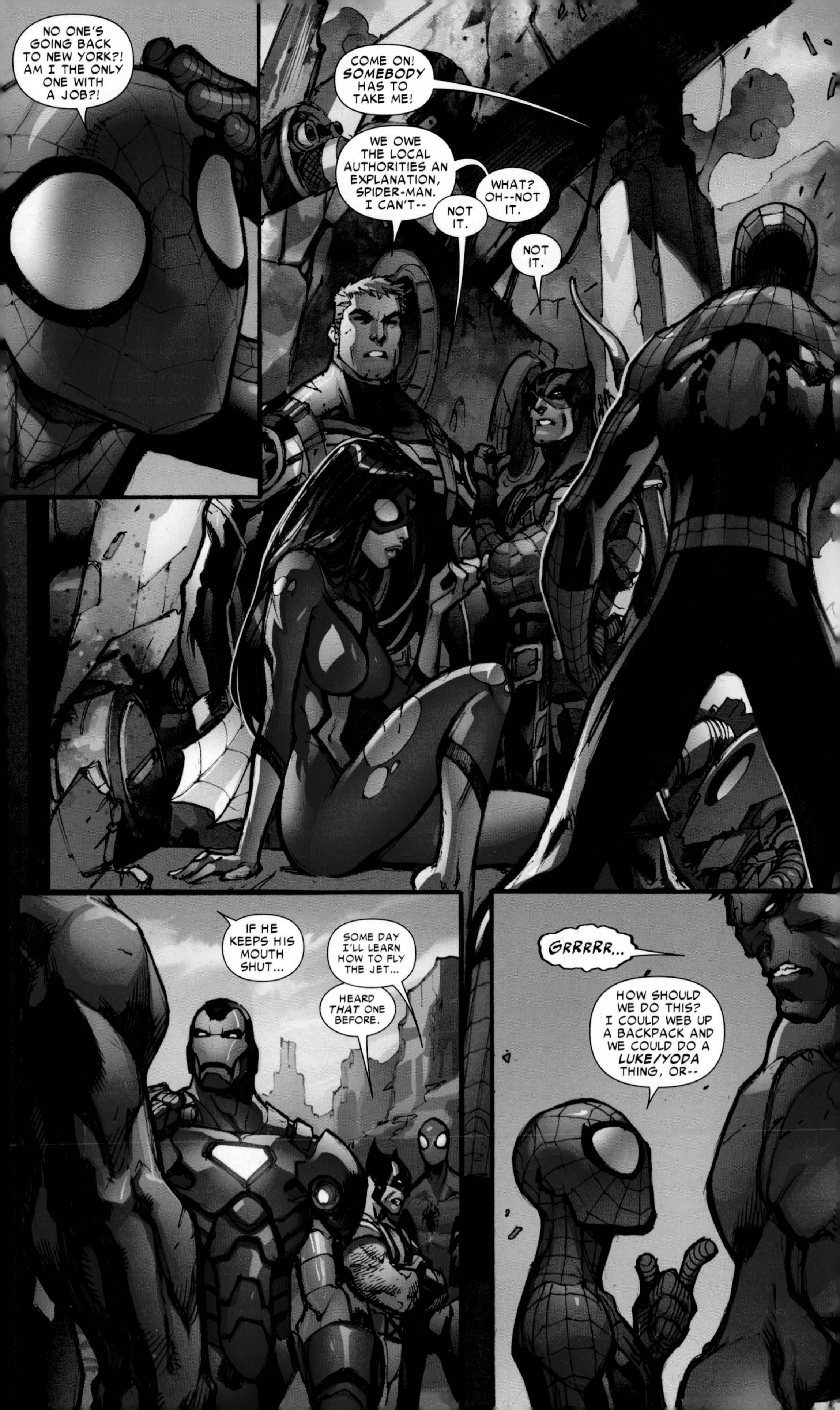
NO ONE'S GOING BACK TO NEW YORK?! AM I THE ONLY ONE WITH A JOB?!
COME ON! *SOMEBODY* HAS TO TAKE ME!
WE OWE THE LOCAL AUTHORITIES AN EXPLANATION, SPIDER-MAN. I CAN'T--
NOT IT.
WHAT? OH--NOT IT.
NOT IT.
IF HE KEEPS HIS MOUTH SHUT...
SOME DAY I'LL LEARN HOW TO FLY THE JET...
HEARD *THAT* ONE BEFORE.
GRRRRR...
HOW SHOULD WE DO THIS? I COULD WEB UP A BACKPACK AND WE COULD DO A *LUKE/YODA* THING, OR--

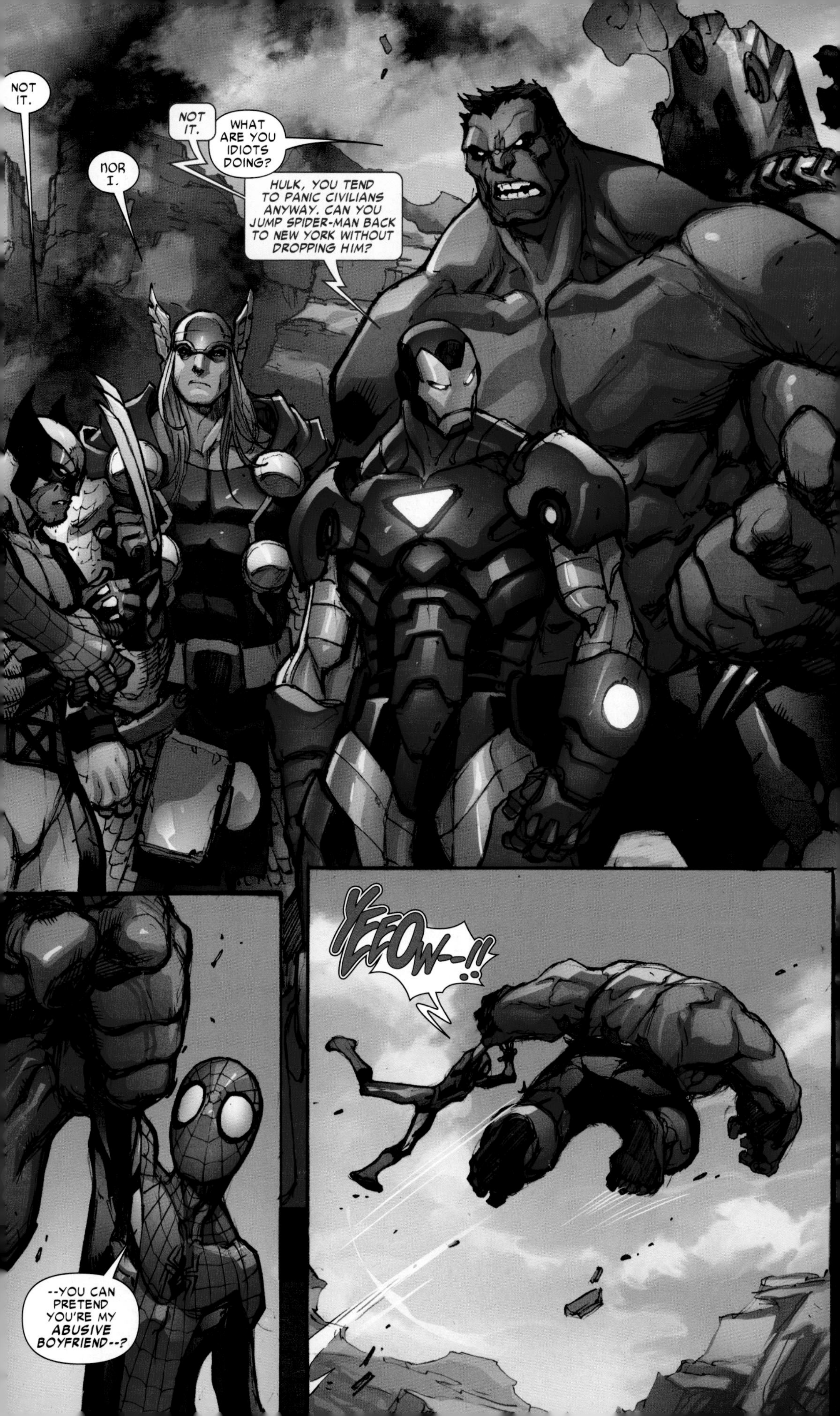
NOT IT.
NOT IT.
NOR I.
WHAT ARE YOU IDIOTS DOING?
HULK, YOU TEND TO PANIC CIVILIANS ANYWAY. CAN YOU JUMP SPIDER-MAN BACK TO NEW YORK WITHOUT DROPPING HIM?
--YOU CAN PRETEND YOU'RE MY ABUSIVE BOYFRIEND--?
YEEOW--!!

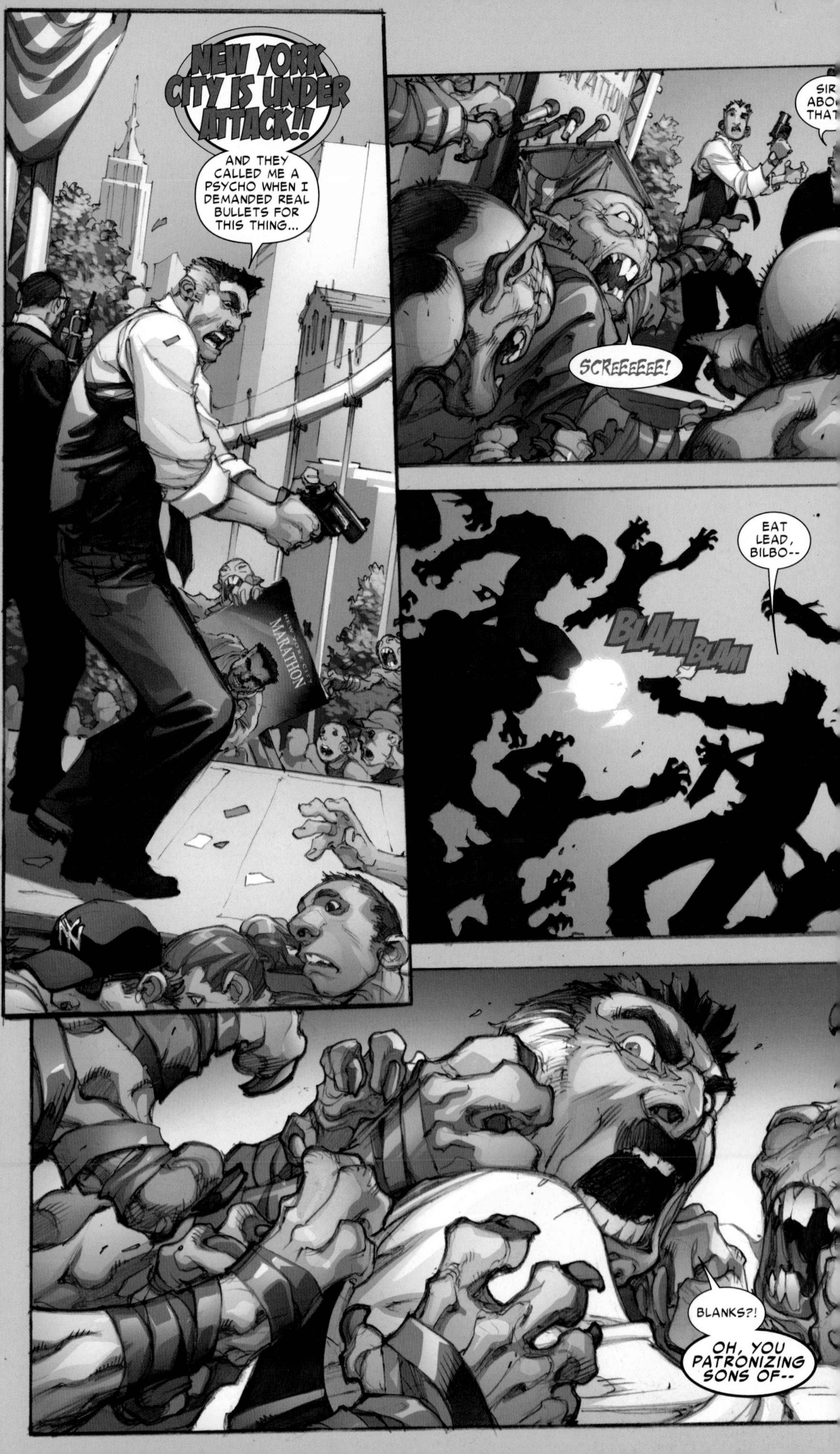

NEW YORK CITY IS UNDER ATTACK!!
AND THEY CALLED ME A PSYCHO WHEN I DEMANDED REAL BULLETS FOR THIS THING...
MARATHON
SCREEEEEEE!
SIR
EAT LEAD, BILBO--
BLAM BLAM
BLANKS?!
OH, YOU PATRONIZING SONS OF--

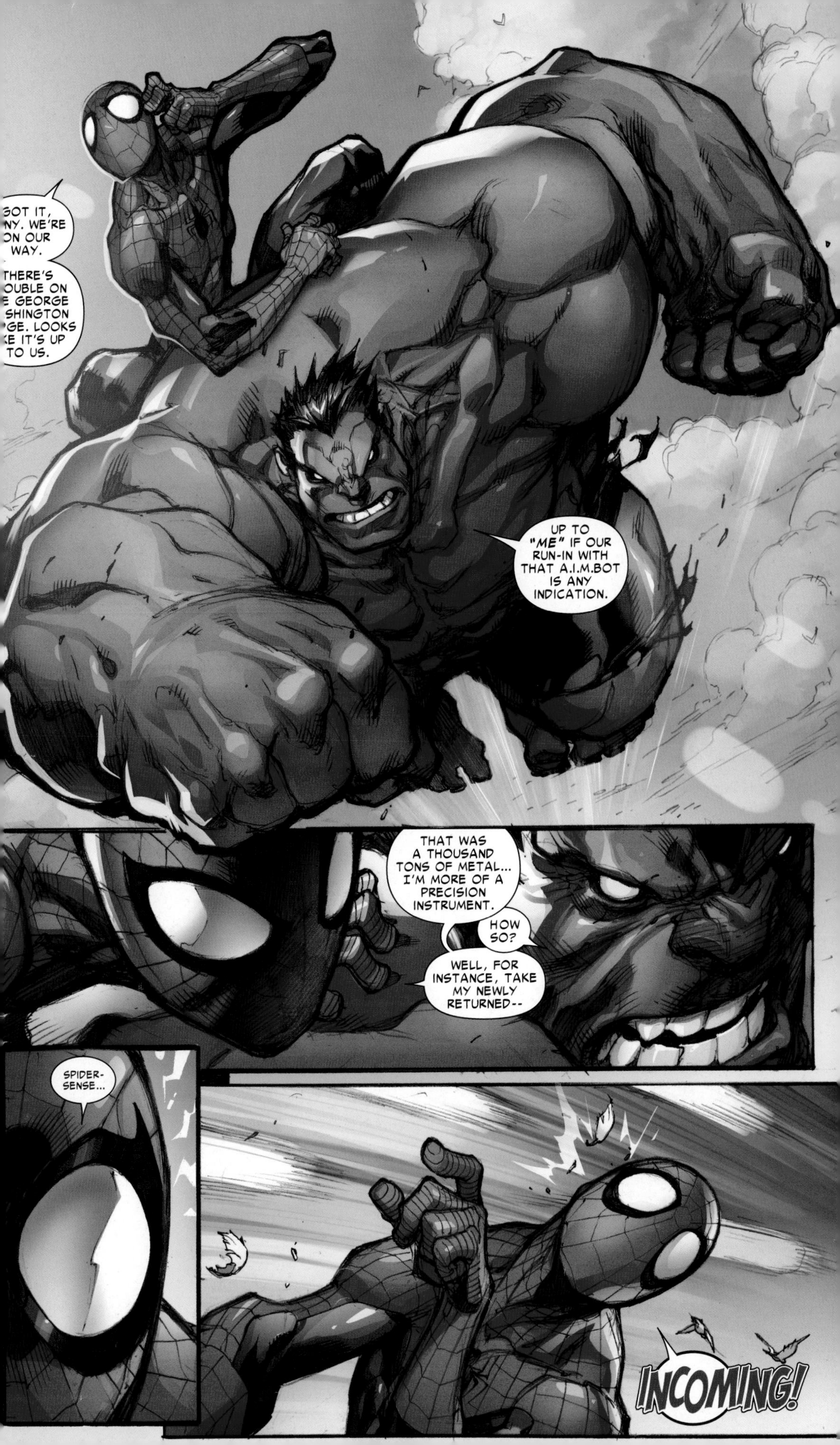
GOT IT, NY. WE'RE ON OUR WAY.
THERE'S OUBLE ON E GEORGE SHINGTON IDGE. LOOKS KE IT'S UP TO US.
UP TO "ME" IF OUR RUN-IN WITH THAT A.I.M.BOT IS ANY INDICATION.
THAT WAS A THOUSAND TONS OF METAL... I'M MORE OF A PRECISION INSTRUMENT.
HOW SO?
WELL, FOR INSTANCE, TAKE MY NEWLY RETURNED--
SPIDER-SENSE...
INCOMING!

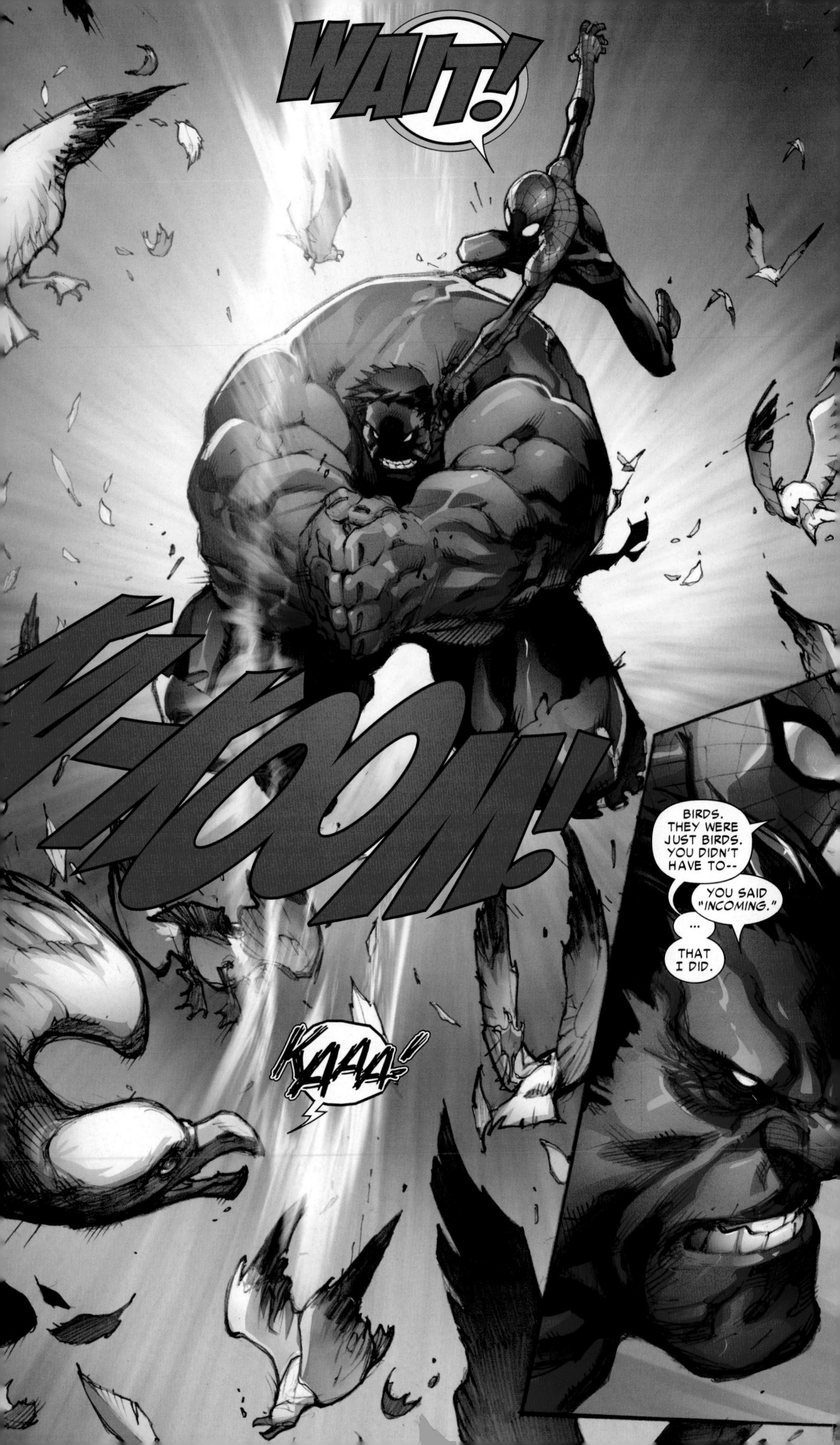
WAIT!
WHOOM!
KAAA!
BIRDS. THEY WERE JUST BIRDS. YOU DIDN'T HAVE TO--
YOU SAID "INCOMING."
...
THAT I DID.

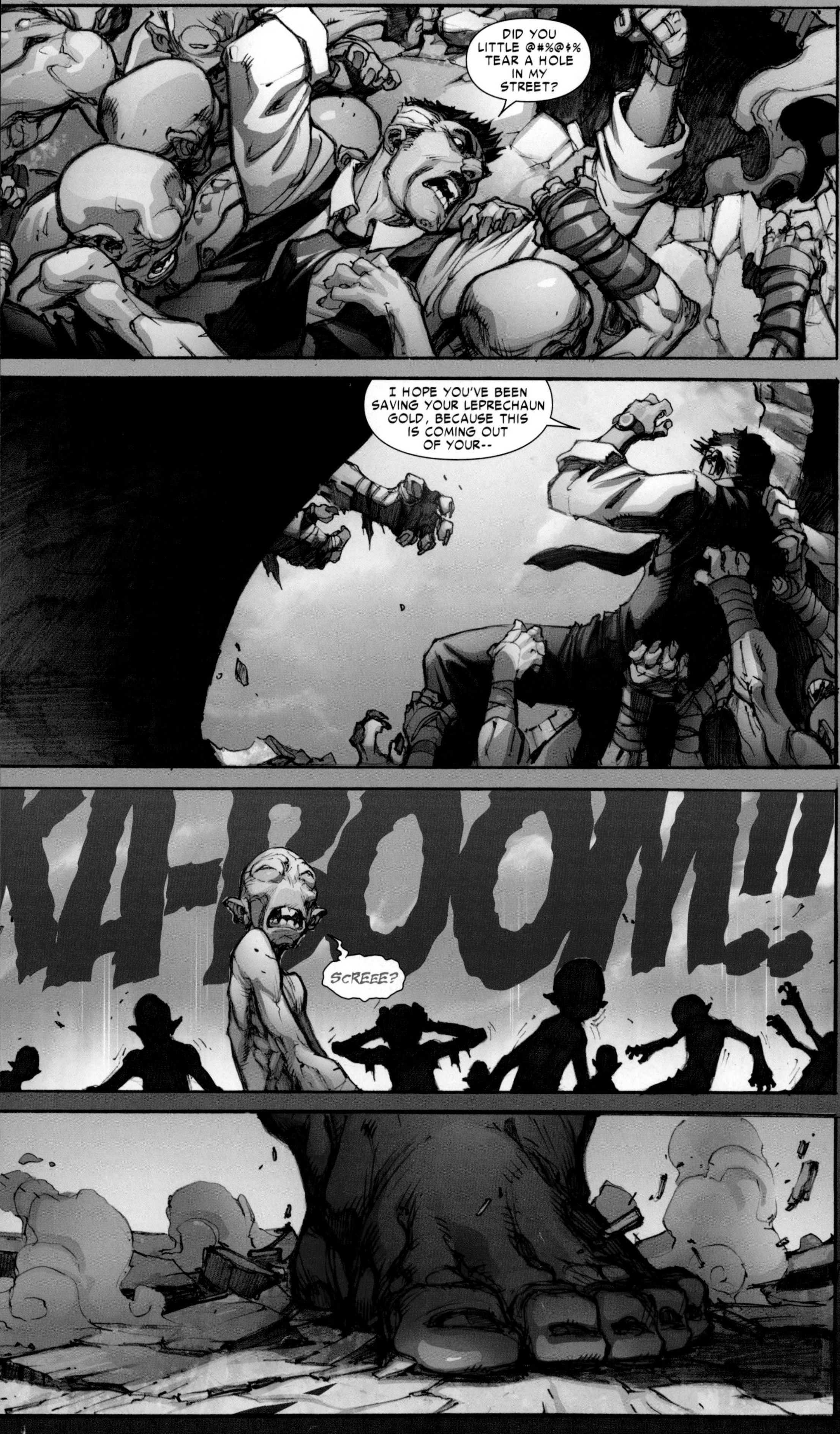
DID YOU LITTLE @#%@$% TEAR A HOLE IN MY STREET?
I HOPE YOU'VE BEEN SAVING YOUR LEPRECHAUN GOLD, BECAUSE THIS IS COMING OUT OF YOUR--
SCREEE?

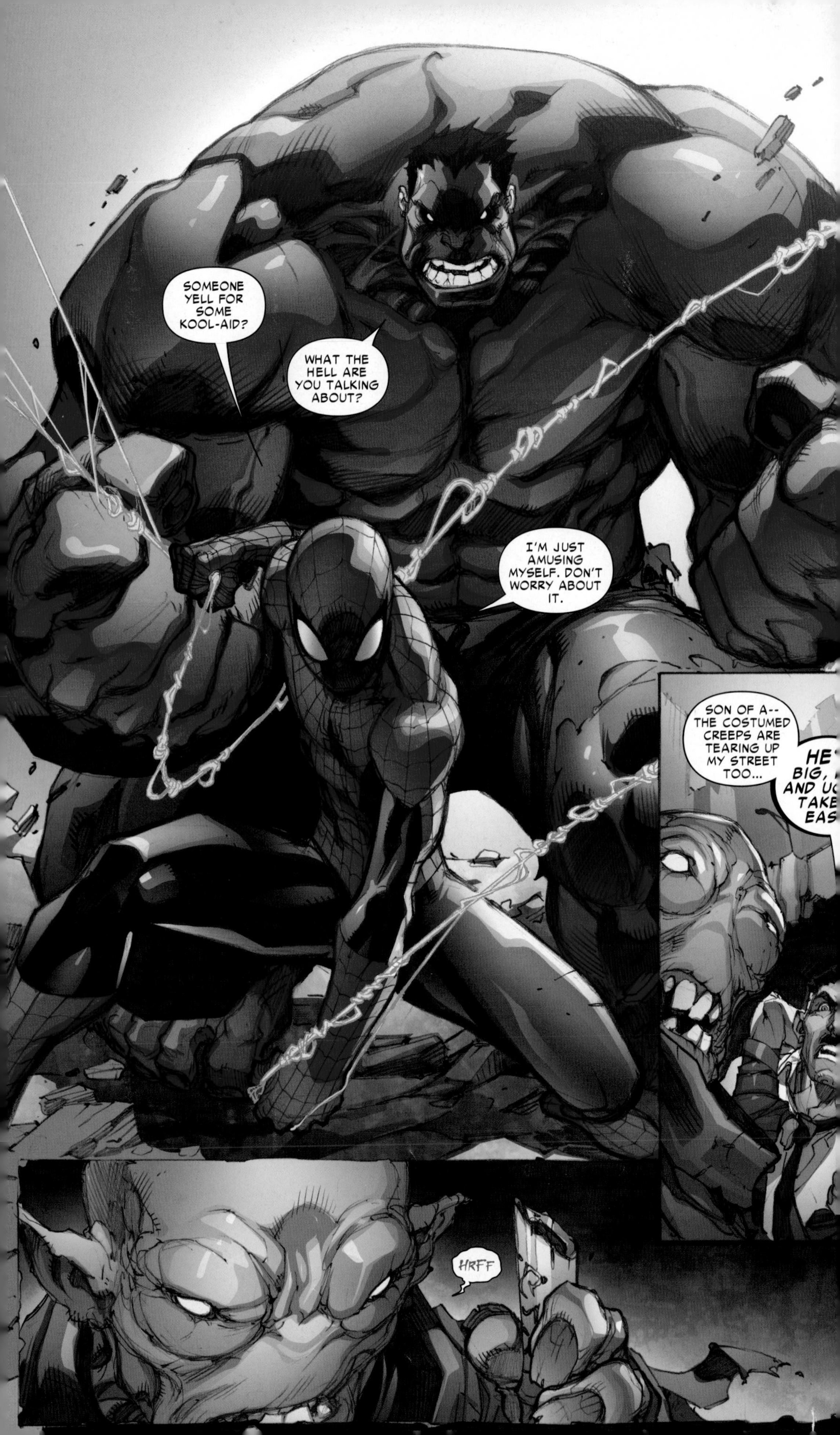
SOMEONE YELL FOR SOME KOOL-AID?
WHAT THE HELL ARE YOU TALKING ABOUT?
I'M JUST AMUSING MYSELF. DON'T WORRY ABOUT IT.
SON OF A-- THE COSTUMED CREEPS ARE TEARING UP MY STREET TOO...
HRFF

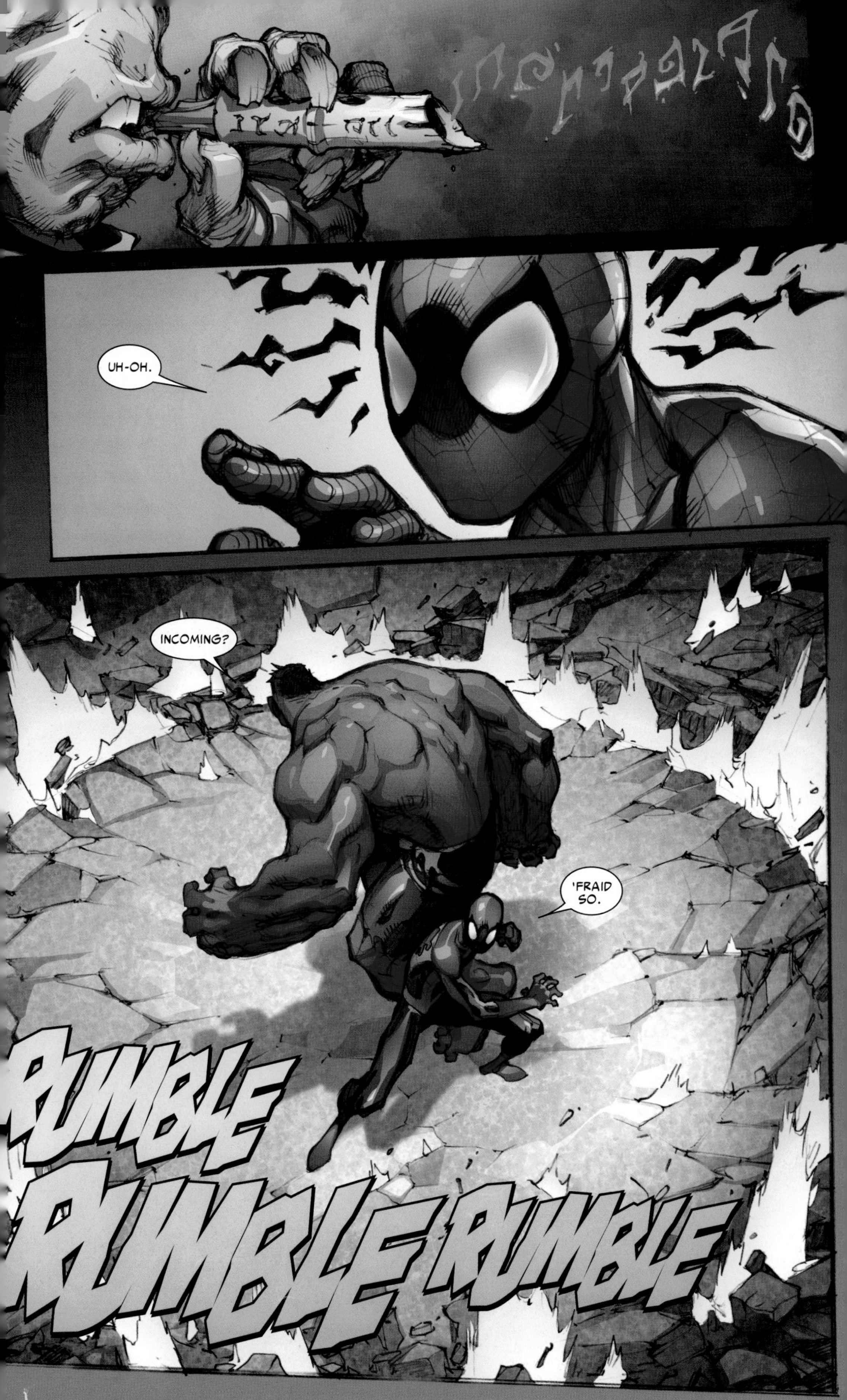
UH-OH.
INCOMING?
'FRAID SO.
RUMBLE
RUMBLE RUMBLE

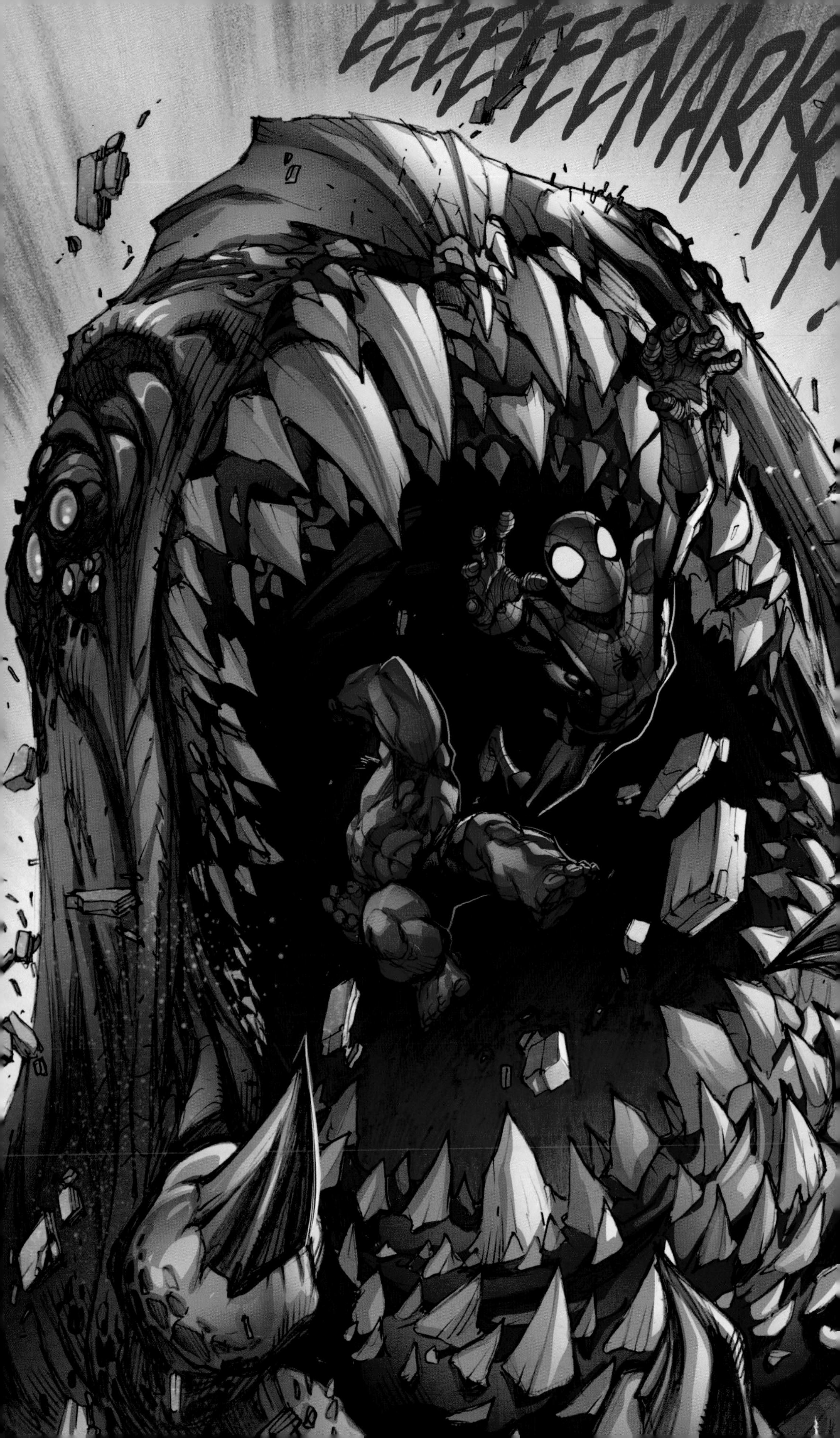
EEEEEENARR

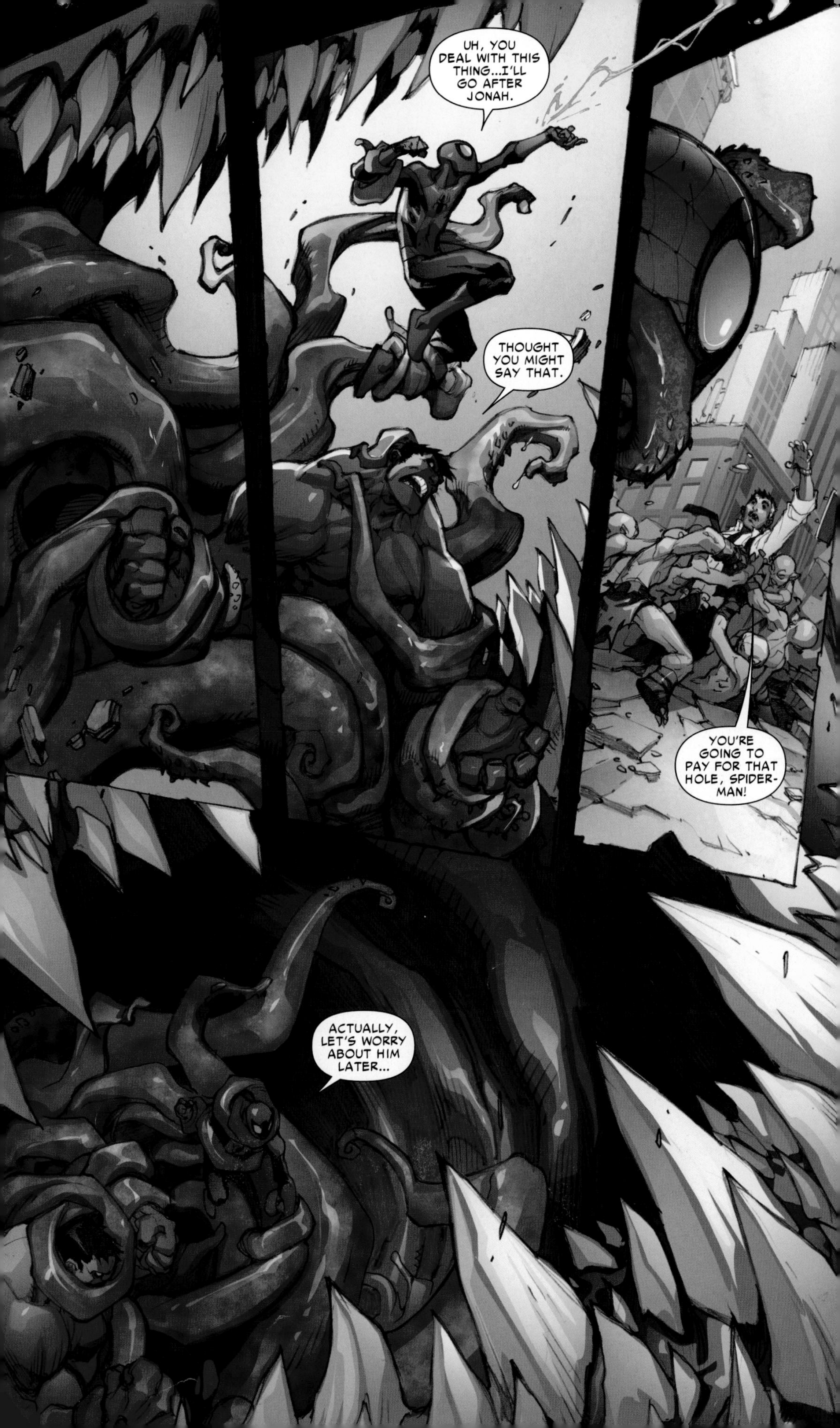
UH, YOU DEAL WITH THIS THING...I'LL GO AFTER JONAH.
THOUGHT YOU MIGHT SAY THAT.
YOU'RE GOING TO PAY FOR THAT HOLE, SPIDER-MAN!
ACTUALLY, LET'S WORRY ABOUT HIM LATER...

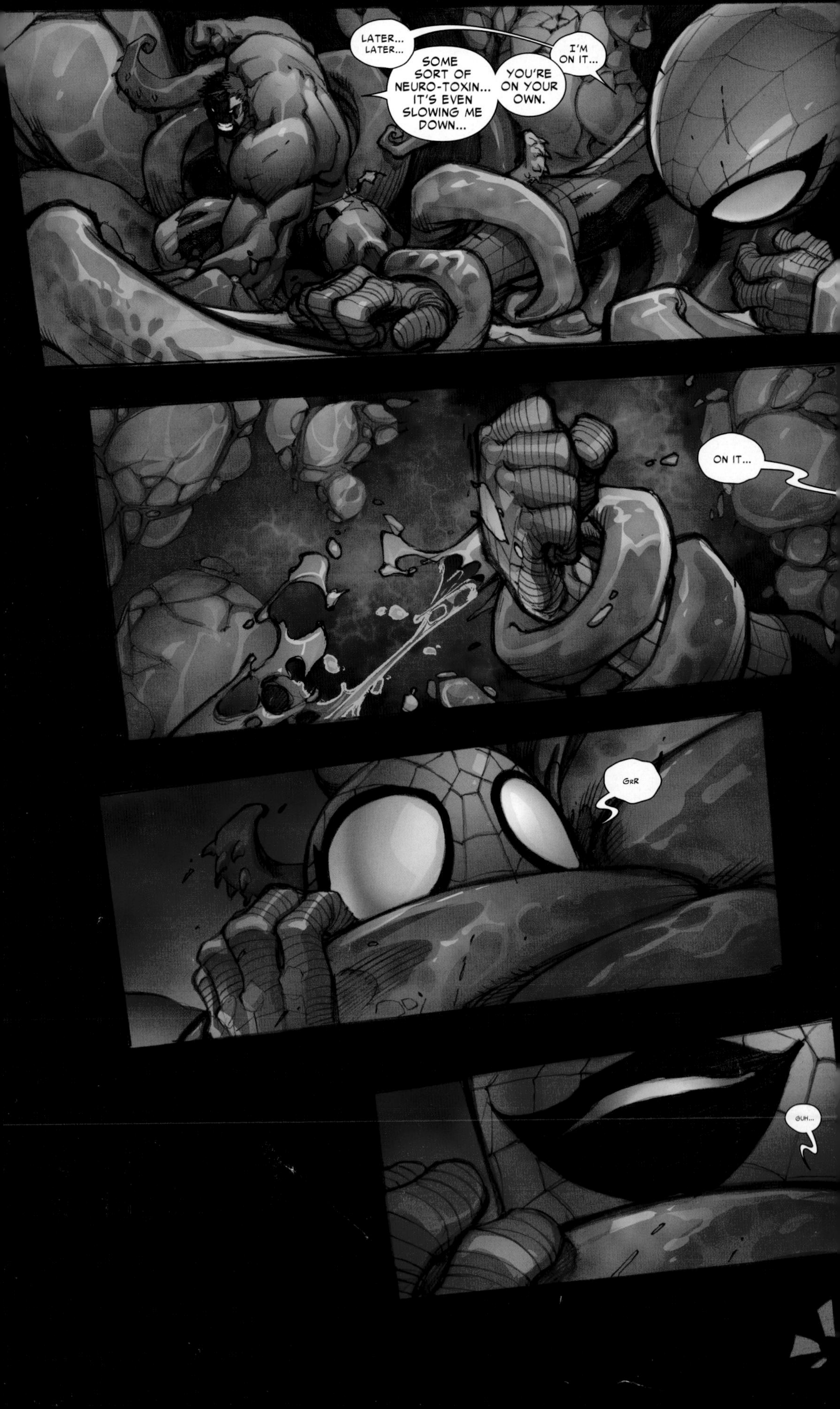
LATER... LATER...
SOME SORT OF NEURO-TOXIN... IT'S EVEN SLOWING ME DOWN...
YOU'RE ON YOUR OWN.
I'M ON IT...
ON IT...
GRR
GUH...

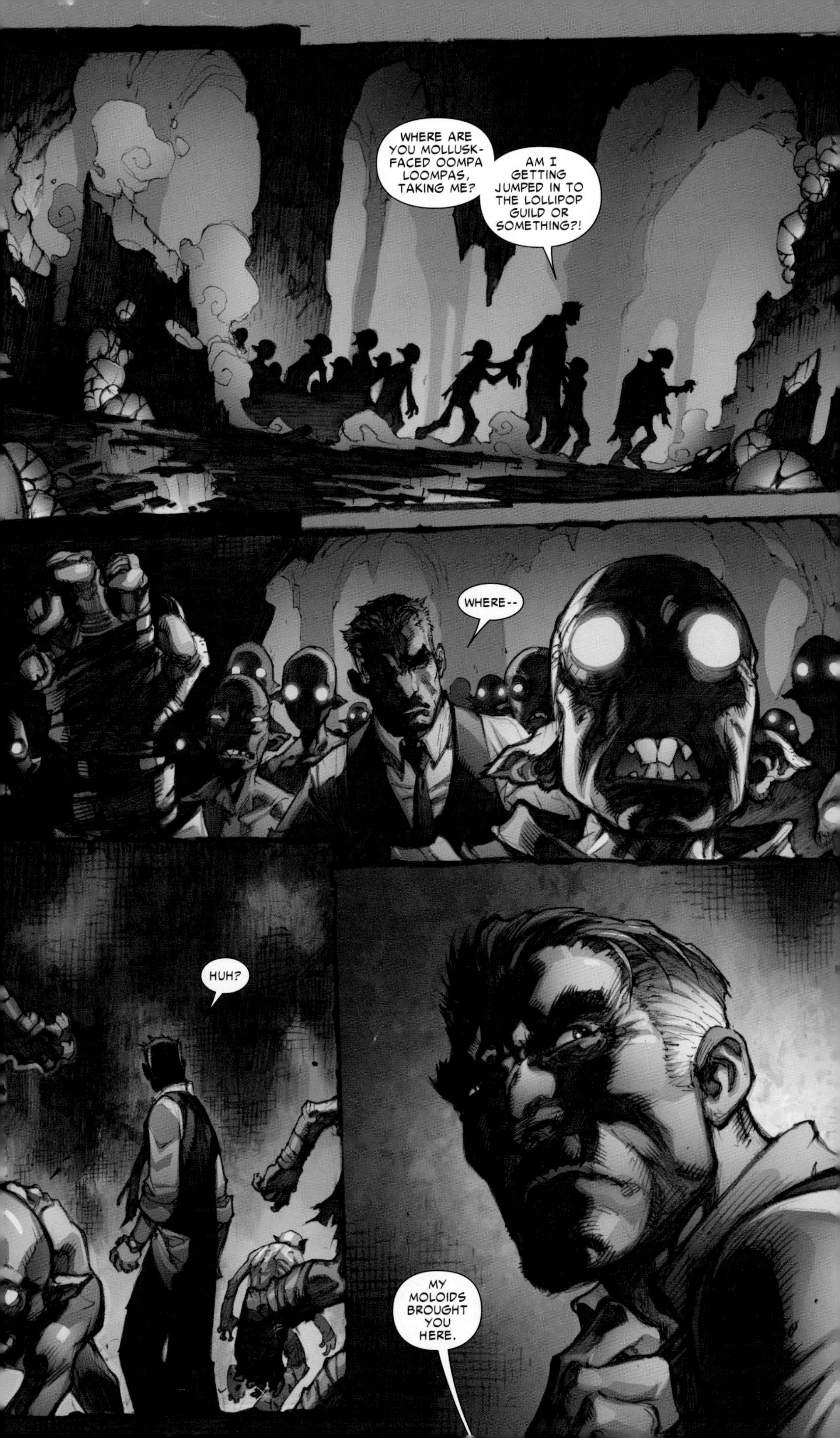
WHERE ARE YOU MOLLUSK-FACED OOMPA LOOMPAS, TAKING ME?
AM I GETTING JUMPED IN TO THE LOLLIPOP GUILD OR SOMETHING?!
WHERE--
HUH?
MY MOLOIDS BROUGHT YOU HERE.

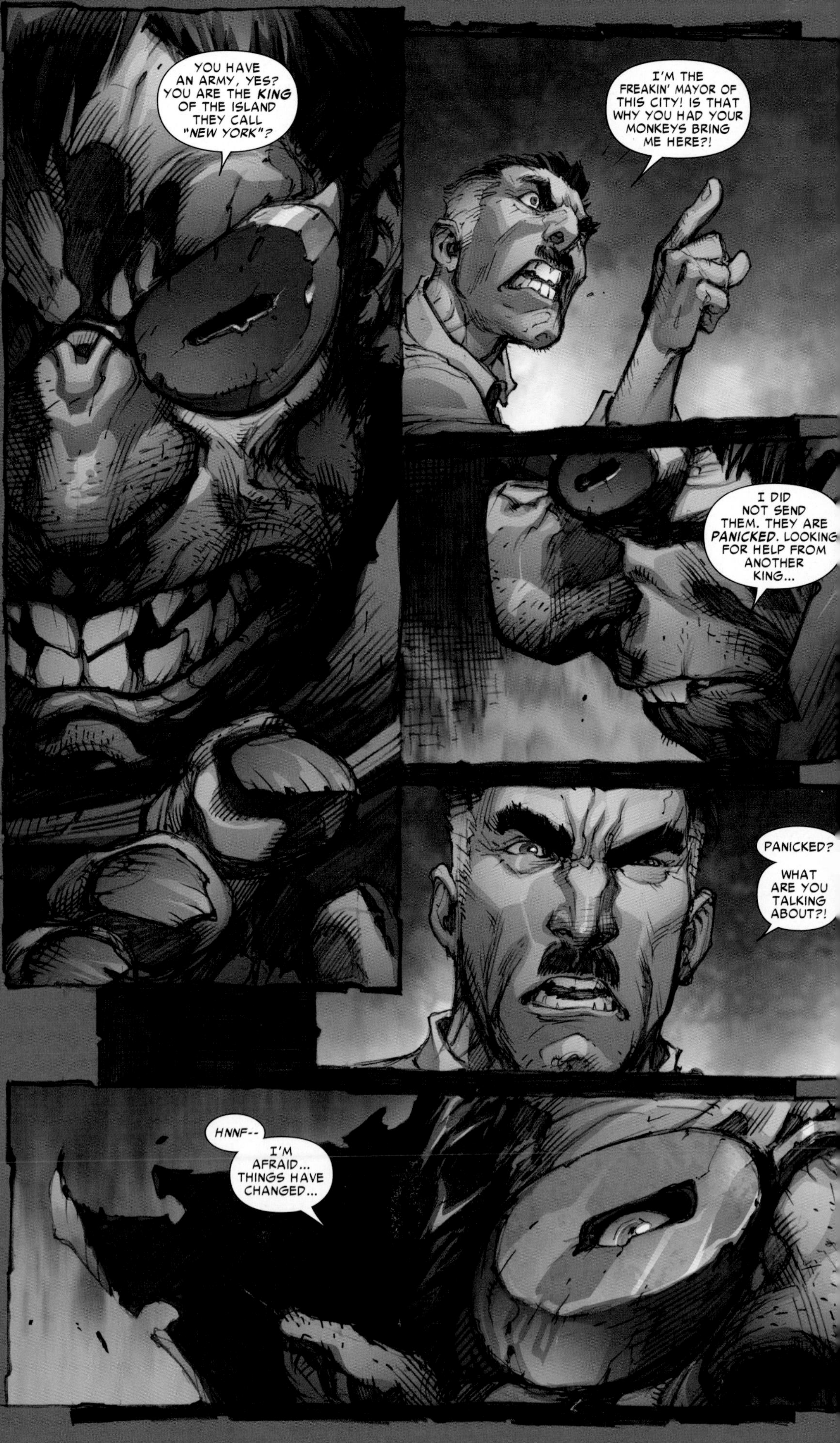
YOU HAVE AN ARMY, YES? YOU ARE THE KING OF THE ISLAND THEY CALL "NEW YORK"?
I'M THE FREAKIN' MAYOR OF THIS CITY! IS THAT WHY YOU HAD YOUR MONKEYS BRING ME HERE?!
I DID NOT SEND THEM. THEY ARE PANICKED. LOOKING FOR HELP FROM ANOTHER KING...
PANICKED?
WHAT ARE YOU TALKING ABOUT?!
HNNF--
I'M AFRAID... THINGS HAVE CHANGED...

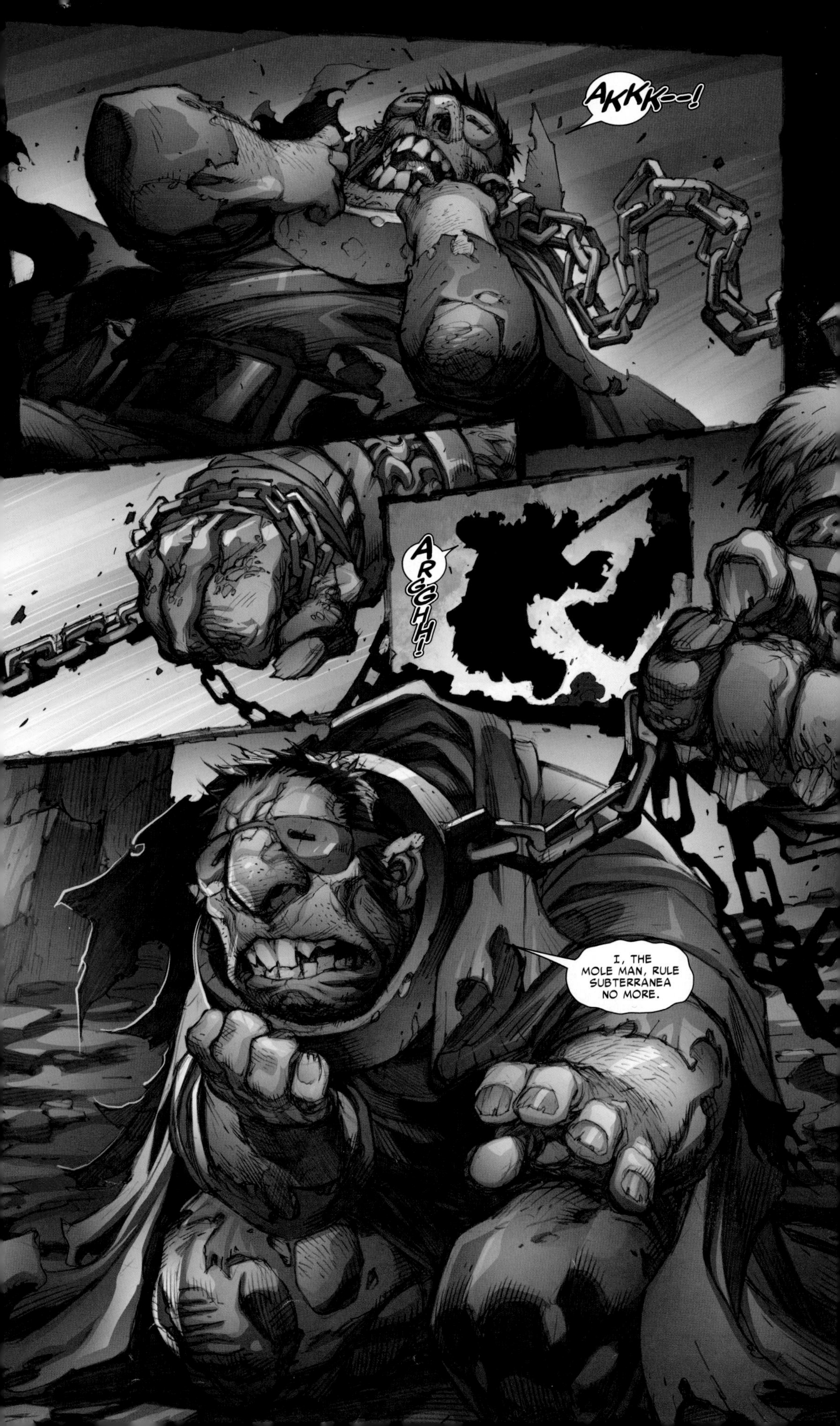
AKKK--!
ARGGHH!
I, THE MOLE MAN, RULE SUBTERRANEA NO MORE.

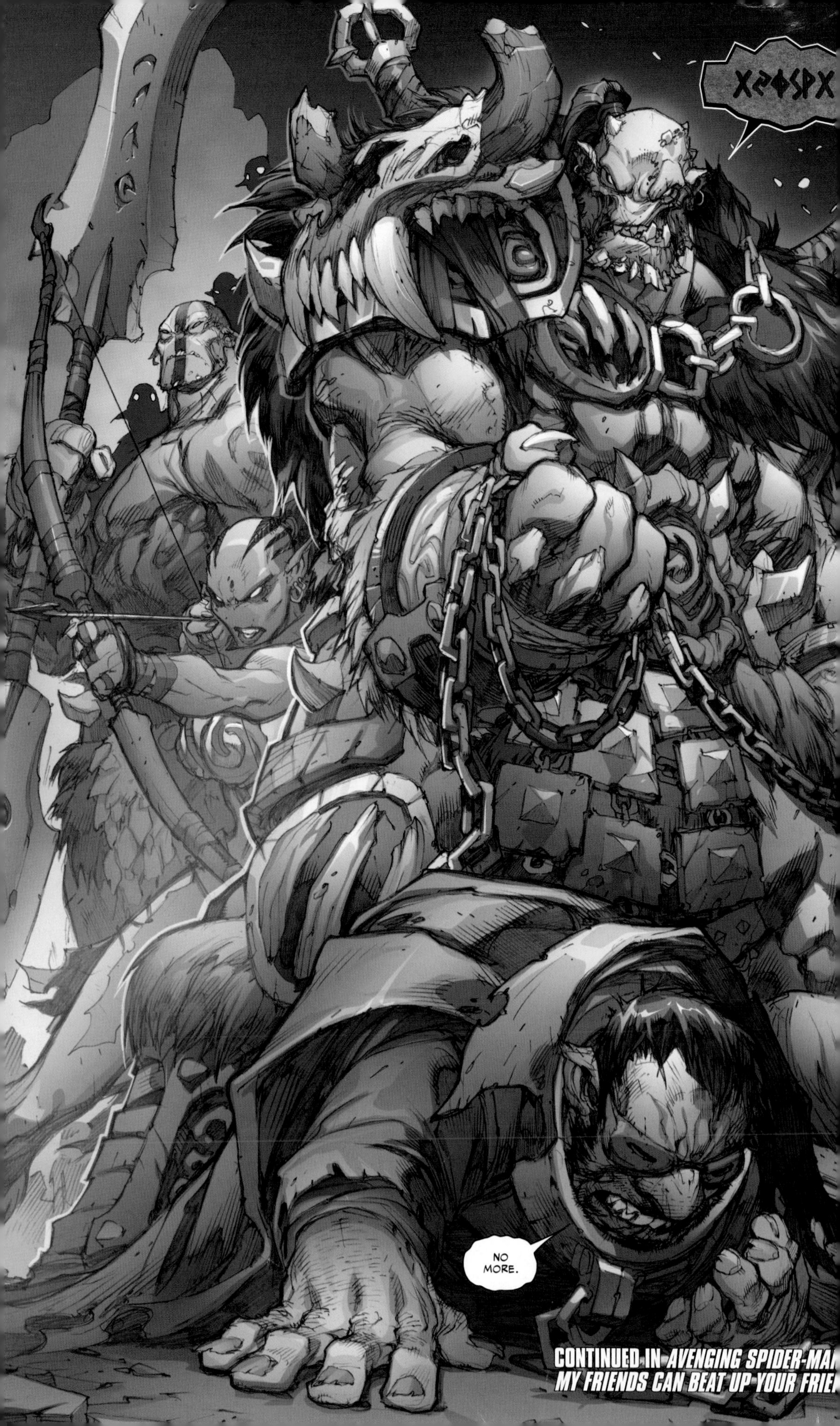
NO MORE.
CONTINUED IN AVENGING SPIDER-MA
MY FRIENDS CAN BEAT UP YOUR FRIE

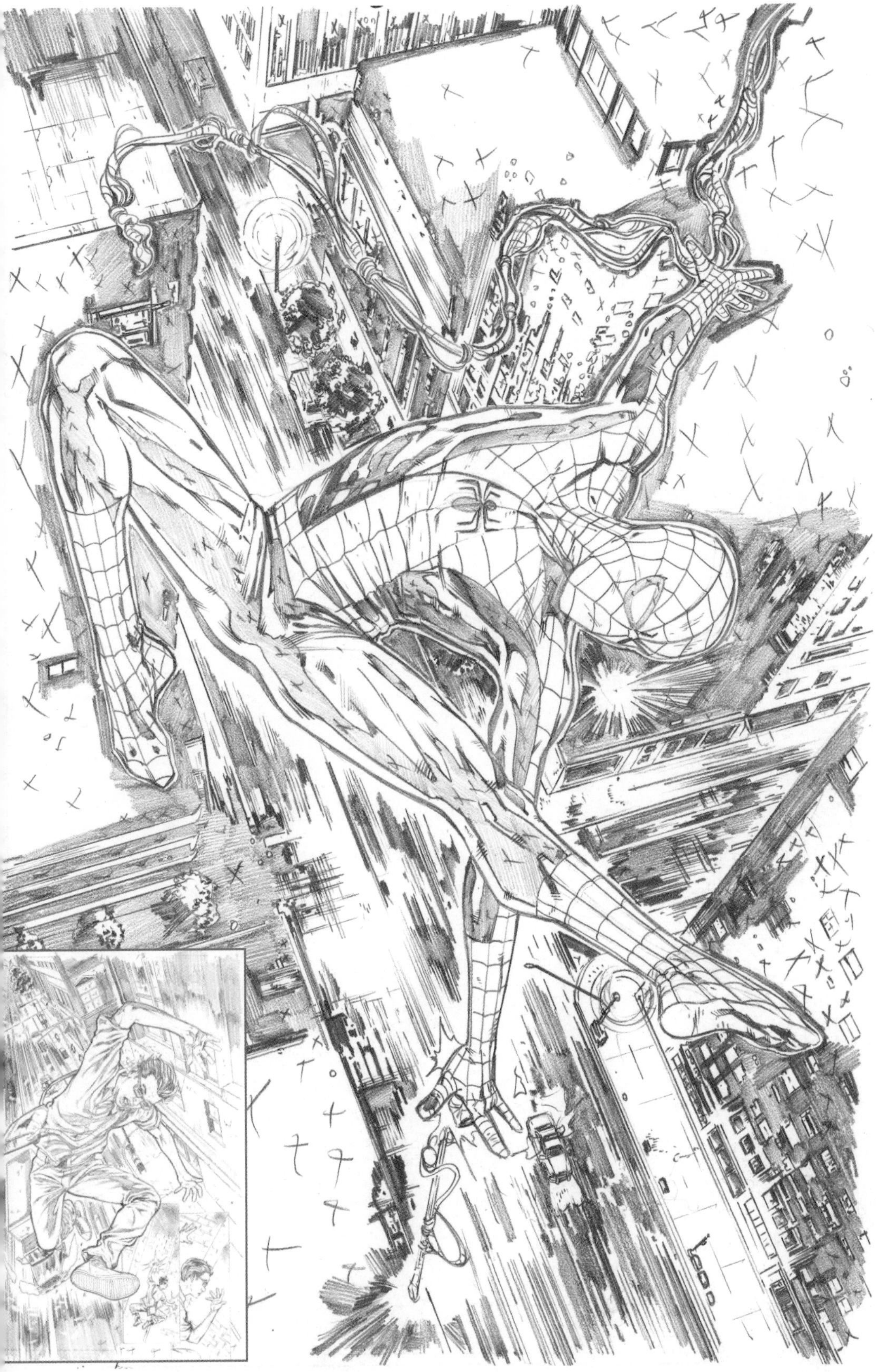

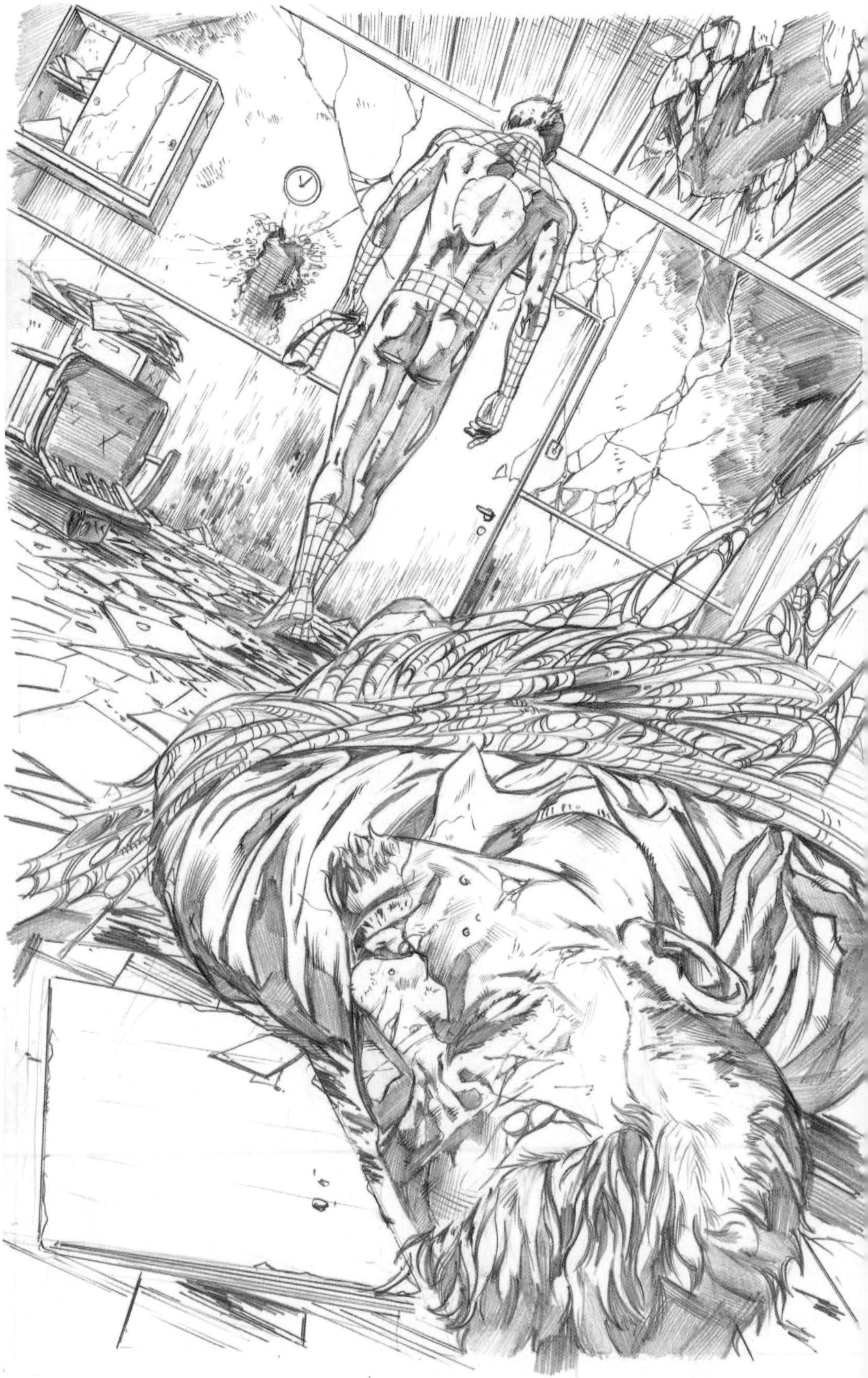

PENCILS BY NEIL EDWARDS, INKS BY KARL KESEL

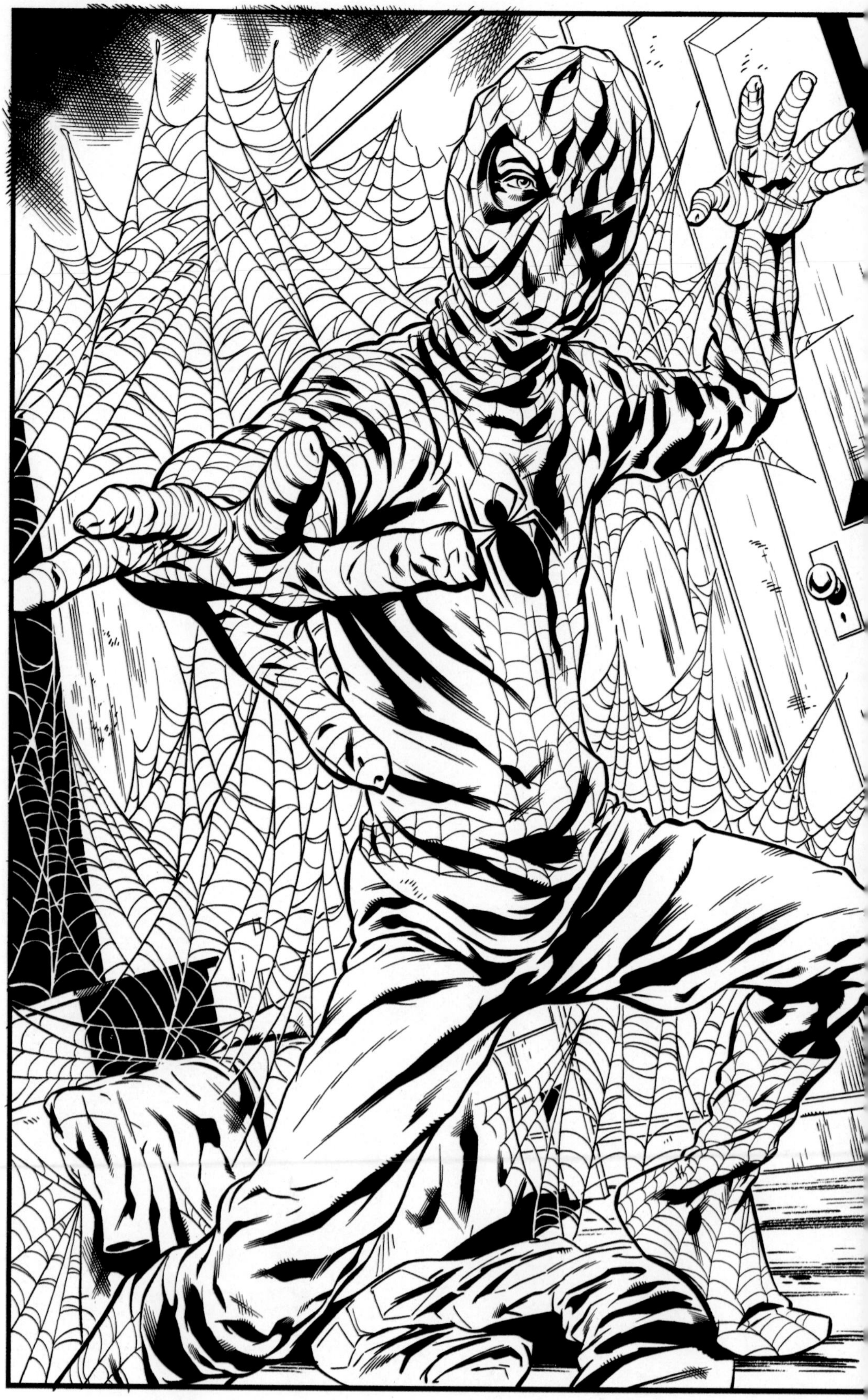

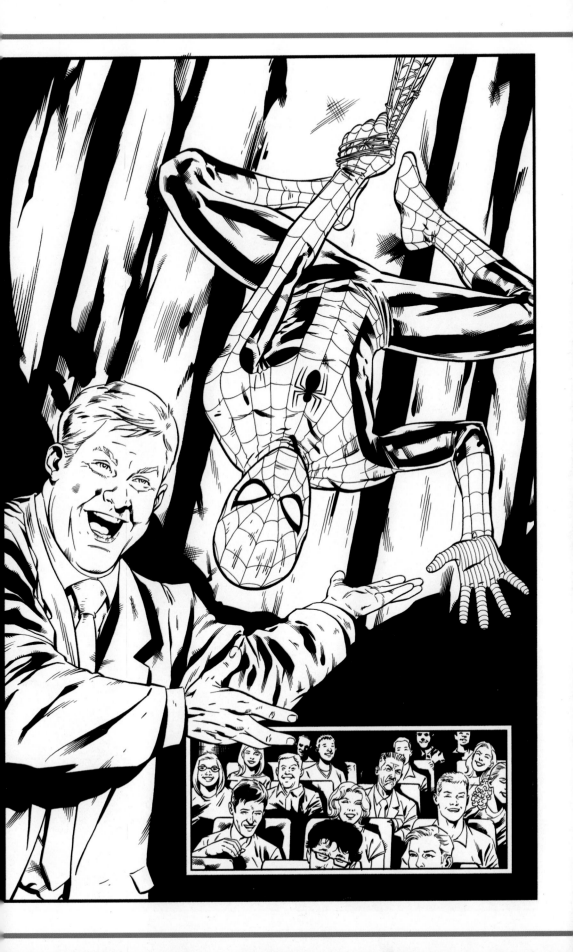

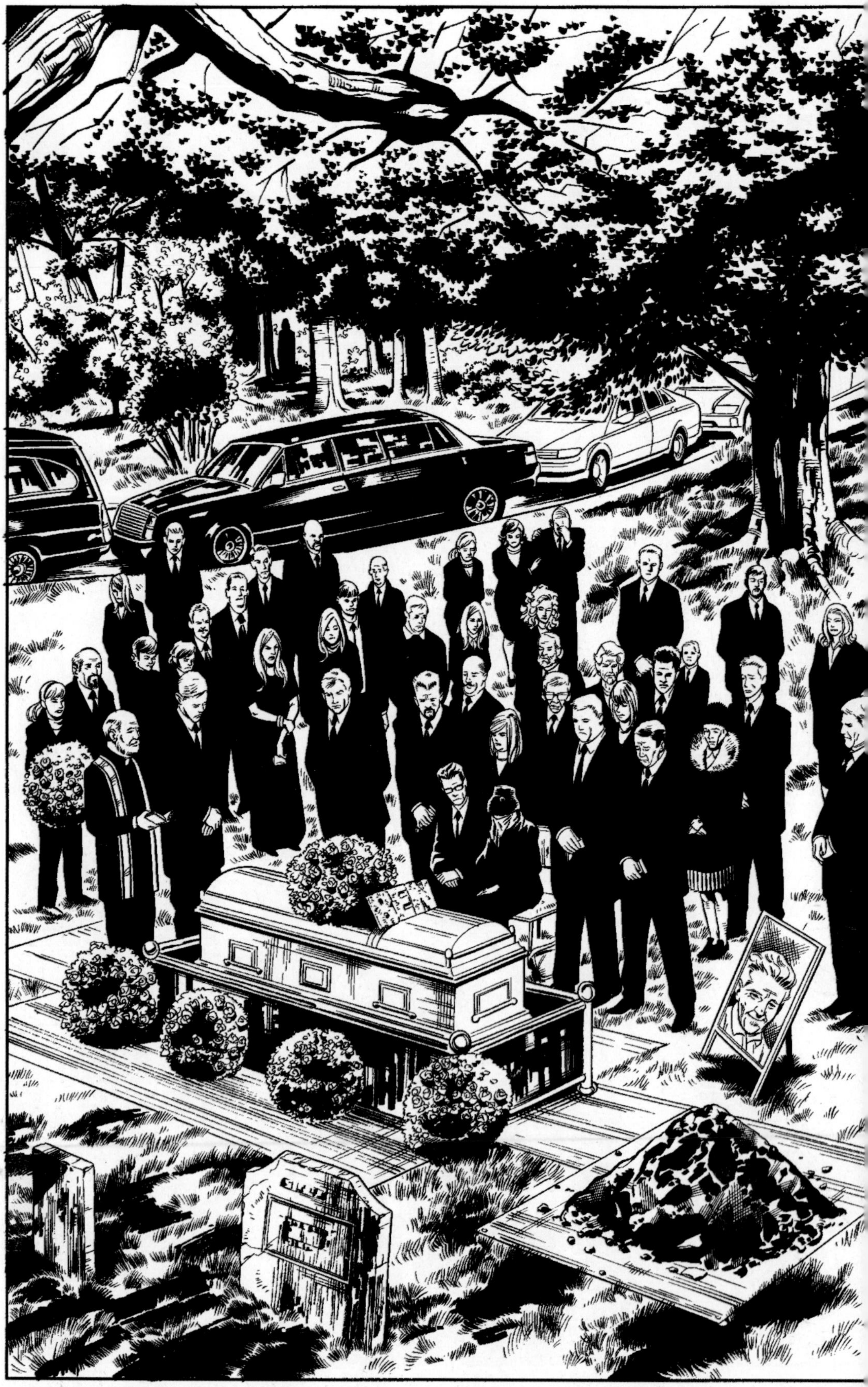

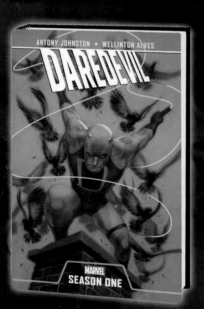

MARVEL

SEASON ONE

TOM DEFALCO • HORACIO DOMINGUES
ANT-MAN
MARVEL
SEASON ONE

ISBN # 978-0-7851-6386-2

GREG PAK • EMMA RIOS
DOCTOR STRANGE
MARVEL
SEASON ONE

ISBN # 978-0-7851-6388-6

FRED VAN LENTE • TOM FOWLER
HULK
MARVEL
SEASON ONE

ISBN # 978-0-7851-6387-9

AVAILABLE WHEREVER BOOKS ARE SOLD.

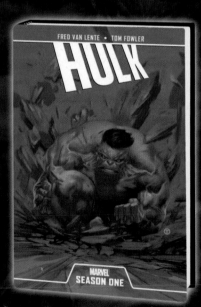